D1879424

ISLAM, AMERICA AND SOUTH ASIA

ISLAM, AMERICA AND SOUTH ASIA

M. Saleem Kidwai

GYAN PUBLISHING HOUSE
NEW DELHI - 110002

Islam, America and South Asia

Rs. 640

© M. Saleem Kidwai

ISBN : 81-212-0870-X

All Rights Reserved. No Part of this book may be reproduced in any manner without written permission.

Published in 2005 in India by
Gyan Publishing House,
5, Ansari Road, Daryaganj,
New Delhi-110002
Phone: 23261060, 23282060
Fax: 91-11-23285914
Email: gyanbook@vsnl.com
Web-site: http//www.gyanbooks.com

Lasertype Setting by: Tact Computer Graphics, Delhi
Printed at: Salasar Imaging System, Delhi

Contents

Preface

Islam happens to be one of the most misunderstood and misinterpreted religions of the world. On the one hand there are elements who are anti-Islam through and through. They deliberately portray a distorted picture of Islam. Maligning Islam is their objective in which they have achieved considerable success after the 9/11 tragedy. On the other hand there are Muslims who have tarnished the image of Islam either intentionally or unconsciously by their rhetoric and actions. Thus, Islam is facing problems both from the foes and friends. Consequently, Islam is being depicted in the media and even in the academic circles as the religion of war, vengeance hatred and destruction. It is misconstrued as a fanatical religion which is intolerant of other faiths, which establishes a male-dominated society and which encourages and promotes terrorism. Islam as a world civilization has been reduced to Islamic fundamentalism.

Islam is not a religion in the limited sense of the term. It is a complete code of conduct, a comprehensive and all embracing way of life. It covers all aspects of human existence. Like all other world religions Islam promotes peace, love and harmony among people. Islam is essentially a set of revealed values designed to guide humanity on the path of enlightenment and virtue. It emphasises liberal values such as religious tolerance, freedom of conscience and speech, civil liberties, social justice, public welfare and intellectual development. However, it has been appropriated by political and extremist groups that are using it as an ideology to pursue a counter hegemonic agenda both within the Muslim world and against the non-Muslim world, especially the US. Extremist interpretations of Islam by *jihadis* are not only creating a global fitna (crisis) but are also corrupting the essence of Islam and worsening the social, political, economic and cultural crisis in the Muslim world.

Recent developments have placed Islam at the forefront in America. Interest in the Muslim world as a whole and Islam as a religion and a political system has grown tremendously. But despite greater interest and a seemingly never-ending stream of politicians and seminars, understanding of Islam and Muslim world remains limited and selective. This selective analysis adds to ignorance instead of knowledge, narrows perspective instead of broadening understanding and reinforcing the problem instead of opening the way to new solutions. Consequently, Islam and Muslims have been reduced to stereotype of Islam against the west.

After the 9/11 tragedy I felt strongly about the distorted image of Islam in the western world. I sincerely desired to do something in this regard. Heart's earnest and pure desires are quite often fulfilled. Dame luck smiled at me and I was selected under the Visiting Specialist Programme: Rapid Access to the Muslim world. Thus new initiative on the part of US Department of State Bureau of Educational and Cultural Affairs is designed at expanding the knowledge and understanding of Islamic people and countries on the part of American students, faculty and communities. During my six weeks sojourn in America in 2004 I was specifically asked to speak on themes like Islam and Democracy, Islam and Human Rights, Islamic concept of *Jihad*, Islam and Women, US Misperceptions of Islam etc. all these presentations were followed by lengthy and lively discussions. The underlying presumptions in most of the questions put to me whether in classroom or at public engagement reflected American stereotypes of Islam. Even ostensibly informed discussion ended with a depressing conclusion that Islam, democratic and enlightening it might have been in the beginning is now hopelessly out of tune with concepts of democracy, individual freedom, free speech and gender equality. People have reason to ask? Why does this violence keep on happening in the name of peaceful religion? It was conveniently glossed over that most of the Muslim societies are the outgrowth of their own history and regional culture and have deviated from the prescribed Islamic values and norms. Most discussion of the so-called Islamic threat demonstrated a dearth of information and lack of discrimination concerning the nature of diversity of Islamic resurgence. On the positive side, it was evident from the many questions that there is a strong desire for people to understand Islam. People, by and large, especially students who are future leaders displayed a genuine concern about the widening gulf between America and the Muslim world. One thing that emerged very clearly was that the US must engage more actively in the process of analysis and dialogue with the Muslim world and also with the local Muslim communities. The need for better understanding of Islam and Muslim societies is greater than ever before. The US should try to better understand the outlook and perceptions of people in the Muslim world. On the basis of both values and interests, the natural relationship between Islam and America is one of friendship and cooperation. Historically, the US played a constructive role in the development of the Muslim world. There is no reason why the US should not continue to play such a role. What binds America and Islam is much more powerful than what divides them. The US should try to better understand the outlook and perceptions of the people in the Muslim world. In the aftermath of the 9/11, a great deal needs to be done to build bridges between America and the Muslim world.

Most of the chapters of the book are based on my presentations at various US academic institutions and forums. It is hoped they will be of some use to the policy makers, academics, students of international relations and general public in this vital area of relations between America and the Muslim world. I must thank my publisher for making this manuscript into a piece presentable to the wider readership. I must acknowledge the help and cooperation which the Gyan Publishers, particularly its dynamic Director, Mr. Amit Garg extended to me in bringing out this volume. Hopefully, the support extended in publishing this book will go a long way in bridging the gulf between Islam and western world headed by United States of America. Any omissions and communions, however, are entirely mine.

1
Islam and Democracy

Is liberal democracy basically compatible with Islam? Can democracy function in a society inspired by Islamic beliefs and principles and shaped by Islamic experience and traditions? Is Islam by its very nature antithetical to the development of democratic institutions? Is it possible for the Muslims to evolve a form of government that will be compatible with their own historical, cultural and religious traditions and yet will bring individual freedom and human rights to the governed as these terms are understood in the free societies of the world? What kind of political system does Islam legitimate? What is Islam's concept of man and the rights of individual? How the accountability to God can be combined with the accountability to the people in a government? An attempt is being made here to find answers to these and similar questions.

Problems of Methodology

In order to address these questions, one should first resolve a problem of methodology. In Islam as in other religions and philosophies, there is always a room for different interpretations. How is one to judge Islamicity, the representativeness of these different interpretations. The answer to this question lies in the fact that at the heart of Islamic principles, values and laws, are two sources viz the Quran and Hadith (saying of the Prophet) Islamic culture throughout the centuries has been centered on these two sources.

Democracy

The term democracy indicates both a set of ideas and principles and a political system, a mechanism for governance and a politico-legal culture. The philosophical roots of democracy lie in the concept of popular sovereignty. The real test for democracy is its principle of legitimacy, laying down that the power is legitimate only when it is derived from the authority of the people and is based on their consent. The other dimensions of democracy relate to a variety of forms of self government and popular participation in political decision-making. The substance of democracy seeks expression in the vision of a government that is chosen by the people, operates in the service of the people in accordance with their wishes and preferences, and is accountable before them. The democratic world is not monolithic. It contains several different forms of government. Republics and monarchies, presidential and parliamentary secular states and established churches and a wide range of electoral systems – but all of them share certain basic assumptions that mark the distinction between democratic and undemocratic governments.

Nature of Islam

Islam is not a religion in the limited sense of the term. It is a complete code of conduct, a comprehensive and all-embracing way of life. It covers all aspects of human existence. The Islamic political system is not something independent or self-contained. It is part of Islamic way of life and is inseparable from other aspects of religion. It provides a world view, a vision and a set of values and leaves enough room to work out details to meet all the emerging challenges of time. Since the teachings of Islam insist on the unity of man's life and reflects separation between God and Caesar, most students of political Islam tend to classify an Islamic government as necessarily a theocratic government. The confusion in this respect results from another principle of Islamic government, namely, that the laws of a Muslim land should always be derived from or at least conform to the principle of Islamic law (the Shariah). Political scientists and constitutional lawyers should distinguish two separate issues: the basis of political power and authority on the one hand, and the sources of the legal system on the other. The political system as envisaged by Islam has nothing to do with theocratic government. The Islamic state is characterized by the supremacy of shariah yet it is diametrically different from theocracy. Theocracy, as it has been known in history stood far divine rule through an ecclesiastical class whose word became the law, undisputed and indisputable. In clear contrast to western concept of theocracy, Islam was a revolt against all anthromorphic implications in the realm of faith. The long western struggle between church and state is quite alien to Islamic thought; for Islam does not authorize any material form, human or institutional, that could claim to be representative of God. In Islam there is no provision of priestly class or religious intermediaries between God and man. Prophethood ended with Prophet Mohammad. The guidance has been perfected Allah's will is clearly available in the form of Quran and Sunna. The Shariah is a known quantity and not a divine secret known only to the priesthood. Islam does not establish a clergy and scholars of theology and Islamic laws are ordinary people. Islam does not call for a government whose authority is based on a divine will. Nor does it call for a government of clerics. According to the consensus of Muslim Sunni jurists the legitimacy of any government derives from the consent of the people. Rulers have no divine rights of any kind and are bound by rule of law. In Islam there is no possibility of any group of people imposing their personal will or preferences over others in the name of God. In brief, there is no theocracy in Islam for it does not confer Divine Rights on any elected or hereditary class.

The fact that the source of Islamic law is divine inspiration, revealed more than 1500 years ago may raise doubts regarding its ability to adjust to contemporary needs. It is worth noting that neither the Quran nor the Hadith contain all the legal norms necessary for the organization of society. In certain spheres of law, they only enunciate broad principles and basic values which need to be concretized and implemented through man made laws and conventions. It is community which has to understand and implement the Divine Guidance in the light of changing scenarios. It is through an open process of debate and discussion that the law is developed.

Quran and Form of Government

Some of the verses which provide a clue for the organization of Islamic state are:

(i) "And their rule is by counsel amongst themselves" (42:38)

(ii) Pardon them and seek protection from them and take counsel from them in the affairs of the state" (3:158)

(iii) Allah commands you to make over trust to those worthy of them and when you judge between people, you judge with justice (4:38)

(iv) "Oh! David, we have made thee a Khalifa in the land, so judge the people with justice and do not follow thy desires" (38:26)

(v) "Obey Allah and obey the messenger and those in authority from among you and if you quarrel about anything, refer it to Allah and its Messenger" (4: 58 & 59).

The first two items highlight the necessity of having a democratic consultation and the duty of taking counsel between the believers; items 3 and 4 create the obligation of the people to repose their trust in those who are worthy of their trust and to abide by the duty to do justice when it comes to judging the relative claims of various persons. The last item lays down the unconditional obedience which is to be shown to the word of God and the Sunna of Prophet and those who are in authority over the affairs of believers. It is with reference to these ideas that Muslim polity is to be organized. There is no fixed form or specific structure of society which is prescribed. A religion that claims to be universal and therefore valid for all times could not very well have given a fixed formula for designing the machinery of actual form of government.

Character of Islamic Polity Under Prophet

So long as the Prophet lived, he was the religious and political head of the government. He was not elected or selected by anyone but was chosen by God, the absolute sovereign, as messenger as well as the ruler of the state which he established at Madina, soon after his migration from Mecca. Prophet Mohammad had established a system that was representative and consultative, transparent, accountable and accessible to everyone. He had voluntarily limited and circumscribed his political administrative powers. The polity in Madina was based on principles of limited government, devolution of executive powers, and compassionate sharing of economic resources and social fraternity. Philip Hitti, the well-known historian in his celebrated work the History of Arabs beautifully summarizes the manner in which the Islamic State functioned under the Prophet: "This Islamic society or the commonwealth which the Prophet (of Islam) set up, was based on perfect equality and justice for all with divine sovereignty as its cardinal principle".

Principle of Consensus

After the demise of the Prophet, the first caliph Abu Bekr was democratically elected by the people of Madina at a conclave.

Interestingly most of the participants were Madinites while the caliph elected was a migrant from Mecca. It was through consensus. The second Caliph Umar was nominated by the first Caliph as his successor. But his selection was not treated valid till approved by the congregation in a mosque. Umar on his turn set up a council of six persons charging them with the duty of electing one of themselves as the Caliph by appeal to the majority principle. Last Caliph Ali was elected by the majority. The very fact that each Caliph was appointed with reference to different methods of selection was consistent with the principle that the right to choose Caliph belongs to the entire body of Ummah and it is entitled to do so by resort to any method it sees fit. The first four Caliphs popularly known as Khufa-e-Rashideen or Pious Caliphs were elected by the community though the methods of selection and approval differed. The common principle was the consent and confidence of the community and accountability. The first caliph Abu Bekr in his first sermon had admitted the right of people to control the caliph. If I do well, support me; if ill, put me right, obey me as I obey the Lord and His Prophet; where in I disobey, obey me not". In fact, the Islamic tradition of rules limiting the powers of the sovereign is much older than the concept of constitutional law in the western democracies. One can all an Islamic state a republic since the sharvat law rules out usurpation and succession as grounds of political legitimacy. The Prophet himself had evolved a system of consultation and consensus building and the Pious Caliphate was subject to the supremacy Quran and Shariah. Here the practice of bayth deserves a little elaboration. The word comes from an Arabic root meaning to "barter", hence to "buy and sell", and originally referring to the clasping on slapping of hands with which in ancient Arabia a deal was normally concluded. The essence of baya is free public consent. Therefore, those who make this contract on behalf of the people should be their trusted and followed representatives rather than their oppressors and intimidators. The best possible way to reach this goal in a contemporary Muslim society is the public vote. The bayth was thus conceived as a contract by which the subjects undertook to obey and the Caliph in return undertook to perform certain duties specified by the jurists. If the Caliph failed in those duties and Islamic history shows that this was by no means a purely theoretical point- he could subject to certain conditions, be removed from office. Thus, according to Sunni Muslim doctrine, the relationship between the Caliph and his subjects was contractual. According to this doctrine the Caliph was to be elected by those qualified to make a choice. The electorate was never defined, nor was any procedure of elections was ever devised or operated but the elective principle remains central to Sunni religious jurisprudence and that is important.

Key Elements of Islamic Political System

1. In Islam, sovereignty belongs to God alone. He is the Creator, the Master, the Law-giver and the Guide. All human beings are equal before the Lord and subject to the same Law, He has ordained. The Islami political system is based on the principle of sovereignty of Allah and the supremacy of the Shariah. The legitimacy of the system comes from the loyalty and obedience to Allah and commitment to follow and establish the Shariah.
2. A human is a vicegerent, Khalifa and representative of God on earth. The concept is one of popular viceregency, shared by all believers. The authority is endowed, not in any chosen persons, family, tribe or group but on all Muslim men and women and it is they who have to exercise power in accordance with the Islamic principle of shura or consultation. The theory that follows from inspirations of Quran and Hadith lays down two cardinal principles:
3. first God's sovereignty and second of the popular viceregency of the believers. Hence, legitimacy in the Islamic political order comes, first and foremost, from accepting Allah as the sovereign and His laws, shariah as the supreme law and secondly, the governance of society by and in accordance with the will of the people. Those in authority must enjoy the confidence and support of the Ummah, the real repositories of Caliph. According to Quran:

"Allah has promised to those among you who believe and do righteous deeds that He will assuredly make them to succeed (those who rule and grant them regency in the land just as made those before them succeed (others)" 2455.

It is clear from the verse that authority or assignment to rule over the earth has been promised to the entire community of believers and not to any particular person, family, class or group All are equal as members of the society and criteria for leadership is tied to their qualities of trustworthiness, competence, God consciousness, dutifulness and sense of accountability. Accountability is not only before God, it is also before the law and the people.

Concept of Consultation

It has great significance in the political system of Islam. The process of consultation has been recommended in the Quran. It says: "And who respond to (the call of) their sustainer and are constant in prayer; and who rule (in all matters of common concern) in consultation among themselves." (42:38). Significantly, the Prophet himself was asked to consult his companions in important matters. According to Quran:

"And take counsel with them in all matters of common concern." (3:159). The Quran makes it very clear that mutual consultation is highly desirable and requires no less a person than the Prophet himself to consult his companions. The Prophet on his part implemented the Quranic teachings meticulously. For instance, decision to release prisoners of war during the Battle of Badar was taken by the Prophet after consultation with his companions. It is worth recalling that during the period of Pious Caliphate whenever a new law was to be enacted and enforced, it used to be done after careful deliberations and extensive consultations among the knowledgeable companions of the Prophet. The decision used to be taken democratically through consensus within the framework of basic principles of Quran. Hence, the principle of democracy was deployed by Islam right from its inception. To quote another eminent historian Bernard Lewis. "According to Islamic principle of consultation, a ruler should not make arbitrary decisions by himself but should act only after consultation." Prophet himself instituted a system of consultation and consensus building. Later this consultative process was almost developed into an indirect representative institution called Majlis-i-Shura (consultative council). The Majlis-i-Shura comes closest to a modern day parliament. The concept of shura implied that the people must directly participate in the government. It is mandated in the Quran and modern application of this Quranic mandate is a form of democracy very similar to that seen in the western world based on "one person-one vote" as the expression of the mutual consultation of the people. Clearly if the concept of shura is understood to mean a broad-based consultation which is then binding upon the ruler, then the remitting system is democratic in character.

Separation of Judiciary from Executive

Separation of judiciary from the Executive and its total independence at all levels has been a cardinal feature of the Islamic polity. Rule of laws and access to justice for all remained inalienable aspects of Muslim Society. The judiciary was vested in the Qazis so much that even the Caliph had no immunity from the judicial process. He could be summoned in a judicial forum to answer the charge should it brought against him, at the instance of anybody who felt aggrieved by what he did or failed to do. The principle of separation of powers, established as it was during the Pious Caliphate, continued in later periods, despite certain degeneration in the system. The supremacy of the constitution i.e. Islamic law remained on integral part of the Muslim experience. The entire legal system developed outside the corridors of political power and once established, the rulers were as much subject to this law as were commoners. Needless to say this had worked as a great check on arbitrary power and entrenched the true credential of participatory democracy in a Muslim society.

Social Security

Another cardinal feature of Islam relates to the system of social security based on Zakat. The Prophet defined Zakat in these words. "God has laid down on them a tax which is taken from the rich and returned to the poor. (Bukhari, Kitab-al-Zakat, vol. vi, p. 187). Here phrase returned to the poor is very significant. It indicates that the wealth taken from the rich belongs, in fact, to the poor. Islam instituted the system of Zakat to ensure that no individual falls below a certain minimum of material well-being. The income from tax was distributed to the poor and needy section of society. This led to the establishment of an egalitarian socio-economic system, enabling all members of society to seek a respectable living. The economic organization of society was such that it enabled the weaker section to stand up and participate in political and economic processes. After consolidating his state in Madina, Prophet took steps towards ensuring that no orphan remained unsupported and no family whose bread earner had died remained unhelped. Thus every effort was made to ensure economic equality without which political equality is meaningless.

Islam and Human Rights

According to the Quran, man is the vice-regent of the Almighty. The human race is the chosen vehicle of God. Prophet Adam and his descendents are elevated above all other creatures, and respect for their dignity is a cornerstone of Islamic morality and social organization. From this concept of man stems the entire theory of human rights. These include the sanctity and protection of human life, absolute freedom of thought, and basic freedom of opinion. The Quran and Sunnah having made in several occasions references to the rights of different sections of society. These rights are also extended to the enjoyment of non-Muslims in an Islamic state. In other words, Islam granted a full-fledged Bill of Rights which is to be accepted throughout the globe. The Quran lays down fundamental values which were applied to the then society by the jurists. The value pronouncements of the Quran-religious justice, equality of all irrespective of colour, race and ethnicity, gender equality, just distribution of economic resources – are amongst the most modern and it is these pronouncements which are fundamental to Islam. Each universally accepted human right finds correspondence in Quranic pronouncements. The Quran unequivocally stipulates the protection of these rights in the most categorical manner.

Islam insist on the protection of human rights and its universal application. It rejects the selective application of the principles of human rights governed by political exigencies. Unfortunately Islam is being mixed up with Muslim societies in different Muslim countries. It is conveniently forgotten that these Muslim societies are the outgrowth of their own historical and political backgrounds and may not be exactly representative of the Quranic value system.

Tolerance

Islam also accepts principle of tolerance and pluralism. It gives to all human beings the right to belief and profession. It accepts the multiplicity of cultures and community styles. Almost from the outset, the Islamic world demonstrated on astonishing diversity. Extending over 3 continents, it embraced a wide variety of races, creeds and cultures which lived side by side in reasonable harmony, Sectarian strife and religious persecutions are not unknown in Islamic history but they are rare, and never reached the level of intensity of the great religious wars and persecutions. Not only the Muslims advised to respect freedom of religion and conscience, they are even expected to be magnanimous to those non-Muslims who do not fight against themselves in the cause of religion. The Quran says: "All forbiddeth you not respecting those who warred not against you on account of religion and drove you not out of your homes that ye should shown them kindness and deal with them. Lo! Allah loves that jirst dealers" (60:8) When Mecca came under the sway of Muslims and Prophet Mohammad entered Mecca, then no one was asked to accept Islam as part of the settlement. As far as inter-faith relations, Quran and Hadith are explicit about the desirability of good relations between peoples. Non-Muslims are given the right to regulate their private life education and family life by adopting their own family laws. More important Muslims are morally bound to relate to non-Muslim minorities positively Muslims have a moral obligation to be fair and friendly in their person-to-person conduct towards non-Muslim citizens, and will be ansawerable to God for that. They must treat them with trust, benevolence and equity.

The Prophet himself set an example of religious toleration when he established a city-state at Madina. He drew up its constitution, which was committed to writing at his instance. This constitution included two significant passages: first Muslims will have their religion and Jews will be entitled to their religion; secondly, Muslims and Jews will together constitute a community. This convenant was extended at a later stage to the Christians of Najran and the pagan Arabs. Thus, the Pan Islamica included not only Muslims but also Jews, Christians and pagan Arabs, and guaranteed to their religious, cultural and judicial autonomy. In fact the Islamic State assumed responsibility for the maintenance and even defence of Jewish, Christian and pagan identities. The charter of rights and assurances issued to the Christian population of Najran by the Prophet included the following passage; "An assurance in hereby extended, on behalf of God and the Prophet to the people of Najran that their lives, religion, lands and wealth will be protected. No change in their existing condition will be affected. These rights will not be violated. Their commercial caravans and delegations will be protected. No cardinal will be dismissed from his position, nor will an ascetic be denied the right to his way of life. The custodians of churches will face no interference in respect of their functions. At the state level freedom of religion, was seen as a paramount pillar of Islamic state. Special care was extended to ensure this freedom for the state's non-Muslim citizens. The state guaranteed protection of the life, property, honour and freedom of conscience of all its non-Muslim subjects. When Jerusalem came under the rule of the Muslims, Caliph Umar himself went to accept the surrender. He immediately granted to its people what was known as the Charter of Rights in the year 638 AD. This charter stands as a living testament of the basic principle of liberty, security, and freedom of faith which Islam offers to all people. It reads: "In the name of God, the Merciful, the compassionate. This is the security which Umar, the servant of God, the commander of the faithful, grants to the people of Aylia. He grants to all, whether sick or sound, security for their lives, their possessions, their churches, and their crosses and for all that concerns their religion. Their churches shall neither be changed into dwelling places nor destroyed, neither shall they, nor their appurtenances, nor any of their possessions, be in any way diminished; nor shall they any constraint be put on them in the matter of their faith, nor shall any one of them be harmed".

Acceptance of Dissent and Opposition

Last but not the least, another important feature of Muslim experience relates to its acceptance of dissent and opposition – individual as well as collective – as something authentic and as part of the tradition – and not something outside it. The Prophet once said: "If anyone sees an evil, he should get it right with his hand; if he is unable to do so, then with his tongue; and if he is unable to do even that, then let him denounce it in his heart. But this last is the weakest form of faith."

On another occasion Prophet observed "The best form of Jihad is to utter a word to tyrannical ruler." Thus, right to criticize the government has been recognized in an Islamic state. Of course, a distinction was made between ikhtilaf (differences) and fitna (rebellion) but it is significant that at least in certain major schools of Islamic laws, opposition that involves even armed rebellion (khruj) is accepted as legitimate.

The above features are illustrative of the Muslim tradition of governance and constitute significant pointers towards the development of a distinctly Islamic model of democratic governance. The picture that emerges from these guidelines is quite clear. This is a faith based society. Its sheet anchor is loyalty to God. There is however, no room for any privileged or priestly class. All have equal rights and obligations. All are equally responsible before law. The rulers do not enjoy any arbitrary power. Freedom and equality are the very breadth of this society. Consultation and participation in decision-making is the way. The concept of an Islamic state reveals that most of the modern theories of constitutional government like social contract, separation of powers, checks and balances, rule of law, natural justice, equality before the law, government as a trust, welfare of the people were known to Muslims from the earliest times. The example of four caliphs who succeeded Prophet at the inception of Islam proves that democratic methods of succession and governance were necessary for Muslim world and in line with Islamic teachings. The four rightly guided caliphs sought to win the people by the example of moral excellence and did not impose their will upon their followers.

Historical record clearly belies the assertions of those who maintain that Islam and democracy are incompatible. In fact there is no incompatibility between Islam and truly democratic system based on people's participation and power sharing. On the contrary, democratization in the sense of freedom of people, fundamental rights and people's participation are natural callories. If democracy means rights of a people to self-determination and self-fulfilment, that is what Islam stands for. There is no contradiction between Islam and democracy. Whatever despotic or arbitrary rule exists in Muslim lands is part of an alien and imposed traditions, against which forces of Islamic resurgence are fighting. Dictators reigning in the West Asia are not the results of Islamic principles. They are more a result of global economics and the aftermath of European imperialism. Islam and democratization are the two sides of the same coin. As such democratic processes and Islam would go hand by hand. Islam prescribes the principles and values of Islamic political order but not its form. Forms are human creations. Man is invited to use his reason and intellect to carve out forms based on conceptual frame of Islam. Democracy is a form of political set up, that is human creation and safely be preferred over other political systems. Muslim world needs to adopt a form of democracy suited to its own nature and become democratic world partner without needing to be exactly the same as western societies.

To sum up, there can be no great difficulty in establishing an Islamic state within the framework of modern democracy based on political theories of the present day statecraft. The ideals of freedom for all human beings, of human brotherhood, of the equality of all men before the law; of democratic government by consultation and universal suffrage, the ideals that inspired the French Revolution and the Declaration of Human Rights, that guided the American constitution find their expression in the Quran and Sunnah. Democracy as conceived in the modern west is infinitely nearer to Islamic concept, for Islam maintains that all human beings are socially equal and must, therefore, be given the same opportunities for development and self-expression. If one goes by Quran and Hadith Islam appears to be quite close to democracy. To quote Bernard Lewis, "Islam offers the best prospects for western style democracy. Historically, culturally, religiously, it is closest to the west, sharing much-though by no means all-of the Judeo-Christian and Greco-Roman heritage that helped to form our new civilization".

Historically, for a variety of reasons, Islam tended towards autocratic governments. Greater stress was placed on obedience to ruler than consent of the governed or consultation with them in political decision making. It may be due to the fact that initially, united fiercely independent nomadic tribes in Arabia lived with no central authority. It is worth remembering that when the basic institutions of democracy were being developed in the west, most of the Muslims world was under the grip of colonialism. This to a large extent, precluded a similar development within the Muslim world. Hence, there is no historical representative democratic precedent in Muslim world upon which to rely. However, the dictators reigning in the Middle East are not the result of Islamic principles. They are more a result of global economics and the aftermath of European colonialism.

However, in recent years many Muslims have came to accept the notion of democracy. The Islamization of democracy has been based on a modern process of reinterpretation of traditional Islamic concepts of politics deliberation or consultation (Shura), community consensus (ijma) and personal interpretation (ijtiad) or reinterpretations to support notions of parliamentary democracy and elections. Many Islamic activists have Islamized parliamentary democracy and have appealed to democracy in their opposition to incumbent regimes. Islamic organizations such as the Muslim Brotherhood in Egypt and Jordon, Jamat-i-Islami in India Pakistan, Bangladesh and Kashmir, Turkey's Refah party. Malaysia's ABIM and PAS, Indonesia's Muhammadya and Nadhatual Ulama among others have advocated the principle of democratic elections and where permitted, have participated in parliamentary elections. There appears to have emerged a general agreement among mainstream Islamists that democracy is the spirit of the Islamic governmental system even though they rejected the philosophical assumptions of western democracy that sovereignty rests with the people. They maintain that since the Quran commands Muslims to conduct their collective affairs through mutual consultation (shura) and grants the privilege of God's viceregency (Khalifa) to the entire Muslim community rather than to a group or class of people, the selection of a Muslim ruler must be based on the free will of the Muslim masses. With this concept of popular viceregency, Islamists reject the institution of Kingship and monarchy as un-Islamic. Maulana Maududi's Caliphate and Monarchy and Khomeni's Islamic government constitute the most devastating critiques and condemnations of monarchs and absolutists rule from an Islamic perspective in modern Islam. Significantly, Islamic movements in Pakistan, Malayasia and North Africa define the governmental structure of an Islamic state in terms no different from a Westminster type of parliamentary democracy, universal adult suffrage, periodic elections, guaranteed human rights, civil liberties, equal political and rights of minorities, an independent judiciary, the rule of law and multiple political parties. Interestingly, the well-known political thinker and leader of Islamic movement in Sudan, Hasan Turabi who is vilified in US as an extremist, entirely incompatible with western thinking is of the view: "In a large Islamic state, consultation would have to be indirect and undertaken by representatives of the people. It follows that an Islamic form of government is essentially form of representative democracy". Thus, across, the ideological spectrum of liberal to conservative scholars, Muslims have reached the same conclusion: the cultural expression of Islamic political principles in some form of representative democracy.

History shows that religious traditions are capable of having multiple ideological interpretations on reorientations. The Judeo-Christian institutions, which once supported political absolutism and divine rights of monarchs was reinterpreted to accommodate democratic idea. The same may be true in the case of Islam also. Democracy has became an integral part of modern Islamic political right and practice. It has been accepted in several Muslim states. However, dissimilation in the Muslim world does not necessarily mean uncritical acceptance of western from of democracy. Historically democracy in the west has taken many forms adopting itself to local conditions. Not unexpectedly, the record of Islamic democratic extremists has been diverse and incongruent what is important is not that they are corrupted but that they are part of a process of real attempts at reconciling Islam and democracy. Some may fool others, as has been the card in the west, may lead it morpe.

2
Islamic Concept of Jihad–Myths and Reality

There exists great misconception about the duty of Jihad in Islam. It is supposed to be synonymous with 'holy war', a usage the media has popularised. However, the term holy war is alien language in Islamic literature. It does not have a counterpart in Islamic glossary and Jihad is certainty not its translation. According to Islamic teachings it is unholy to start a war. As a matter of fact the term holy war was coined in Europe during the Crusades, meaning the war against Muslims.

Literally, the Arabic word Jihad means struggling or striving. It applies to any effort exerted by anyone. The word Jihad has nowhere been used in the Quran to imply war in the sense of launching an offensive. It is deployed rather to mean struggle. In its primary sense it is a spiritual struggle within one's self to rid one from debased action or inclination. The action most consistently called for in the Quran is the exercise of patience. Jihad in Islam requires the believers to do whatever they can towards popularising, defending and keeping alive and flourishing as the best and truest life the way of Islam and servility to God. The Quran and Hadith (sayings of Prophet) use the world Jihad in several different contexts. It can take several forms depending on the circumstances varying from time to time and place to place. For instance to carry the divine guidance to those that are ignorant of it and make an earnest effort to persuade them to accept it is a form of Jihad. Then, to speak a just word, before a tyrannical ruler – be a Muslim or a non-Muslim – is, again a form of Jihad. According to Hadith, it has been termed as the best form of Jihad. Significantly, military action is just a sub-group of Jihad and not its totality. Jihad is not a declaration of war against other religions. Not everyone can declare a Jihad. It is a collective struggle to defend self, property, religion not just a vigilante movement.

Rigorous Conditions: Islam imposes strict conditions for waging a Jihad. First, such a step must not be motivated by any personal or national or self-interest, greed or enmity. It should be taken solely to carry out the command of God and to serve the cause of His Faith. Secondly there should be some persons who, by their character and outward appearance look like true slaves of God. Thirdly, owing allegiance to an Ameer, political ruler is a necessary precondition for carrying out a Jihad for the sake of God. If the force is used without the fulfillment of these conditions, it will not be Jihad according to Islam but wanton wickedness and mischief.

Jihad and Terrorism: A distinction must be made between Jihad and terrorism. They are antithesis of each other. But those who do not understand Islam and those who have a vested interest in distorting truth about the religion of Islam, have been trying to make the word terrorist and terrorism synonymous to Jihad. While terrorism is a violent act that violates international law and intends to intimidate civilians, and influence government policies through coercion. On the other hand, Islam condemns killing of civilians for political purposes. Terrorism is a secret act by a group of politically motivated individuals but Jihad is an announced strategy that calls upon armed battalions to conduct a war. Inward and outward peace is the goal of Jihad, while terrorism seeks only more conflict and chaos. Islam never allows an individual or group to take another person's life without ample justification. Murder is so much detested in the eyes of Allah that murder of one innocent person has been held as equal to the murder of entire humanity. Indeed no condemnation of a killer could be stronger than of holding him guilty of having killed all humankind. When a single such killing is regarded as serious as this, one can imagine how heinous will be the killing of large number of people. Islam awards death penalty for such a crime, intending to act as a deterrent. Terrorism means indiscriminate killing but Islam forbids violence against innocent civilians, women, children, the elderly and the environment in Jihad. Jihad in Islam does not include striving for individual or national power, dominance, glory, wealth, privilege and pride. Any aggressive act which leads to the killing of the innocent, irrespective of religion, community and colour is strictly forbidden in Islam and is deemed a heinous sin. In the light of outright condemnation of the shedding of blood of the innocent, Islam cannot and does not support acts of terrorism in any form. Similarly, there is no Quranic support for suicidal bombing. Significantly, suicide as such is prohibited in Islam and whoever commits suicide will be denied a place in heaven. Therefore, acts of terrorism performed by the Muslims will have to be viewed in the historical and political context and not as licensed by Islam.

The very word Islam is the negation of the concept of violence. Islam means, surrender to the will of God on the one hand, and establishing peace, on the other. Prophet of Islam was born at a time when an atmosphere of militancy prevailed in the Arab society. But Prophet Mohammad always opted for avoidance of conflict. For instance, in the campaign of Ahzab, Prophet advised his companions to dig a trench between them and the enemies, thus prevented a head-on-clash. Another well-known example of prophet's dislike for hostilities is the Hudaibiyah peace treaty made by accepting unilaterally all the conditions of enemy. On all occasions prophet tried to accomplish his aims by peaceful rather war-like means. Throughout the history of Islam, armed struggle was controlled and limited to a specific purpose, which is to fight those who fight against the Muslims. Jihad in Islam is striving in the way of Allah by pen, tongue, hand, media and if inevitable with arms. Islam abhors wars of aggression, and the killing of innocent people. Defensive wars are permitted. Islam does not allow the killing of people merely because they embrace a different faith, nor does it allow Muslims to fight against those who disagree with them on religious questions. Islam as a religion is totally against terrorism meaning senseless murder of innocent people.

It is really unfortunate that today the focus is on Islamic terrorism. It is argued that Islam as such has something to do with terrorism and that Muslims can not live in peace with other communities and faiths. Ever since the 11 September tragedy, attempts are being made at the behest of vested elements to tar Islam with the terrorism brush. This is atrocious and alarming. A thief is not referred by his religion. There is nothing like a Muslim thief, Hindu thief or a Christian thief. Terrorism as an act of violence has been committed by people from all religions and political backgrounds. None of these groups represent the true religions of the Jews or the Christians as these terrorists represent Islam. Terrorism has never been endorsed by any religion, least of all by Islam.

One may ask why so great a contradiction exists between the principles of Islam and practices of a section of Muslims. Well, Muslim societies are the outgrowth of their own history and regional culture and have deviated from the prescribed Islamic values and norms. Significantly, terrorism was introduced to the Muslim world by Zionists who founded the state of Israel. The very terrorism unleashed by the state of Israel has become the "role model" for the outbreak of Arab and some other Muslim terrorism. The volatility of that part of the world is not necessarily caused by Islamic activity as such. It is much less a manifestation of religious fervour than of political and economic justifications. The problem is that some Muslim activists are carrying out their militant campaign in the name of Islam and people perceive these movements as acts approved by Islamic tenets. Nothing could be farther from the truth if one goes by Islamic teachings. Islam has to be assessed on the principles enunciated and values promoted in the Quran and the traditions of Prophet who is remembered as the harbinger of kindness and mercy for the entire universe. Islam is definitely opposed to the culture of bullets and bombs. It teaches peace, compassion and forgiveness. Unfortunately a label of Jihad is put on every conflict. This is simply bringing out bad name to Islam and misuse of pious and holy word of Jihad in the path of God. Liberally every struggle is a Jihad. But Jihad in the way of God is something else and its terms and conditions are different. Jihad in the path of God will take the form of a battle only if certain conditions are fulfilled.

3

Islam and Human Rights

Quran and Fundamental Rights

At the outset, references may be made to some of the verses of the Holy Quran wherein principles in the nature of fundamental rights have been enunciated:

Equality of All Persons:

O' mankind; We have created you male and female, and have made you nations and tribes that you may know one another. The noblest of you, in the eyes of Allah, is the best in conduct (H9:13)

Mankind was one single nation (2:213)

Freedom of Conscience

Let there be no compulsion in religion (2:256)

Rule of Law

If ye judge between mankind, that ye judge justly (4:58)

Deal justly, that is nearer to your duty (5:9)

No Liability for the action of others

No bearer of burdens can bear the burden of another (6:164)

Right of Privacy

O'ye who believe! Enter not houses other than your own without first announcing your presence and invoking peace upon the folk thereof (24:27).

Injunction Against suspicion and spying

O'ye believe! Shun much suspicion for lo! Some suspicion is crime. And spy not, neither backbite one another. Would one of you love to eat the flesh of his dead brother? (49:12)

Free Trade

O'ye believe! Squander not your wealth among yourselves in vanity, except it be a trade by mutual consent (4:29)

According to the Quran, man is the viceregent of the Almighty. The human race is the chosen vehicle of God. Prophet Adam and his descendents are elevated above all other creatures, and respect for their dignity is a cornerstone of Islamic morality and social organization. From this concept of man stems the entire theory of human rights. These include the sanctity and protection of human life, absolute freedom of thought, and basic freedom of opinion. The Quran and Hadith (the prophet's saying) have made in several occasions references to the rights of different sections of society. These rights are also extended to the enjoyment of non-Muslims in an Islamic state. In other words, Islam granted a full-fledged Bill of Rights which is to be accepted throughout the globe. The Quran lays down fundamental values which were applied to the then society by the jurists. The value pronouncements of the Quran-religious justice, equality of all irrespective of colour, race and ethnicity, gender equality, just distribution of economic resources – are amongst the most modern and it is these pronouncements which are fundamental to Islam. Each universally accepted human right finds correspondence in Quranic pronouncements. The Quran unequivocally stipulates the protection of these rights in the most categorical manner.

The right of life is an important aspect of the UN Declaration of Human Rights. The Quran also stresses that one cannot take the life of any person, including non-Muslims, without a just reason and due process of law. The Quran says, "Whoever kills a person unless it be for manslaughter or for mischief in the land, it is as though he had killed all mankind and whoever saves a life, it is as though he had saved the lives of all men". (532) Laying emphasis on the sanctity of human life prophet Mahammod in his last pilgrimage message says, "O, you people, be aware that your blood, your property and your honour are protected from aggression amongst you. They are as sacred as the culmination day of pilgrimage in the sacred city of Mecca". Significantly, in Islam capital punishment is reserved for only three crimes, one of which is the killing of another human. Islam ensures the sanctity of life through imposing ban on killing man except on reasonable grounds.

According to the Quran and Sunnah (the body of Islamic custom) speech or the use of the word is not simply a freedom but also an obligation on every believer. The duty of inviting to the good and warning against the evil is a religious and moral duty of first priority in Islam. According to the Quran witnesses are enjoined to give testimony and are warned against refraining there from. It says: the witnesses should not refuse when they are called on (2:282). It further says: "conceal not evidence, for whoever conceals it, his heart is tainted with sin". A witness is by an explicit Quranic verse-protected against any harm he may suffer because of his testimony. The writer of his opinion or of someone else's testimony receives equal guarantees. Right to criticize has been recognized in an Islamic state.

The Quranic statement that there is no compulsion in religion is quite significant. It says: "there is no compulsion in religion, truth stands clear from error" (2:256). The Quran also upholds the right of individual to worship the way he/she desires even if it be an idolatrous way of worshipping. The right to worship in one's way is emphasized in several verses of the Quran. The protection of freedom of belief is carried to extremes, as manifested by the Quranic verse regarding believers to give refuge to those who associate a different God than Allah with the Almighty, if they seek such a refuge. A Muslim is required moreover to guide such a refugee until he reaches a safe place. Regarding the rights of non-Muslims, Islam is very liberal and it extends them full freedom to observe their respective religions. It ensures all types of social rights to the non-Muslims. Non-Muslims enjoy full security of their lives and property. Likewise, they enjoy full rights of educational facilities. They enjoy maximum political rights.

It is generally believed that Islam is unfair to women and their rights. This is far from truth. It is necessary to differentiate Islamic principles from the state of affairs prevailing in various Muslims countries. The Quran is most categorical in pronouncing the equality of men and women. In fact, the Quran is the first revealed book which defines women's rights concretely in respect of marriage, divorce, inheritance and property. In the marriage contract, a woman has an equal right and, in fact marry on her own conditions. The Quran gives women the right to free themselves from marriage by compensating the husband for the *mehr* given by him at the time of marriage. As far as Quran is concerned, polygamy it is permitted in exceptional circumstances and on rigorous condition of justice and equality between all wives. If one reads the two verses on polygamy, it becomes clear that polygamy is allowed in extraordinary circumstances. The right of men to divorce their wives is not an absolute right. Women are not deprived of the right to stipulate a similar right at the time the marriage contract is executed. Women have the right to property by way of inheritance or her own earning. She retains her complete financial independence from her husband and her wealth and property remains her after her marriage. The Quranic norm is clearly sexual equality, not male superiority. It is clearly stated in verse 2:228 wherein her rights are equated to what is held against her i.e., her duties. It is even more explicitly stated in the verse 33:35 which leaves no one in doubt about the Quran's concept of sexual equality. Islam places women at the same level as men with respect to property, honour, marriage, education etc. it ensures her right to life by protecting in strong language the then prevailing practice of burying the new born female infants. Because of the Taliban action in Afghanistan, the impression is being created that Islam discriminates against women. In fact, the Quran nowhere deprives women of their right to earn their own livelihood, let alone confine them to their homes.

Equality of all people regardless of their race, colour, sex and language is in fact the foundation of Islam's concept of human relations, on both the individual and the collective levels. Islam rejects all distinctions of birth, class, race, colour and language. Anyone who believes in one Allah as his Lord and accepts the guidance of the Prophet as the law of this life can be a member of the Muslim society. A convert from a humble origin can enjoy the same rights and privileges as one who belonged to the noblest. Islam recognizes the right of every person irrespective of caste, creed and religion to meet their basic economic needs life, food, shelter clothes, education etc. In respect of employment and earnings, equal opportunities are open to all. Everyone is allowed to adopt any profession or service according to will and ability. If anyone fails to meet his basic needs through personal income, despite his best efforts to do so, he is exhibited to financial assistance from the society. Besides special grants are also offered by the state to the unemployed, the disabled and the family of the diseased person. In this way Islam offers complete security of basic needs to the society. Contrary to the claims of orientalists, slavery is not an Islamic social institution. Slavery was a social institution in the Arabian peninsula prior to the advent of Islam. Islam gradually but in a most effective manner-liquidated that inhuman institution. Islam created a radical transformation in the status and position of slaves. The prophet spoke of slaves as brothers since they all are descended from the same father,

Adam. In this way slaves in Islam enjoyed ranks and position unparallel in world history.

The unity of mankind is repeatedly stressed in the Quran. For instance it says: O, mankind be conscious of your sustainer, who has created you out of one living entity, and out of it created its mate, and out of the two a broad multitude of men and women. And remain conscious of God, in whose name you demand (your rights) from one another and of these ties of kinship. Verily God is ever watchful over you (4:1). In another verse while stressing the unity of mankind the Quran demolishes completely racial discrimination and asserts that piety and noble deeds alone raise the status of persons in the eyes of Allah. They alone are treated with honour and dignity. Allah does not give any weight to the wealth, worldly position and status if they are not accompanied by virtuous deeds (49:13).

Islam insist on the protection of human rights and its universal application. It rejects the selective application of the principles of human rights governed by political exigencies. Significantly, the legal 'jurisdiction of Islamic law encircled every section of the society and nobody enjoyed the preferential treatment of any kind in this regard. Once a rich woman called Fatima, stole money from a destitute and impoverished person. Prophet Mohammood issued an amputation verdict against her. Some of Prophet's associates requested the nullification of the sentence on the grounds that it would restore tranquility among the rebellions numbers of the influential tribe to which the rich woman belonged. This suggestion infuriated the prophet who expressed his anger in these words: "you are asking me to release this rich woman Fatima from he implementation of the Islamic law. If my own daughter Fatima had engaged in act of theft, I would have amputated her hand also. The nations before you were destroyed only due to the reason, that whenever an influential person in their society committed a misdemeanor act he was released from the punishment and when a person of lower social status acted the same way, he was immediately punished.

Islam not only guarantees human rights and fundamental freedoms but at the same time provides a procedure for the enforcement of these rights if and when they are infringed upon by any person. The enforcement procedure are dual in alternative. One will be conducted by the state machinery and the court, and another will be conducted in the next world. If any right is infringed by any party, the aggrieved person has the right to petition before the court for the enforcement of this infringed right. Another procedure has been provided in the Quran that if anybody does mischief, infringes upon the right of others, he will be punished in the next world.

Despite the lofty ideals of Islam, it is evident that the status of human rights in the Muslim world has been poor. The chief reasons for the human rights abuses in the Muslim countries appear to be at the hands of radial governments and not to Islam per se. The three factors which contribute to the poor record of human rights and the Muslims states are: a) The lack of genuine democratic governments among the majority of Muslims nations, and the lack of incentives for serious human rights reforms, which would erode the power of most rulers b) The lack of an effective Islamic human rights voice c) The role of the US vis-v-vis its allies. The US has continued to support various friendly governments in the Muslim world despite atrocious records in the areas of human rights.

It is clear that Islam recognizes human rights and along with them the procedure for enforcement. The procedures are unique which are not found in the modern system. As a matter of fact, the concept of human rights originates not from American constitution as is generally believed but from the last sermon, which Prophet Mohamood delivered after the successful conquest of Mecca in 630 AD (14 centuries ago). His sermon which is now called Mohammad constitution constitutes the first and the only foundation of the concept of human rights, peace and justice and equality. In his historic sermon Prophet Mahammed declared: "blacks and whites are equal, Arabs and non-Arabs are equal. Rich and poor are equal. Nobody has any superiority of any kind upon the other. Islam recognizes and grants no superiority to anybody and grants a complete equality to all you all originate from Prophet Adam are subsequently all equal". Thus, civic equally, freedom from fear, freedom of belief and religious practice, freedom of teaching, freedom of trade and commerce were conceded in the Mohammad's constitution. Islam's appeal for human rights was able to prove its worth and effectiveness as it was addressed to all human beings without distinction to race, sex, clan or creed. The contribution of Islam in the field of human rights is such that to any student of Quran not one word in the Preamble or in the objectives of the UN Charter and not a single article in the text of UN Declaration of Human Rights will appear unfamiliar. While in the modern instruments human rights have been interpreted and explained which are comprehensible to common man. But the words of holy Quran are very much brief, sometimes they are symbolic in nature which are not comprehensible to the ordinary man. Consequently misunderstanding is created with regard to interpretations of some particular verse or verses of the Quran.

4
Islam and Terrorism

Many in the west easily merge the fanaticism of hostage-takers, attacks of Palestinian terrorists and military threat by Iran and Saddam together to constitute a single mental picture of Islam. To many, Islam is seen in terms of killing and bombing by extremist groups. The mass media in the west has played a most damaging role in this by portraying Islam as a primitive, rigid and inhumane culture that is alien to the basic principles of western civilizations. Explicitly and implicitly, Islam is depicted in the media and even in academic literature as the religion of war, vengeance, hatred and destruction. Islam is misconstrued as a fanatical religion which is intolerant of other religions and therefore encourages terrorism. However, the very world "Islam" is negation of the concept of violence. Islam means, surrender to the will of God on one hand, and establishing peace, on the other. While Islam means establishment of peace, Muslim means one who establishes peace-through his action and conduct.

Any aggressive act which leads to the killing of the innocent, irrespective of religion, community and colour is strictly forbidden in Islam and is deemed a heinous sin. There is a clear Quranic injunction against the shedding of the blood of innocent:

"We did ordain into the children of Israel that if anyone slays a human-being unless it be (in punishment) for murder or for spreading corruption on earth – it shall be as though he had slain all mankind; whereas, if anyone saves a life it shall be as though he saved the lives of all mankind. And indeed there came into them our apostles with all evidence of the truth yet, behold, notwithstanding all this, many of them go on committing all manner of exercises on earth". (5:32)

In the light of this outright condemnation of the shedding of blood of the innocent, Islam cannot and does not support acts of terrorism in any form. Similarly, there is no Quranic support for suicidal bombing. Suicide as such is prohibited in Islam and whoever commits suicide will be denied a place in heaven. Therefore, acts of terrorism performed by the Muslims will have to be viewed in the historical and political contexts and not as licensed by Islam.

Moreover, Islam ensures the security of human life through imposing ban on killing man except on reasonable grounds. According to Quran "kill not one another" (4:10). Laying stress on the sanctity of human life, Prophet Mohammad in his speech at his Farewell Pilgrimage said:

"O, your people, be aware that your lives, your properties and your honours are protected from aggression amongst you. They are as sacred as the culmination day of pilgrimage in the sacred city of Mecca."

Mercy is the foremost quality praised by Islam and it is the first quality of Allah. A Muslim repeats everyday dozens of times Bissmillahir Rahman al Raheem (in the name of Allah, most merciful most compassionate Allah says in the Quran that he has inscribed for Himself the rule of mercy (6:12). The Prophet has been described by Allah as Mercy into the worlds (21:107). So this religion cannot sanction the murder of innocent people under any pretext.

Significantly, in Islam, capital punishment is reserved for only three crimes, one of which is the killing of another human. Morally terrorism is contrary to the spirit of Quran because "God loves not the aggressors".

Islamic societies all these 14 centuries did not experience the phenomenon of terrorism. Only once in the annals of Islam, terrorism raved its ugly head. It was in the eleventh century when Imam Ghazali, hailed as the Resurrector of Islam" warned the faithful that if they did not destroy terrorism, terrorism would destroy them. The warning was well taken and for centuries thereafter nothing of this kind happened.

Muslim societies are being mixed up with Islamic societies. While there are Muslim movements and organizations that advocate violence and follow revolutionary path, they are by no means representatives of the political attitudes of the majority of Muslims. Unfortunately, acts of violence and terrorism committed by bodies like Hamas, Islamic Jihad, Hizbullah, Harkatul Asrar, Hizbul Mujahideen etc make headlines and overshadow moderate statements made by leading Islamist thinkers. It is necessary to distinguish between illegitimate use of religion by individuals and the faith and practice of the majority of world's Muslims. A distinction has to be made between the beliefs and activities of the majority and a minority of extremists who justify their aggression and violence in the name of religion, ethnicity and political ideology. No religion should be vilified on account of fanatical conduct of some elements or groups. It is true that some Muslim governments are supporting terrorist organizations as instruments of their own foreign policies. But non-Muslim governments are equally found guilty of the same.

The tendency to judge the actions of Muslims in splendid isolation, to generalize the actions of the few to the many, to disregard similar excuses committed in the name of other religions and ideologies is unfortunate. The analysts without regard to the diversity of Islamic organizations and specific social and political contexts conclude that the so-called Islamic fundamentalism is inherently a major global threat. The selective presentation and analysis of Islam and developments in the Muslim world fails to tell the whole story, to provide the full context for Muslims attitudes, events and actions and fails to account for the diversity of Muslim practice. It is a partial light which obscures the full picture. The selective presentation of most analysis of Islamic activism omits, downplays or dismisses the reasons given by the activists for their actions. Consequently, Islam is reduced to stereo types of Islam against the west, Islam's war against modernity, or Muslim rage, extremism, fanaticism and terrorism. The terms "fundamentalism" and "terrorism" have become linked in the minds of many. Viewing Islam and events in the Muslim would primarily through the prism of violence and terrorism has resulted in a failure to see the breadth and depth of contemporary Islam.

Muslim societies are the outgrowth of their own history and regional culture and have deviated from the prescribed Islamic values and norms. The growth of fundamentalist and extremist Islam has been manifested in different ways and over different local issues in each nation. Its roots have been nourished by a confluence of economic, cultural and political factors. The politics of the Muslim would emanates from the complex factors. The political dimension of Islam became more prominent after the creation of the state of Israel. The rise of Islamic movements in Egypt, Lebanon and other parts of the Muslim world was motivated by uprooting of three million Palestinians in order to implant a Jewish state based on fundamentalist Biblical grounds. The humiliation caused to the Muslim/Arab psyche with the loss of Palestine was a great significant contributing factor to Islamic extremism and terrorism. Islam reemerged as a political global force in Muslim politics during the

1970's and 1980's. 1967 proved to be a year of catastrophe as well as historic turning point. Israel's quick and decisive defeat of Arab forces constituted a devastating blow to Arab/Muslim pride, identity and self-esteem. Most important, the loss of Jerusalem would not be regarded as a regional (Arab) cause but rather as an Islamic cause throughout the Muslim world. The aftermath of the 1967 war witnessed a sense of disillusionment and soul searching that gripped both western-oriented secular elite as well as the more Islamically committed, striking at their sense of pride, identity and history. The governmental use of Islam was illustrated by a great spectrum of leaders in the Middle East and Asia; Libya's Muammar Qaddafi, Sudan's Gaffar Nimererie, Egypt's Anwar Sadaat, Iran's Ayatollah Khomeni, Pakistan's Ziaul Haq and Bangladesh's General Ershad. Most rulers and governments became aware of the potential growth of Islam shown concerned sensitivity to and anxiety about Islamic issues. The Iranian revolution of 1979 focussed attention on Islamic fundamentalism and for more than a decade Iran represented the embodiment of Islamic threat. Few leaders in the Muslim would have captured the attention of the West and symbolized "Islamic radicalism and terrorism" in the 70's and 80's more stridently than Libya's Qaddafi. While the western media found it attractive to speak of Libya's Islamic fundamentalist state and to level much of what Qaddafi did as Islamic Laws, Islamic bombs, Islamic terrorism, Qaddafi subordinated Islam to his interests and used Islam to export his influence in the Muslim world. Contrary to stereotypes, Qaddafi's Libya was not an Islamic fundamentalist state. He practised what his critics regarded as a radical Islam that rejected key aspects of Islamic tradition to support Libya's populist state and his Third Universal Theory. Qaddafi set Islamic law aside. His Green book replaced the traditional comprehensive role of Shariah. Qaddafi's authority and legitimacy was challenged by Islamic movements such as Muslims Brotherhood and Islamic Liberation Organisation. Because of the early identification of Libya as a fundamentalist Islamic state, owing to the implementation of Islamic laws, Libyan state-sponsored terrorism regardless of its motives, came to be indiscriminately associated with Islam whether the actors were the Irish Republican Army, Arabs or Palestinian organizations, Maoists or Islamic extremists. Libya's reputation as an Islamic fundamentalist state led to the identification of Qaddafi and terrorism with Islam and the equation of all Islamic activists with radicalism and extremism. For the Reagan Administration Qaddafi and Khomeni became symbols of worldwide terrorism. Libya's influence and its effective export of Islam waned in the 80's as its oil reserves dried up. Likewise radical Islam epitomized by Iran and Sudan failed to make any impact on the Muslim world. The attempts of these two regimes to export their revolutions failed because there is no such monolithic movement as Islamic fundamentalism.

Islam already stigmatized in the west, is once more equated with violence and terrorism. Though Muslim ideologues have pertinently declared that terrorism has no sanction in religion, the entire community carries the awesome burden of dispelling the false notions about the meaning and significance of Jihad. Undoubtedly, fundamentalist ideas exemplified by the Taliban and Al Qaeda inspire certain segments of Muslim communities. But such elements do not represent Islam's authoritative voice. One should do well to take into account the silent majority's passive equanimity. Today resistance, and terrorist movements vigarously deploy the call for Jihad alike to legitimize their cause and motivate their followers. But it has few takers among more than a billion Muslims living across the globe. Islam is eventually a religion of peace and moderation. If is does not appear to be today, this is not due to the teachings of Islam but to misinterpretation made by those who are not qualified enough to do so in order to suit their own vested interests.

Significantly, terrorism was introduced to the Muslim world by Zionists into founded the state of Israel. The very terrorism unleashed by the state of Israel has become the "role model" for the outbreak of Arab and some other Muslim terrorism. The volatility of that part of the world is not necessarily caused by Islamic activity as such. Rather this increased Islamic activity is a manifestation of deeply rooted underlying problems in the region that have contributed to this type of response. It is much less a manifestation of religious fervour than by political and economic frustrations.

Fear of Islam is not new. Islamic revivalism, Islamic resurgence, Islamic movement are not new. They are as old as Islam itself. Islam is nothing short of an endless revolution, the eternal quest to reach out to God. In most Muslim countries, decades of repression of nationalist liberal and Marxist trends left a wide open, depoliticized society, a political and intellectual vacuum, that is now filled mainly by Islamist militants. In considering why Islam is becoming more of a world force today once needs to explain what is happening to Muslim countries. The problem is that some Muslim activists are carrying out their militant campaigns in the name of Islam. Ironically most of these movements are regarded as the representative movements of Islam. Generally the people perceive these movements as approved acts of Islam and start believing that Islam is a violent religion. Nothing could be farther from Islamic teachings. Islam is essentially a peace-long religion. Islam has to be assessed on the principles enunciated and values promoted in the Quran and traditions of the Prophet, who is remembered as the harbinger of kindness and mercy for the whole universe. He is a messenger of kindness and not of violence. Islam is clearly opposed to the culture of bullets and bombs. In fact, it teaches peace, compassion and forgiveness. Terrorism is repugnant to the Quranic teachings. Terrorists who quote some of the more viloent passages of the Quran to justify their actions ignore the exhortions to peace and mercy that almost invariably follow. Fundamentalist Islamic terrorism, therefore, is not an inevitable outcome of the teachings of Quran. It is the result of several factors-failure to remove the corrupt, oppressive and anti-democratic regimes of the Muslim world and to end Israeli occupation of Palestine and hatred towards the US for its support to these regime and Israel.

Religious extremism remains a threat today as it was in the past but it is not restricted to or inherent in any one religion. As former President of the US Bill Clinton rightly observed. "when it comes to terrorisms there should be no dividing line between Muslims and Jews, Protestants and Catholics, Serbs and Albanians, developed societies and emerging countries. The only dividing issue is between those who practice, support or tolerate terror and those who understand that it is murder, plain and simple. "The spector of attacks by terrorists motivated by ethnic, religious or ideological beliefs and grievances is real. The challenge today is to avoid any easy answers yielded by stereotyping or the projection of a monolithic threat, to distinguish between the beliefs and activities of majority (whether be Hindus, Muslims Sikhs, Christians, Jews, Tamils and Buddhists) and a minority of extremists who justify their aggression and violence in the name of religion, ethnicity and political dialogue. It is equally important to distinguish between the aspirations and demands of legitimate political opposition groups and those of extremist groups. There cannot be peace without justice. The Muslim world is full of injustices and hence of violence. Islam laid great stress on justice and peace but a section of Muslims particularly. Muslim rulers perpetrated injustice and violence. Thus the blame for violence lay on the doors of some Muslims and not on Islam. As far as Islam is concerned justice and peace are integral parts of its teachings. No peace is possible in the world unless more equitable and just international system is ushered in which all have a stake.

5
Islam and Women

Introduction

It is generally believed that Islam has treated women unjustly. It enjoins upon them to cover their bodies from top to toe and thus force them to confine themselves behind four walls of their houses. It does not give them the right to divorce. It permits their husbands to keep four wives simultaneously. It accords them half of the share in inheritance of property as compared to men. In order to have a correct assessment of the status and role of women in Islam one must look into the basic sources of Islam viz., the Quran and Hadith (Prophets' sayings).

Equality of Treatment

The Quran does not distinguish between man and woman. According to Quran, "the most honoured of your in the eyes of Allah is the most righteous of you." (49:13) It is on the basis of their righteous deeds and sinful acts that man and woman will be rewarded or punished. There will be no discrimination on the grounds of sex, colour or ethnicity. This is explicitly stated in a verse: "Whoever works righteously, man or woman, and has faith, verify to him, we will give new life, that is good and pure, and we will bestow on such people their reward, according to their best of actions." (16:97) This equality of treatment is reiterated in another verse: "He that works evil will not be requited but by the like thereof. And he that works righteous deed whether man or woman and is a believer will enter the Garden of Bliss." (40:40) The Quranic verses and sayings of the Prophet repeatedly stressed on the equality of their rights. For instance man and women enjoyed equal rights in granting asylum to their relations seeking refuge. The equality of status between man and woman is further highlighted when Quran says: "Permitted to you on the night of the fast is the approach to your wives. They are your garments and you are their garments." (2:187) This verse clearly implies both literally and metaphysically that husband (man) and wife (woman) are the protectors of each others dignity and honour. It is clear that the Quranic view of women is no different from that of a man. They both are God's creatures whose sublime goal or on earth is to worship their Lord, do righteous deeds, and avoid evil and both will be assured accordingly. The Quran never mentions that man is created in God's image, and that all men and all women are his creatures.

Intellectual Status

Having established beyond question the equality of man and woman in Islam, Prophet Mohammed said: "The search for knowledge is a duty for every Muslim (male or female)" and "seek knowledge from the cradle to grave". "Knowledge for a Muslim is not divided into sacred and secular and the implications of these sayings of the Prophet, in modern terms, is that every Muslim boy or girl, man or women, should pursue his or her education as far as it is possible, bearing in mind the words of Allah in the Quran: "Only those of His servants who are learned truly fear God" (35:28) In Islam, therefore, both men and women are credited with the capacity for learning and understanding and teaching, and one of the aims of acquiring knowledge is that of becoming more conscious of God. It is worth pointing out that one of the most famous women in the history of Islam is Aiysha, the Prophet's wife. And the quality for which she is remembered primarily is that of her intelligence and outstanding memory. She is recognized as one of the most reliable sources of Hadith (Prophet's sayings) by virtue of these qualities. She is regarded as one of the greatest teachers of the Hadith. It is also worth recalling that one of the most famous mystics in Islam Rabi'a al Basari was a woman. According to the Quran, a woman's role on earth is not limited only to childbirth. She is required to do as many good deeds as any man is required to do. The Quran does not state that no upright woman had ever existed. To the contrary, the Quran has instructed all the believers, women as well as men, to follow the example of those ideal women such as the Virgin Mary and the Pharoah' wife (66:11-13).

Elevated Status

One should consider the pathetic tales of woe with which women were subjected to in non-Islamic societies prior to the advent of Islam. In the male dominated societies, birth of female child was regarded a disgrace. Hence they were invariably buried alive soon after their birth. Islam demolished the superstitions prevailing in the then Arab society and stopped the killing of innocent newborn female babies. Quran condemned strongly and clearly this brutal practice: "Kill not your children for fear of want, we shall provide sustenance for them as well as for your verily the killing of them is a great sin." (17:31) Besides women were not treated as human beings but were considered as chatter to gratify the needs of the owners. They were openly traded in market places like goods. Widows were abhorred, their heads were tonsured and they were forced to sit on the pyre of their husbands to be burnt alive. Right of female child to life and right of her proper upbringing and education like the male child under the strict Quranic injunctions was granted with the advent of Islam. Right of inheritance, of acquisition, ownership and disposal of property were conferred on women by Islam centuries ago while it was 12 centuries later in 1881 that UK, supposed to be cradle of democracy, adopted this institution of Islam and an Act was passed called the Married Women's Act. The elevated rank of women is borne out by the Quranic verses and sayings of the Prophet. For instance the Quran speaks eloquently about the birth of Mary (Mariyam), the mother of Prophet Jesus. Mary's mother expressed grave disappointment of giving birth to a female child but she was unequivocally told that a female child like Mary was far superior to any male child. And Allah knew best what she brought forth. And no wise is the male like the female." (3:36). This verse ought to dispel the inferiority complex among women if any. Mary the mother of Jesus is presented in the Quran as a model of chastity, integrity, honesty and righteousness. Prophet Mohammed treated women with great respect. Once a person asked, "who among the people is most deserving of fine treatment from my hand?" Prophet Mohammed replied, Your mother, then who is the next one. He (the Prophet) said: again it is your mother". He again asked them who? Thereafter he said: Again it is your mother. He again asked then who? Thereafter he said: Then it is your father. Thus the status of mother is far above that of the father.

Women and Inheritance of Property

Before Islam among the pagan Arabs, inheritance rights were confined exclusively to the male relatives. The Quran abolished all these unjust customs and gave all the female relatives their first share. A woman's right to property is enshrined in the Quran. Islam has assigned half share to women from the paternal property as compared to men because they are not obliged to look after anyone from their property. It is their sole property. Whereas on the other hand, men are duly bound to maintain their families which include wives, children and even their aged parents. It should have been utterly unjustified if both men and women were treated equally in the inheritance of property. Moreover, women get a handsome amount of money at the time of their marriage which is their own property. So if one looks at the wisdom behind the Islamic Law of inheritance, one would find that women are in no way treated unfairly. In fact they are duly compensated. Prophet Mohammed advised the rich parents to leave enough for their children including daughters in order to sustain them during their lifetime with honour and dignity.

Marriage and Women

Islamic marriage is a kind of contract between two adult and sensible human beings of the opposite sex for a happy wedded life. The women are at liberty to have this clause included in the martial contract (nikahnama) that in the event of unbearable circumstances, they would be obliged to seek divorce. Islam grants women the right to seek divorce in the form of Khula. If women are not satisfied with their married life they can seek divorce from their husbands by making them to agree to divorce by financially compensating them. This is known as Khula. Islam has not given this right directly to women but to hold that it has denied this right is nothing but ignorance from the wisdom of Islam. The law of Islam does not compel couples to stay together, but its procedures help them to find a basis on which they can be reconciled with each other. If reconciliation is impossible the law does not impose any unnecessary delay or obstacle in the way of either partner's remarriage.

Polygamy

A very common criticism against Islam is that it has done injustice to women by granting men the right to have four wives simultaneously while compelling them to be content with one husband at a time. It is worth pointing out that polygamy is a very ancient practice. Bible did not condemn polygamy. The Old Testament frequently attest to the legality of polygamy. So far as the Quran is concerned it allows polygamy but not without certain stringent conditions. It says: "If you fear that you shall not be able to deal justly with the orphans, marry women of your choice, two or three or four but if you fear that you shall not be able to deal justly with them, then only one" (4:3). The Quran contrary to the Bible limits the number of wives to four under strict condition of treating the wives equally and justly. It does not imply that the Quran exhorts the believers to practice polygamy or that polygamy is considered an ideal. In fact the Quran has tolerated or allowed polygamy and no more. The wisdom behind the permission to allow four wives at a time is that man by nature is promiscuous. Mostly, he is not satisfied with one partner. He wants change. The existence of prostitution, world over, the mushrooming of sex outlets and the rising level of sex industry is proof enough of man's promiscuous behaviour. Thus Islam has provided a sensible limit of four wives because Islam wants to eradicate corruption from the society and not to pave way for it.

Islam is Egalitarian

This egalitarian streak plays itself out in relations between sexes. The Quran laid out a set of marriage laws that guarantee married women their family shares, their own possessions and capital, the right to agree upon when they will marry, and the right to initiate divorce. Significantly, in Islam's early period, women were professionals and property owners, as increasingly as they are today. The basic democratic spirit of Islam emancipated women from bondage of men. Islam teaches that men and women have come from the same essence, possess the same soul and have been equipped with equal capabilities into equal capabilities for intellectual, spiritual and moral attainments. Far from wage less slave subordinated to the male, a child bearing machine and a source of enjoyment as was her almost all over the world, the women in Islam got her rights centuries ago as an individual, as also socially. It was centuries earlier that Prophet of Islam had proclaimed that women are twin halves of men. Rights of women are sacred. He commanded his followers to see that women got the rights granted to them. During his 23 years as a prophet and leader, he always included women in all key decisions pertaining to important socio-political issues. He encouraged women to excel in religious and social and natural sciences. He even gave permission to Umm Waraqa to organize religious services in her neighbourhood during his absence from Madina when the battle of Badr was about to take place. Religiosity and conservatism must be distinguished from one another. One must acknowledge problems of Muslim women are related to the clause structure of Muslim society, and the differential level of their consciousness of the rights granted to them in Islam. Most of the disabilities that Muslim women suffer from derive from the vested interests of the bigots. Socio-cultural milieu of Muslim societies leave its imprint on the surface structure of Quranic message.

Muslim women make up over 50 percent of the Muslim world population. The majority of them are illiterate and denied any role in Muslim public life. As long as they remain in this situation, the socio-political progress of the community will always face impediments and obstacles. It is time that the genuine Quranic teachings about the role of women that was the foundation of the Prophet's time is applied in changing attitude about women. Muslim men must fulfill their responsibility towards women in general. They must ensure that all those instruments that perpetuate a culture of discrimination and injustice are removed.

6

Is There a Church in Islam?

It is in institutional terms that Islam most differs from Christianity. While the overarching institutions of Christianity are formal those of Islam are informal. Islam has evolved formal institutions only for the performance of specific functions. Majority Sunni Islam lacks any overarching, formal, corporate institution that might be identified as a church, Islam differs from Judaism and Christianity because it has no system of priests. The Ulama and muftis are not in any sense priests but rather scholars, akin to the New Testament doctors of the law.

In Islam, the three most important varieties of authority are material, doctrinal and spiritual. Ritual authority is of little significance in Islam, contrary to Christianity and other religions. The Christian churches have considerable authority since in most cases many of the important forms of Christian worship are impossible to perform without the presense of a priest or Minister. In contrast there are no ritual actions in Islam that cannot be carried out by any sane adult Muslim.

Since the teaching of Islam insist on the unity of man's life and rejects separation between God and Caesar, most students of Political Islam tend to classify Islamic government as necessarily a theocratic government, implying that the laws of a Muslim land should always be derived from or at least conform to the principles of Islamic law (shariah) Political scientists and constitutional lawyers should distinguish between two separate issues; the basis of political power and authority on the one hand, and the sources of the legal system on the other. The political system as envisaged by Islam has nothing to do with theocratic government. The Islamic state is characterized by the supremacy of shariah, yet it is diametrically different from theocracy. Theocracy, as it has been known in history stood for divine rule through an ecclesiastical class whose word became the law, undisputed and indisputable. In clear contrast to the western concept of theocracy, Islam was a revolt against all anthropomorphic implications in the realm of faith. The long western struggle between church and state is quite alien to Islamic thought. For Islam does not authorize any material form, human or institutional, that could claim to be representative of God. In Islam there is no provision for priestly class or religious intermediaries between God and man. Prophethood ended with Prophet Mohammod. The guidance has been perfected. Allah's will is clearly available in the form of Quran and Sunnah (Prophet's traditions). The Shariah is a known quantity and it is not a divine secret known only to the priesthood. Islam does not establish a clergy and scholars of theology and Islamic laws are ordinary people. Islam does not call for a government whose authority is based on a divine will. Nor does it call for government of clerics. According to the consensus of Muslim Sunni jurists the legitimacy of any government derives from the consent of the people. Rulers have no divine rights of any kind and are bound by rule of law. In Islam there is absolutely no permission for any group imposing their personal will or preferences over others in the name of God. The much talked about fatwas are not edicts. They are mere legal opinions which are not binding. Fatwa is a formal legal opinion given by a mufti or cannon lawyer of standing in answers to a question submitted to him either by a judge or by a private individual. It is politics, not religion which inspires declaration of fatwas, exposing, both to ridicule and Islam to misunderstanding and misinterpretation.

However, over the centuries those learned in Islam, the Ulema, gained such authority over the Muslim community that many of them tended to use their considerable influence to gain power for themselves. They became like the priests of other religions. Early Ulemas were knowledgeable in very disciplines besides theology. Today public Ulema are knowledgable only in those parts of the teaching of Islam which seemingly support their public views. Many misinterpret and distort Islam to legitimize their political creed. A favourable view is that only Ulemas can rule a country. These political Ulema reject knowledge that is not specifically religious for fear that people with such knowledge might challenge their authority.

One must score the central Islamic belief that after Mohammad no human being has been or shall be the messenger of God. It follows that there is no divine sanctity to the sayings of the Caliphs, the Ulemas, the Mullahs, and most decidedly not the Osamas and the Abu Graiths. Muslims are free to reject every claim or act as un-Islamic that goes against the spirit of the Quran or the Sunnah of the Prophet. Islam meant to be a simple religion, with repeated stress that every human begin has equal access to God. Besides Mohammad, no one can rightly claim that he/she got any message from God. Islam believes that Herbrew and Christians priests changed the original religion. Islam does not want priests to change Islam. In brief there is no church in Islam for it does not confer Divine Rights on any elected or hereditary class.

7
US and Islam

Americans as a people share certain human and moral values with Islam. The first and foremost, a deep faith in the one Supreme Being. We are all commanded by Him to faith, compassion and justice. We have common respect and reverence for law on the basis of both values and interests, the natural relationship between Islam and American is one of friendship.

Jimmy Carter Former US President

Introduction

At the end of the present century, religion has become a dynamic force all over the world. The recent developments in Eastern Europe and countries of the erstwhile Soviet Union clearly demonstrate that religion remains a potent force despite all the efforts to suppress it. More than other world religions, Islam is making its presence felt in various parts of the world. Islam as a world religion is characterized by unity. Islam is the only monotheistic religion that offers not only a set of spiritual beliefs but also a set of rules to govern the society. The commonality of belief structure gives Islam a strength that is not characteristic of other religions having multinational presence.

Islam has the second largest following in the world. It is the principal religion that extends from Morocco on the Atlantic through North and East Africa and into sub-Saharan Africa, across the broad expanse of central and South-West Asia to the headwaters of the Indus in the tableland of Tibet, and Southward to the Java sea. Such an extensive area, apart from the Arab core area, is subdivided into regional civilizations and local cultures: Turkish, Caucasian, Central Asian, Persian, African, South And Southeast Asian, and European. There are about one billion Muslims all over the world. They constitute more than eighty five per cent population in thirty two countries, between twentyfive and eighty five per cent in 11 more countries, and significant populations in another 47 countries. They control most of the oil and occupy world's most strategic areas where politics is enmeshed with religion.

Early Contacts

The history of Islam is very long compared to that of the United States. However, from the outset, the US has enjoyed close and valued ties with the Islamic world. Significantly, a Muslim state, Morocco, was the first to recognize American independence. The Sultan of Morocco signed a Treaty of Peace and friendship with US in 1787, and thereafter the new republic had a number of dealings with other Muslim countries. During the inter war years, America had a clean image in the Muslim world because of educational and health services organised by American missionaries. The second world war, the oil industry and the post war developments brought many Americans to the Islamic countries; large number of Muslims also came to America, first as students, then as teachers or businessmen or visitors, and eventually as immigrants. The American outreach to the Muslim world developed during the 20th Century driven by both growing importance of petroleum for economic development and the emerging role of the US on the international stage. During his long and historic presidency Franklin D. Roosevelt conducted personal diplomacy with kind Saud of Saudi Arabia and Shah of Iran. Elicit Roosevelt, son of President Roosevelt wrote a full length account of his father's collaboration with Persian Gulf leaders to develop a modern, post-colonial economy and a strategic partnership between these Muslim states and the US.

Cold War Period

After the emergence of US as a prominent power, the American policymakers devoted special attention to West Asia. Prompted by the American oil companies, they tried to cultivate Saudi Arabia to ensure access to oil. However, the US role in the creation of the state of Israel resulted in strong anti-American feelings among the Muslim countries. This also resulted in the emergence of radical groups, some of which were able to attain state power. They adopted anti-American postures. It then became an objective of US diplomacy to ensure that a consolidation of such radical Muslim states did not materialize and a corporate relationship was established with the moderate and conservative regimes in the Muslim world. The US found Saudi Arabia's championship of Islam as a convenient weapon to beat the Arab radicals with. In the wake of Suez Crisis in 1956, which spelled disaster for Britain as a custodian of western interests in the region, President Eisenhower seriously toyed with the idea of promoting King Saud as the Pope of Islam. But the project failed to take off. This was also the period when US was striving to contain Soviet expansionism, which also implied similar containment of 'radical' Islamic states that tended to move closer to the Soviet Union. During the cold war period, American ideologues and strategists tended to view positive side of Islam from their own perspective and ironically concluded that "conservative" Islamic regimes were the custodians of Islamic values which held Communism as an atheistic heretical creed and disapproved of it. Therefore, they considered such conservatism a useful impediment to any unacceptable growth of pro-Soviet radical regimes in the Islamic world.

The US policy in West Asia throughout the cold war era was directed to drive a wedge between the socialist community and the Muslim national liberation movements and to prevent them from establishing friendly relations.[1] Washington was seeking to destroy the very possibility of such relations by arguing that people who supported Marxism could never support Islam. The US tried to impress upon Muslims that there were incompatibilities between the Islamic world and the Soviet Communism. In Washington's view, Islam could play the role of a "barrier" blocking the spread of socialist ideology in the Muslim countries. By and large, American diplomacy achieved considerable success, notwithstanding the occasional setbacks. From the second half of 1970s, Washington began to evince special interest in Islam. It was chiefly due to world energy crisis. The Muslim countries of the Middle East and North Africa at that time provided as much as fifty five per cent of the oil requirement in the western world and exported as much as seventyfive per cent of its oil.

Another important factor was that these oil exporting Muslim countries had built up huge financial strength which enabled their ruling classes to exert even greater influence on the world economy. The US also took note of the growing political and economic weight of the Muslim oil producing countries in the non-aligned movement among developing countries in general and international organizations in particular.

All these factors resulted in an increasing interest in Islam in the US. In January 1979, Zbignew Brzesinski, then Assistant to the President on National Security Affairs, instructed the relevant departments to arrange for an intensive study of Islam and its political role in the world and prepare a detailed report on the situation in various Muslim countries. So, at the turn of Seventies, the issues related to Islam came to figure prominently in the activities of US policy-making bodies. Washington began to view these issues as important components of its foreign policy. In order to legitimize its concern, US extended support to the movements like the one going on in Afghanistan, which according to its perception would be appreciated by the Muslims in other countries.

The "Islamic factor" was also strategically used by US to keep the Soviet Union out of any possible Middle East settlement. According to the reasoning of American diplomats, the "religious affinity" of the two sides, i.e.; the Muslims and the Jews, which was affirmed in the Camp David Accord, should help in enhancing the hostility of the Middle East Muslim countries towards the 'atheist' Soviet Union.

Post Cold War Scenario

The end of the cold war also witnessed the rise of religious fervor in Muslim countries. All over the Muslim world, from Algeria, Morocco, Libya and Egypt to Iran, Pakistan and Indonesia, a persistent undercurrent of religious revival, taking the form of a political ideology is being observed now. In media and among the academic circles, this has been referred to as "Islamic Fundamentalism". The Islamic current is not a novelty of 1990s although it is gaining new heights now. The new burst of activism has reached such proportions that with the demise of international communism, Islam is increasingly being perceived as one of the future ideological rivals to the West, led by the US. After the cold war, Americans are turning in increasing number towards a new enemy: Islam. The American mass media has started sounding alarming signals: Beware of Islamic Fundamentalism,[2] The Muslims are coming,[3] The Roots of Muslim Rage[4], Islamic Fundamentalists call for a Holy war[5] etc. etc.

These headlines were symbolic of the then prevailing negative images of Islam and Muslims in America. It is argued that with the demise of International Communism, Islam's militant strain is on the verge of replacing Communism as the principal adversary of western liberal democracy and the values it enshrines. Some American strategic thinkers view Islamic fundamentalism as a far more serious threat than international communism since Islam is more deeply embedded in the psyche of its adherents than communism. To many in America, Islam is seen in terms of killing and bombing by extremist groups. Explicitly and implicitly, Islam is depicted in the media and even in academic literature as the religion of war, vengeance, hatred and destruction, and a force that is inimical to the orderly conduct of international relations and the progress of society and politics. Islam as a world civilization has been reduced to Islamic fundamentalism. Thus, with the end of the cold war, the new focus for American policy makers is on Islamic fundamentalism. For the American power-elite that is the challenge in the next century. Jean Kirkpatrick, former US ambassador to the UN had said on the CNN as she watched the hammer and sickle go down last time on Kremlin: The next enemy is "Islamic Fundamentalism".

American Phobia

The American phobia of Islam has some justification. A whole succession of memories starting with the Crusades and coming down to the bombing of US embassies in Kenya and Sudan and a huge cultural divide keeps the US and Islam apart. The divide was never that deep and wide between the Americans and the Russians. Both culturally and civilizationally, they were similar even if they were ideologically apart at the political level. In contrast, Islam had confronted the Christianity off and on for centuries. From the battle of Ajnadayn in 634 A.D, military hostility has always defined the crux of Christian-Muslim relationship. Many Americans see the acts of terrorism and the ubiquitous Muslim diatribes against the West as part of a deepening conflict between an aggressive Islam and a defensive Christian civilization. According to Bernard Lewis: "The Struggle between Islam and West has now lasted 14 centuries. It has consisted of a long series of attacks and counterattacks, Jihads and Crusades, conquests and re-conquests. Today, much of the Muslim world is again seized by intense and violent indictment of the West. Recently, America had become the enemy, the incarnation of diabolic opponent of all and specifically for Islam."[6] Explosive headline events and acts of violence make it tempting to view Islam through the prism of religious extremism and terrorism.

Thus, political Islam has become one of the hottest, nastiest themes for debates in academic circles today, mirroring the well-organized and monolithic debate that was going on between Communism and Liberal Democracy. Muslim phobia that took off in 1989 was a byproduct of the orgy of speculation that accompanied the fall of Soviet Union and the liberation of Central Europe. During the cold war period the US had an "enemy". Now it has to create an enemy to instill national purpose into a tottering economy. The end of the cold war sparked a kind of intellectual exercise to identify the biggest and the most credible new enemy. One threat has crystallized well in the public mind: Islamic fundamentalism.

Apart from such historical and cultural divides, there are more recent geo-strategic interests that keep the US and Islam apart. The new antithesis of the West is specially designed to replace communism with Islamic Fundamentalism in popular perception, which would make it easy on the part of the whole American nation to redefine its national and security concerns in terms of this new menace. The strategic thinkers might be speculating that such a redefinition could bring about a new surcharged national solidarity that would serve national interests well in an era of economic crises. Thus, with the end of the cold war, the new focus for the American policymakers is on Islamic nations and movements. As Professor Dallal rightly argues that there is now "an all-out effort to drive a wedge between the US and the Muslim world."

The evidence is clear that Islam is the new enemy and the major flashpoints all over the world involving Islamic people and movements. The threat from the Islamic world is perceived at various levels. At one level Iran, Iraq, Libya and other hostile states are perceived as military forces bent on waging Jihad. At the other level, the overwhelming migration from the Islamic countries to the west during the post-Cold War period, in the event of the rising tide of socio-political upheavals in the Islamic world, has given rise to the fear that the Muslim immigrants may play havoc with the cultural system of the West and subvert the western civilization from within.

Clash of Civilizations Theory

First under Kissinger and then under Z. Brzezinkli, Dr. Bernard Lewis shaped an overhaul of American policy towards the Muslim world. He argued for the inevitability and desirability of a clash of civilization between the west and the Islamic world. However, the most provocative and influential articulation of the position came from Samuel P

Huntington's clash of civilization article in Foreign Affairs, Huntington declared that in the post-cold war period, the clash of civilization will dominate global politics. He identified a confucian-Islamic connection that has emerged to challenge western interests, values, and power, including that 'a central focus of conflict for the immediate future until be between the west and several Islamic-confucian states". He characterized Islam as the age old enemy of the west. Viewing the crescent shaped bloc of nations from Africa to Central Asia and other conflicts between Muslims and orthodox serbs in the Balkans, Hindus in India, Jews in Israel, catholics in Philippines, he concludes that Islam has bloody borders. The phrase explicitly attributes the bloodshed to the religion of Islam and not simply to the actions of some Muslims. However, the idea that the west is destined to clash with Islam found little support in US policy making establishment. For instance, in an important speech in Jordanian parliament in 1994 the then US President Bill Clinton strenuously repudiated the clash of civilization thesis, noting that "there are those who insist that there are impossible religions and other obstacles to harmony; that our beliefs and our cultures must somehow inevitably clash. America refuses to accept that our cultures must collide". Other senior officials followed suit. Notwithstanding such high level repudiation, the idea of an Islamic phalanx has proven remarkably durable, especially to members of western military establishment in the post-cold war era. Willy Claas, the Secretary General of NATO embraced the thesis in mid 1990's when he pointed to the Islamic challenge as the main threat confronting the west (that is NATO). Since 9/11 tragedy, a series of editorials and provocative articles appeared in leading. US newspapers, periodicals and other media legitimizing the clash of civilization thesis. A decade old debate has been renewed about whether the current war on terror is an inevitable, civilization conflict between the forces of Islam and the west. The events of 9/11 combined with the consolidation of power within the Bush Administration by a tight-knit cabal of neoconservatives with deep right wing Zionist view.

Bush Administration and Islam

The realization that the US has international responsibilities in the post-cold war period has shaped the policies of the US Administration towards Islam. The US position was first enunciated by the then Assistant Secretary of state for Near Eastern and South Asian Affairs, Edward P. Djrejian in June 1992. At that time many conspiracy theories

War, the "real" intentions of the US in the region and its "obdurate" attitude towards Islam and Muslims. In such an emotionally charged environment, Djerejian sought to dispel fears that the US government was contributing to the perceptions of a widening gap between western values and those of the Muslim world. He stressed that the US government does not view Islam as the next "ism" confronting the west or threatening world peace and said that "we acknowledge Islam as a historical civilizing force among the many that have influenced and enriched our culture". About Islamic fundamentalist movements, he suggested that "we detect no monolithic or coordinated international effort behind these movements."[7]

One year later, before the House Foreign Affairs Committee, Djerejian detailed the Clinton Administration's position on the subject. He voiced the concern over connections between extremist groups and radical regimes such as Iran and Sudan and noted that "the US parts company with those individuals and governments who seek to advance their agenda through violence, through terror, through intolerance, through coercion. Our quarrel is with extremism, whether in a religious or secular guise"[8]. Reconfirming Washington's stand towards Islam, Robert H. Pelletreau, Sr. Assistant Secretary of State for Near Eastern Affairs said: "We view the religion of Islam with great respect; we respect it as a movement".

On the other hand, Martin Idnyk who had been appointed by President Clinton as the Middle East specialist on the National Security Council, detailed the Administration's Middle East policy blueprint in May 1993. One of the major threats envisaged in Idnyk's NSC blueprint, Islamic fundamentalism, involved extremist groups engaged in terrorism and other violence, such as Hamas and Hezbullah. He recommended that the promotion of democratic political development and free market economic development would presumably counter this Islamic threat.[9]

However, most students of Muslim politics would not accept the claim of a cohesive, transnational Muslim movement. That Muslim parties have done well in the few relatively free elections held in the West Asian countries is worth considering here. The Islamic parties, which favour free market economies, seem to generate support from those strata that suffer the pain of "structured development" enforced by the regimented apparatus of the state. The statements of several Islamic fundamentalist leaders also reveal that they aspire to bring about change peacefully, preserving the broad principles of democracy, rule of law, the majority rule, minority rights, freedom of expression, and political participation. A dialogue with such individuals shall not harm US interests. President Bush promised to make promotion of democracy a more central concern of the US foreign policy. It remains to be seen whether promotion of human rights will become, for the first time, an element of US administration's Middle East policy in the days to come. While the US government has taken great pains to differentiate between its opposition to violence and its respect for Islam, it has nonetheless supported non- responsive governments in Egypt and Algeria that at times use extreme violence to suppress even nonviolent Islamic groups who oppose those regimes.

One has to acknowledge here, nonetheless, that however contradictory or limited Washington's support for democratic movements appear to be, the fact remains that the US is the most powerful promoter of democracy in the world. Yet, perhaps, in Washington's view, the Middle East is not yet ready for democratization. Even attention to human rights, the basic precondition for inculcation of democratic norms, is absent in the official American attitude towards the governments of the Middle East. Washington cannot be indifferent to gross violations in one part of the world while celebrating the rise of democracy everywhere else. The Bush Administration now faces a challenge and opportunity to formulate a new policy towards the Muslim world, which would be free from hatred and vilification, and which would be based on quest for the real solutions. It should be a policy free from the unwarranted fears and imagined enemies and should be motivated by vital US national interests.

Islamic Solidarity - Myth or Reality!

American judgement of Islam has been grossly distorted by taking the extremes to be the norm. Extremism does exist at the fringe and it must be seriously dealt with. It is unwise indeed to judge an entire community on the basis of stray isolated incidents, which inevitably leads to distortions and prejudiced conclusions. There is a regrettable tendency in America to overestimate the influence of the so-called fundamentalist groups in Muslim countries and an even more unfortunate tendency to generalize and assume that any movement raising the banner of Islam will necessarily be fundamentalist in nature. Very often, the entire community of Muslims, lumped together as a single monolithic group, is regarded as a potential threat to the western interests. This hypothesis ignores the diversity among Muslims. A cohesive, transnational Islamic movement simply does not exist. Thinking of Muslims as a single constituency is unrealistic. While there are Islamic movements that advocate violence, oppose the west and follow the revolutionary path, they are by no means representative of the political attitudes of majority of Muslims.

Islam, much like Christianity and Judaism, encompasses far too many perspectives, which often contend among themselves for recognition and influence. As such, while studying a subject as vast and as variegated as the Islamic order, it would not be too helpful to jump into facile generalizations. Iran is as much an example of an Islamic order, as is Saudi Arabia. Similarly, Takir Waal Hijre is as much representative of Islamic fundamentalism as are Afghan Mujahideens–– the erstwhile comrades-in-arm of the US. The US tends to put all these disparate groups into one monolith. There are clear dangers in the US failing to recognize diversity in the unity of Islam. The various Islamic movements should rather be contextualized and examined against the background of domestic and international events that have helped to shape them.

The growth of fundamentalist and extremist Islam has manifested in different ways and over different local issues in different political and administrative units called the states or the nations. The roots of Islamic fundamentalism, like its ideological variants in other cultures, have been nourished by a confluence of economic, cultural and political factors. As far as Algeria, Egypt and Sudan are concerned, a major cause for people turning to Islam and taking to violence for resolving their economic and political problems lies in the denial of opportunities to bring about political change through democratic means. A liberal doze of democracy could bring a semblance of purpose and poise to the institutions of governance in these areas of Islamic conflict. Not all those whom the US denounces as Islamist extremists are in fact true followers of the faith or are even accepted as spokespersons of Islam by Muslims themselves. A case in point is of Col. Gaddafi, whom the US vilified as an Islamic fundamentalist; majority of Muslims also views Gaddafi with skepticism. It was President Reagan, not the Muslim masses, who crowned Gaddafi with the title of "Muslim Leader". The same is true of Saddam Hussein, whom most of the Muslims do not acknowledge as a religious leader, even if they were supporting him in the ongoing crisis.

History bears testimony to the fact that Muslims do not fight non-Muslims with as much passion and determination and as they fight one another. The divisions within Islam are so wide and deep and the conflict among them so acute and insoluble that more blood has been shed by Muslims of the Muslims themselves than of the non- Muslims. There have been endless wars going on between them over the years. For instance, between Malaysia and Indonesia, Pakistan and Bangladesh, Egypt and Saudi Arabia, South Yemen and North Yemen, Libya and Chad, Libya and Morocco and most horrible of all, the ten year war between Iran and Iraq. As compared to these bloody conflicts, there have been hardly any disputes between the Muslim and non-Muslim states, barring the Arab-Israel and India-Pakistan wars.

The Muslims have made futile attempts, no doubt, in modern times, to unite under a single political banner. But all these attempts failed miserably. The Union between Egypt and Syria was a disaster. Today, every Muslim State guards its sovereignty zealously. No one is prepared to share even a bit of it and each one is determined to preserve its own identity, howsoever small and economically unviable it might be. Their differing national interests are more important for them than their loyalty to Islam.

Terrorism

It is true that some Muslim governments are supporting terrorist organizations as instruments of their own foreign policy. Some are also found guilty of human rights violations. But non-Muslim governments are equally found guilty of the same. No religion should be vilified on account of tyrannical conduct of some governments. Morally, terrorism is contrary to the spirit of Quran. Islam enjoins Muslims not to initiate hostilities, because "God loves not the aggressors"[10].

The US in its legitimate concern about terrorism worldwide, and particularly in the Middle East, should know that terrorism was introduced to the Arab world by Zionists who founded the state of Israel. If Americans are really concerned about terrorism in West Asia, then by all means they should try to curb the Israeli State-run terrorism. The irony, perhaps, is lost on Americans that the very terrorism unleashed by the state of Israel has become the "role model" for the outbreak of Arab and of some other Muslim terrorism.

The volatility of that part of the world is not necessarily caused by Islamic activity as such. Rather, as Robertson correctly observed: "...this increased Islamic activity is a manifestation of deeply rooted underlying problems in the region that have contributed to this type of response. It is much less a manifestation of religious fervor than of political and economic frustration." Many Americans easily merge the fanaticism of hostage-takers, attacks of Palestinian terrorists and military threat by Iran and Saddam together to constitute a single mental picture of Islam. The US should recognize that the problems of the Muslim world emanate from the complex factors; for some of which former US policies were responsible. The political dimension of Islam has become more prominent after the creation of the state of Israel. The rise of Islamic movements in Iran, Egypt, Lebanon and other parts of the Muslim world was motivated by uprooting of three million Palestinians in order to implant a Jewish state based on fundamentalist Biblical grounds. The failure of the US policymakers to give this fact due recognition and their attempt to skirt it does not alter its vital importance. The humiliation caused to the Arab psyche with the loss of Palestine has been a significant contributing factor to Islamic extremism and terrorism.

Muslims in the US

Fears about a Muslim influx have more substance than the worry about Jihad. It is argued that the Muslim immigrants will subvert Western civilization from within. The argument further runs that the Muslim immigrants bring with them a chauvinism that augurs badly for their integration into the mainstream of western societies. Is Islam the primary identity of American Muslims? Whether they are moving towards the formation of a distinct community? American Muslim community is a quilt of cultures; about twenty five percent are of South Asian descent. Arabs represent another twelve percent and nearly half of them are converts: primarily, African-Americans. Some six million strong America's Muslim population is fast increasing on account of immigration, conversion and inter-faith marriages. America's Muslim population is set to outstrip its Jewish Community by the year 2010, making Islam America's second largest faith after Christianity[11].

Multicultural democracy, with its guarantees of religious freedom and speech, makes life easier for Muslims in America than in many Muslim states in West Asia. Unlike other western countries, the US faces less of a problem thanks to a long tradition of immigration and healthy attitudes that go with it. Being an American depends far less on ancestry than on shared values, and this encourages enfranchisement. Meritocratic ethics and an open educational system are also important. Should the fundamentalist Muslims move to migrate to the US and choose to remain outside the mainstream of culture, that too can be accommodated, as the Amish Mennonites of Pennsylvania and the Hasidic Jews of New York city make clear.

Religion is not a basis of conflict in American public life. Instead of being divisive, it is a binding force. It helps in the regeneration of values that produce an integrated character and culture, making America a stable society. American society allows Muslims to strip away the cultural influences and superstitions that have crept into Islam during the past 1400 years. By going back to the basic texts, the Muslims are rediscovering Islam founded on tolerance, social justice and human rights. It is a generation committed to maintaining its Islamic heritage while finding a niche in the New World.

Anti American Sentiments in the Muslim World

The US has never exercised imperial authority over the Islamic world. But since the US is the legitimate heir of European civilization and the recognized and unchallenged leader of the west, the US has inherited the resulting grievances and has become the focus for the pent-up hate and anger in the Muslim world. Nowhere in the Islamic world, in the Middle East or elsewhere has American policy suffered such disaster or encountered problems comparable to those in South East Asia or Central America. There is no Cuba, no Vietnam in the Muslim world. But there is a surge of hatred that distresses, alarms and baffles the Americans. The most important cause for anti-American feelings among Muslims is American support for Israel. Another reason is American support for hated regimes, seen as reactionary by radicals, as impious by conservatives, as corrupt and tyrannical by both. Many Islamic radicals regard the US as hypocritical in not supporting their quest for traditional American values: elections, civil liberties, human rights etc. America's indifference to the issues of domestic governance in the Middle East is based on the claim that preconditions for liberal political reform cannot be found in Islamic societies.

The end of the cold war has not changed the US view on the feasibility of democratization in the Middle East. Washington continues to maintain that nations of the region are not ready to institute democratic rule. Among the rationale offered to justify this contention is the claim that Islam, the dominant belief system in the region, is resistant to democratic practices and thus any effort—particularly by outsiders— to break this resistance is likely to be counterproductive. This claim is based on a prejudice rather than on an informed observation. An examination of empirical evidence strongly suggests that it is not Islam but pervasiveness of despotism that hinders democracy's advance in the region.

International Stability

Muslims constitute majority in about fifty countries from Africa to Southeast Asia and by virtue of its large population and strategic location, the Islamic world is of vital significance to the security of the world. It is unfair to pit such vast and populous areas of the world against the peoples of the United States. For the US to make a strong economic recovery and compete with other industrial nations successfully, it needs the markets of these regions. Many of the Muslim countries posses important natural resources, such as oil and gas, which are essential to many American industries. Hurling insults at a religion of one billion adherents is dangerous in that it is certain to destabilize a vital and volatile region. To make Islam an enemy of the US is to declare a second cold war that is unlikely to end in the same resounding victory as the first. Challenging an ideology is one thing; demonizing a century's old faith and culture is yet another matter.

No Tangible Strategy

It is rather unfortunate that despite the strong evidence of Islam's political appeal and its future potential, the US still has no tangible strategy to contend with Islam. American popular stereotyping of Muslims as inferior people and as terrorists complicates the US Administration's efforts to deal with the populist Islam throughout West Asia. Time has come for the US to chart out a new course in its foreign policy towards the Muslim world. Past policies based on erroneous premises should be reexamined. The US should recognize that the problems of the Muslim World emanate from the complex factors for some of which former US policies were responsible. Only by recognizing errors committed in the past will the US be able to avoid repeating them.

Two Alternatives

There are two alternatives available to the US. One is to press Muslim dominated areas of the world towards political pluralism and then to accept the results of free and fair elections. Having sided with democracy from an early stage, the US would be in a strong position to hold new Muslim governments accountable, if they abuse or give up democratic principles— without being seen as anti-Islamic.[12] The other alternative which the US is right now adopting is to try to counter or contain Islamist movements by backing or aiding governments that suppress them. But such a policy could become as expensive and prolonged as fighting Communism, and potentially more difficult.[13] Washington's perceived reluctance to promote genuine democracy among its allies in Saudi Arabia, Egypt and elsewhere has led the opinion makers throughout the Arab world to criticize Washington for being reluctant to press for political liberalization, notwithstanding its pro-democracy rhetoric. It is rather unfortunate that the US is not applying the most important lesson of the cold war period that cooption is far more effective than confrontation in undermining a rival. Any attempt to limit or control Islam appears counterproductive and may help the rise of Islamic fundamentalism.

Americans should understand that it is possible to encourage democracy in the Muslim would without being perceived as enemies of Islam in West Asia. The US interests would also be better served by encouraging democratic forces that include the conservative forces rather than propping up authoritarian systems that seek to exclude them. Given the growing sense of interdependence between the Muslim world and the industrialized world, the US can play a significant role in providing the pro-democracy forces with the much-needed confidence to carry on the struggle. The instability and uncertainty likely to result from this strategy should be weighed carefully against the probable consequences of alliances with dictators. The fate of Washington's ties with Saddam Hussein only confirms how unpredictable and costly the collaboration with dictators can be.

Conclusion

Fundamental structural changes in the international environment have directly affected the nature of the Muslim world's relations with the US and profoundly altered its approach to the question of regional balance. The collapse of the Soviet Union transformed the bipolar regime in the direction of a unipolar order. The US attempt to fill the strategic vacuum that this restructuring has created has imposed severe constraints on the regional actors in West Asia. Islam's role as a source of legitimacy and a potential influence on domestic and bilateral stability needs, therefore, has to be closely investigated keeping this fact in mind. Within this investigative framework, one may then be able to analyze the dynamic linkage between the domestic, religious, political and socio-economic conditions in the Muslim world and the international environment.

The end of communism is by no means "the end of history" as Francis Fukuyama claimed. The clash of Civilizations as propounded by Samuel Huntigton is also not inevitable. The current challenge can be met peacefully if reconciliation takes place between Islam and Western secular modernity. After the Second World War, Islam had been considered as a bulwark against communist threat. However, after the end of the cold war, Islam has been seen as an expansionist and as the only ideological opponent to the West. Islamic fundamentalist ideology does not challenge either the US or the west on its own turf. Fundamentalism is not a global ideology like communism or capitalism and hence, it should not trigger alarm bells in Washington. The more the US foreign policy seeks global power and greater the demand for an international system of liberal democracy, the greater will be the threat posed by an Islamic fundamentalism that adamantly and violently rejects hegemonistic influences. If the goals of the US remain relatively limited and it attends to issues such as global prosperity and domestic security with sincerity, then Islamic fundamentalism should not be regarded as a threat to the US. There is no unitary Islamic fundamentalism any more than there is a unitary Christian fundamentalism. The US policy needs to be tailored to meet the needs of the local conditions, with an 'imaginative understanding' of what can be realistically attained in each society.

It is a mistake to assume that a fanatic version of Islam is shared by majority of Muslims. Generalizations, libels and stereotypes blunt the kind of awareness that could help the US to play a positive role in the future development of the Muslim world. It is worth pointing out that majority of Muslim governments cooperate with the US rather than threaten it. For instance, Turkey is a member of NATO. Morocco and Jordan have long worked with the Western governments. So have the rulers of Tunisia, Pakistan, Saudi Arabia and Indonesia. The Saudis have invested so much so heavily in the West that their interests are directly tied up with Washington. The picture is hardly of uniform hostility.

The US officials have been at pains to stress that the US does not view Islam or Muslims in adversorial terms except when Muslims engage in extremism or seek to undermine US objectives. For instance President Bush in a speech to the American Congress declared: "The enemy of America is not our many Muslim friends; it is not our many Arab friends. Our enemy is a radical network of terrorists, and every government that supports them. Our war on terrorism begins with Al-Qaeda. The terrorists practice a fringe form of Islamic extremism that has been rejected by Muslim scholars and the vast majority of Muslim clerics – a fringe movement that perverts the peaceful teaching of Islam". But it cannot be denied that in the US there is a tendency to use brush of extremism to paint those who simply oppose its policies, especially in West Asia. When an Under Secretary of Defense speaks about a clash between the west and 'Satan', as Lt. General William Baykin did, it only reinforces the predominant view in the Muslim world that the US war on terrorism is essentially a war against Islam/Muslims.

Recent developments have placed Islam at the forefront. One unfortunate aspect of this increased attention has been the manner it strengthened ugly stereotypes of Islam and Muslims already prevailed in the West. This occurs despite the existence of moderate Islamic segments and secular movements that are more influential than radicals in the political life of Muslim countries. Even though the vast majority of the world's Muslims oppose terrorism, religious intolerance and the oppression of women, these remain the most prevalent images of the Muslim faith throughout the western world. Clitches about Muslims and their attitudes have taken on the standing of truisms but virtually none stands up to serious reflection. Much American commentary on the Muslims world draws heavily on classical writings as well as on the rhetoric and ideology of contemporary Islamist movements. Consequently, little attention is paid to the overwhelming majority of Muslims who do not support or join Islamist movements and also who do not favour any single interpretation of Islam. Muslims reside in a world of independent states and these states are riven by conflicting interests in the international scene as well as by the pressures of domestic cultural diversity. The rigidity or flexibility of Islam as practiced varies widely by social laws, region and political system. The complexity of the Muslim world bedevils any attempt to create a ground stra'egy for dealing with it. The US should have no "one size fits all" policy for the Muslim world.

In the aftermath of 9/11, a great deal needs to be done to build bridges between America and the Muslims world. Traditional presentation of Islam has been woefully inadequate. The point to stress is that the

Muslim world is neither a unified entity nor it is inimical to the west. Conversely, western ideas and institutions are not antithetical to Islam. The need of the hour is to move beyond facile stereotypes and readymade images and answers. The tendency of the US media to equate Islam with extremism, terrorism and anti-westernism would surely hamper understanding and condition of responses. A combination of ignorance and stereotyping, history and experience as well as religious cultural chauvinism often blind even the best intentioned American scholar while dealing with the Muslim world. The challenge today is to appreciate the diversity of Islamic actors and movements to ascertain the causes and reasons, behind confrontations and conflicts, and thus to respond to specific events and situations with informed, reasoned responses, rather than predetermined presumptions and reactions.

Muslims make up one-sixth of the world's population and for this reason no major government can afford to ignore the world of Islam not least of all the US government in its moment of undisputed power. A more energetic promotion of central US foreign policy themes-especially freedom, democracy and human rights – world undermine Muslim critics of US policy and underscore that the future holds great opportunity for continued American cooperation with the Muslim world rather than conflict. Through mutual exchange of ideas and experiences ground work must be laid for enhanced understanding between the US and Muslim world. America is not a commodity to be sold to the Muslim world. American public diplomacy should be directed mainly at spheres of daily life. Washington should put its money into helping American doctors, teachers, business, religious leaders, sportsmen and entertainers to provide the sorts of services people of Muslim world are eager for. The US must engage more actively in the process of analysis and dialogue with Muslim world and also with the local Muslims communities. A dialogue can serve to rectify any negative images that both have of each other and to build mutual trust. There is urgent need to appraise Islam as it has flourished during the past 1500 years, not only since 9/11, 2001. Teaching of Islamic studies in American educational institutions needs to be strengthened. American teachers of Islamic studies undergo regular orientation courses to be conducted by scholars in the Muslim world. For students of Islamic studies, a semester abroad in a Muslim society be made compulsory. More and more moderate Islamic figures scholars and others should be included in US – funded academic and cultural exchange programmes. What is needed is a culture of tolerance.

True tolerance requires that one should learn to know and understand better those who are different. Historically, the US played a constructive role in the development of the Muslim world. There is no reason why the US should not continue to play such a role, which could be mutually beneficial, particularly for foreign trade. What binds America and Islam is much more powerful than what divides them. On the basis of both values and interests, the natural relationship between Islam and America is one of friendship.

References

1. Kislov A and R Zemenkov, USA and the Islamic World, New Delhi, Sterling Publishers, 1984, p. 2.
2. US News and World Report, March 22, 1993.
3. The National Review, November 19, 1990.
4. The Atlantic Monthly, September 1990.
5. World Press Review, June 1993.
6. Lewis, Bernard, "The Roots of Muslim Rage", The Atlantic Monthly, September 1990, p. 49.
7. US Department of State Dispatch, June 8, 1992.
8. US Department of State Dispatch, Vol. 4, No. 32, August 9, 1993
9. Michael C. Hudson, "The Clinton Administration and the Middle East: Squandering the Inheritance?", Current History, Vol. 93, No. 580, February, 1994.
10. See The Quran, Sura 2, Verse 196, Also Sura 4, Verse 30.
11. Carla Power, "The New Islam", Span, May/June 1998, p. 38.
12. Robin Wright, Islam, "Democracy and the West", Foreign Affairs, p. 144.
13. *Ibid.*

8

US and Muslim World: Impression of Visiting Specialist on Islams

Visiting Specialist Programs

After the 9/11 tragedy, I felt deeply concerned about the distorted image of Islam in the western world. I sincerely wished to do something in this regard. Heart's earnest and pure desires are quite often fulfilled. Dame luck smiled at me and I was selected under the Visiting Specialist Program: Rapid Access to the Muslim World. This new initiative on the part of US Department of State Bureau of Educational and Cultural Affairs is designed at expanding the knowledge and understanding of Islamic people and countries on the part of American students, faculty and communities. My six weeks sojourn in America included classroom lectures at Jamestown community college in New York state and at Charleston college in south Carolina as well as public engagements. The themes on which I was specifically asked to speak included Islam and Democracy, Islam and woman, Islamic concept of *Jihad*, Islam and Human Rights, US misperceptions of Islam, etc. All these presentations were followed by lengthy and lively discussions.

Retrospective Analysis

Recent events have placed Islam at the forefront in America. Interest in the Islamic world as a whole and in Islam as a religion and a political system has grown tremendously. Of late, a large number of non-Muslim Americans have taken up the study of Islam. English translation of the *Holy Quran* has become hot selling item. Classes in Arabic and Islamic studies have been overflowing. Muslims scholars are being invited by religious, cultural and academic institutions to explain Islam. Open Houses organized by Islamic centres have been well attended. Innumerable seminars, and conferences have been organized about Islam and Muslim world. US media, often perceived as hostile by Muslims has given fair exposure to the Muslim viewpoint. Informative programmes like the PBS documentary "Empire of Faith" and Oprah Winsfrey's "Islam 101" highlighted aspects of Islamic beliefs and history. However, despite greater interest and a seemingly never ending stream of publication and conferences, understanding of Islam and Muslim world remains limited and selective. The selective analysis fails to tell the whole story. Selective and biased analysis adds to ignorance, instead of knowledge, narrow perspective instead of broadening understanding and reinforcing the problem instead of offering solutions. Ironically, most of the experts on Islam were trained in area studied by professors with little real expertise in the Islamic religion. In history and politics courses Islam was treated primarily as part of a cultural legacy. Islamic studies was studied textually and historically rather than contextually oriented with little relevance on the social sciences and with minimal attention to the modern world. Consequently, Islam and Muslims are reduced to stereotypes of Islam against the west. Several academicians after listening to my presentations frankly confessed: "We realize how little we know of Islam".

The underlying presumptions in most of the questions put to me whether in classroom lectures or speaking at public engagements reflected American stereotypes of Islam. For many of them Islam self-evidently refers to an aggressive, hostile and anti-American religious traditions and peoples. Arguments on issues ranging from terrorism to oppression of woman centred on an image of a monster community driven by extremism, intolerance and a world view at odds with the values of western civilized world. Even ostensibly informed discussion ended with the depressing conclusion that Islam, however democratic and enlightening it might have been in the beginning is now hopelessly out of tune with excerpts of democracy, individual freedom, free speech and gender equality. People have reason to ask?" Why does this violence keeps on happening in the name of peaceful religion?"

Most discussions of the so-called Islamic threat includes a dearth of information and lack of discrimination concerning the nature of diversity of Islamic resurgence. Integral to the vision of an Islamic threat there is the belief that Islam is anti-democratic and intolerant. Many

Americans perceive that Islam is nothing other than what Muslims appear to be doing. Most of them know Osama Bin Laden, Saddam Hussain, Taliban and Al Qaeda but do not know about all infrastructural and intellectual facilities built by Muslims. None of the virtues in Islam appear obvious to most Americans because of cultural overlays. Positive aspects of Islam are often not taught properly at US educational institutions. Most of the Americans do not know that in Quran God talks exclusively inter alia of Abraham, Christ and Moses and they have been recognized by Islam as Prophet Mohammad. Significantly, Muslims have been exhorted to revere all the prophets and all the revealed books. Islamic concepts like *Jihad* have been grossly misinterpreted by the media. The popular attitudes is also reflected in articles by prominent political commentators. Even though the vast majority of the world's Muslims oppose terrorism, religious intolerance and the oppression of woman, these remain the most popular stereotypes about Islam and Islamic movements are often exacerbated by the media and popular culture.

On the positive side it was evident from the many questions asked by audience that there is a strong desire for people to understood Islam. People, by and large, especially students who are future leaders displayed a genuine concern about the widening gulf between America and the Islamic world. Many of them stood for a better and peaceful relationship between the US and the Muslim world. One thing has emerged very clearly the US must engage more actively in the process of analysis and dialogue with the Muslim world and also with the local Muslim communities. A dialogue can serve to rectify any negative images that they have of each other and to build mutual trust. In this connection role of American Muslims is crucial. It is their duty to make a concerted effort to counteract negative stereotypes and identify where Islam and America have a common ground. The point to stress it that pillars of justice, equality before the law, human rights, independence of judiciary, as they are at the heart of US constitution, were cornerstones of Islamic jurisprudence for a millennium before the framing of American constitution. The Muslims feel quite at home and quite comfortable with the US constitution because it is a familiar echo of the principles which lie at the basis of Islamic law. There is urgent need to appraise Islam as it has flourished during the last 1500 years, not only since 9/11, 2001. Teaching of Islamic studies needs to be supplemented. American teachers of Islamic studies should undergo regular orientation courses to be conducted by scholars in the Muslim world. For students of Islamic studies permit a semester abroad in a Muslim society. Media should stop blaming Islam for whatever any self-styled champion of Islam does or utter-howsoever potentially un-Islamic act might be. Traditional presentation of Islam are woefully a inadequate. It is worth emphasizing that Islamic world is neither a unified entity nor it is inimical to the western world. In fact western ideas and institutions are not antithetical to Islam. More attention needs to be paid to the overwhelming majority of Muslims who do not support or join Islamist movements who do not favour any single interpretation of Islam and its dictates. These Muslims are not as well organized as extremists, but they are a global presence. More and more moderate Islamic figures–scholars and others should be included in US-funded academic and cultural exchange programme. What is needed is a culture of tolerance. True tolerance requires that we learn to know and understand better those who are different from ourselves. The problem today is putting into perspective relations between America and the Muslim world. The need for better understanding of Islam and Muslim politics is as great as ever. The US should try to better understand the outlook and perception of people in the Muslim world. Many currents of anti-Americanism develop not because US is misguided but because it is misunderstood. What shapes US strategic culture today are not the traditional tools of power-military might–but the so-called soft power tools such as economic, trade, cultural relations, education and dialogue. The need of the hour is that cooperation in these spheres should be intensified. On the basis of both values and interests, the natural relationship between Islam and America is one of friendship and cooperation.

In the aftermath of 9/11, a great deal needs to be done to build bridges between America and the Muslim world. Building the bridges understanding is what I sincerely tried to achieve throughout my stay in the US. I felt thrilled and duly rewarded when at the end of my visit, Mamiko Hada, an official from the Fulbright Headquarters, Washington D.C. wrote : "I would like to thank you for being a great ambassador of Islam to the people of US".

9
American Misperceptions of Islam

Never before the image of Islam has been so terribly distorted in the US as after the 9/11 tragedy. Islam is constantly being defined to American public by non-Muslim analysts. Most of them are anti-Muslim through and through. They deliberately present a distorted picture. Maligning Islam appears to be their mission. On the other hand, Islam is defined by a small group of Muslim extremists who lent credence to a distorted image of Islam. Both portray Islam as a primitive, rigid and inhumane culture which is basically alien to basic principles of modern civilization. Islam is depicted in the American media as the religion of war, vengeance, hatred and annihilation. It is misconstrued as a fundamentalist religion which is intolerant of other faiths, which establishes a male-dominated society and which encourages and promotes terrorism. Some of the very common perceptions of Islam and Muslims found in America are:

Islam and Muslim Societies are Same

Many Americans perceive that Islam is nothing other than what Muslims appear to be doing. No distinction is made between an Islamic state and a Muslim state. The term Islamic state implies that Islam is central factor that shapes the dynamics of such societies/countries. In contrast Muslim world or society understood as a plural and concrete identity allows a self-conscious Muslim majority to define their own reality in an inevitably differential and dynamic fashion. Here the emphasis is not on Islam but on Muslims as objects of their societies and cultures. They are never religious by definition as such, no are their cultures mean religion.

Monolithic Islam

The entire Muslim community is lumped together as a single monolithic group. Muslim countries have generally been characterized as a unified single block known as Muslim world. This hypothesis ignores the diversity among Muslims. Islam encompasses for too many perspectives which often contend among themselves for recognition and influence. A cohesive transnational Islamic movement simply does not exist. Thinking of Muslims as a single constituency is unrealistic. It has innumerable currents: violent and non violent, revolutionary, reactionary and middle of the road, socialist and capitalist, democratic and non-democratic Islam as practised in the Middle East is different from Islam is Southeast Asia. The Indian Muslims are different from Muslims of Uzbekistan. The basic principle may be the same but they are affected by cultural ethics of the people of region.

Overestimation of Extremist Islam

American judgment of Islam has been grassly distorted by taking the extremes to be the norm. Extremists do exist at this fringe but it is unfair to judge an entire community on the basis of stray or isolated incidents. There is a regrettable tendency to overestimate the influence of the fundamentalist groups in Muslim countries. Not all those whom the US government and media denounces as Islamist extremists are in fact not true followers of the faith or even accepted as spokespersons of Islam by Muslims themselves. Little attention is paid to the overwhelming majority of Muslims who do not support or join islamist movements and who do not favour any single interpretation of Islam and its dictates.

Middle East True Representative of Islam

One of the most widespread misperception about Islam is that Middle East is regarded as the mainstream or true representative of Islam. It is true that the Arabic language and sacred places in Mecca, Madina and Jerusalem give Arab world a special position. In recent years oil wealth and sheer number of petty Arab states have added to their influence and inflated importance. However, Arabs account only 20 per cent of all Muslims. Interestingly, there are about 100 million more Muslims to the Indian sub-continent alone than in all Arab countries combined. It is ironical that regions like South Asia and South East

Asia, where majority of Muslims live are not taken into account. The global Muslims politics is dictated by events in the Arab world, and not what obtains in other regions. It is due to the Muslims vs others. Syndrome which several ethnic-religious conflicts around the globe brought to reckoning. At the core of this problematic is the extra territoriality of Muslims ethos. In general American diplomats simply do not count religion as a significant factor in formulating policy for non-Middle Eastern Muslim countries like Indonesia and Malaysia. They have an especially hard time seeing Indonesia as a Muslim country, even though it is home to 185 million Muslims which is more than Muslim populations of all Arabs countries combined together.

Islam is Anti-democratic

Many in America believe that Islam is inherently antidemocratic or, at best is not hospitable to democracy. It is argued that the political reality in the Muslim world has more often been one of authoritarianism–monarchies and dictatorships. It is forgotten that the dictators reigning in the Arab world are not the result of Islamic principles. They are more a result of global economics and the aftermath of western colonialism Men, according to the Quran are born free and are equal in dignity, rights and status: their worth and merit are to be measured irrespective of their origin and application; all humans are equal before the law and are entitled equal protection of laws; presumption of innocencc and due process of law are necessary preconditions of justice. The Quran commands Muslims to conduct their collective affairs through mutual consultation (shura) and grants the privilege of God's vice-regency to the entire Muslim country rather than to a single individual or a specific groups or class of people. The selection of a Muslim ruler must be based on the free will of the Muslim masses. Prophet Mohammad had established a political system that was representative and consultative, transparent, accountable and accessible to everyone. It was a government that was based on principles of limited government, devolution of executive powers and compassionate sharing of economic resources, social fraternity and system based on treaties. In fact, the Islamic tradition of rules limiting the powers of sovereign is much older than the concept of constitutional law in the western democracies. One may call an Islamic state a republic since the Islamic law rules out usurpation and succession as grounds of political legitimacy. The Prophet himself had evolved a system of consultation and consensus-building and the pious caliphate followed that. The institution of Majlis-i-Shura comes very close to modern parliament. The Islamic state has to be based on the principle of separation of powers. It ensures the founding of an independent judiciary and no one including the head of state, is above the law.

Islam is Intolerant to Other Faiths

Another common misperception is that Islam is intolerant of other faiths. However, the Quran clearly says that "There is no compulsion in religion". When Mecca came under the sway of Muslims and Prophet Mohammad entered Mecca, then "No one was asked to accept Islam as part of this settlement. The non-Muslims were guaranteed right to their religious convictions, to profess and practice their own faiths. As far as the inter-faith relations are concerned, both the Quran and Hadith (Prophet sayings) are explicit about the desirability of relations between peoples. In the first Islamic state of Madina, there were not only Muslims but jews and others too. All were guaranteed rights to their religious belief, to profess and defend their convictions. More important, Muslims are morally bound to relate to non-Muslims minorities positively. Muslims have a moral obligation to be fair and friendly in their person-to-person conduct towards non-Muslims citizens, and will be answerable to God for that. They must treat them with trust benevolence and equity. According to the Quran Muslims, Christians and Jews are people of the Book". They share a monotheistic vision; a believe in divine God, in the transience of earthly life, in accountability for actions, and in the assurance of life to come. Muslims revere the same prophets as Judaism and Christianity, from Abraham, the first monotheist to Moses, to Jesus.

Islam and Terrorism

After 9/11 tragedy, Islam is seen by many in America as a fanatical doctrine of encouraging and perpetrating violence and terrorism. Islam like all religions is a religion of peace and moderation. If it does not appear to be so today, this is not due to the teaching of Islam but to interpretations made by those who want to exploit Islam to suit their vested interests. Islam clearly abhars wars of aggression and the killing of innocent people. Though Muslim ideologues have persistently declared that terrorism has no sanction in Islam, the entire Muslim community carries the awesome burden of dispelling the false notions about the meaning and significance of Jihad. Doubtless fundamentalist ideas exemplified by Taliban and Al-Qaeda inspire certain segments of Muslim communities. But such elements do not represent Islam's authoritative voice. One should do well to take into account the silent majority's positive equanimity. Today, resistance liberation and terrorist movements variously use the call of Jihad alike to legitimize their cause and motivate their followers. But it has few takes among more than a billion Muslims living across the globe.

Islam and Women

Last but not the least, it is commonly believed that Islam treated women unjustly and wants to create a male-dominated society. Women are not second class citizens when they live in Muslim countries. One should not judge the position of women in Islam by taking the most conservative Muslims states as representative of the whole. The obvious American prejudice is to judge the position of women in Islamic society by the extreme cases. Some Muslim countries like Turkey, Egypt and Syria gave women the vote as early as Europe did its women and much earlier even the Switzerland. In these countries, women have long enjoyed equal pay and the opportunity to play a full working role in their societies. Rights of Muslim women to property and inheritance, to some protection, if divorced and to the conducting of business were rights prescribed by the Quran 14 centuries ago. In fact, some of these rights were novel till 19th century. Islam gave those social and inheritance rights which liberated women in the contemporary world received from their respective governments only in the second half of the 20th century. Women received their instant liberation from the cruel social customs at the hands of Prophet Mohammad in 630 AD.

The need of the hour is to move beyond the facile stereotypes and readymade images and answers. The tendency of the American media to equate Islam with radicalism, barbarism and anti-Americanism would seriously hamper understanding and condition of responses. The challenge before the US today is to appreciate the diversity of Muslim actors and movements, and thus to respond to specific events and situations with informed, reasoned responses, rather than predetermined presumptions and reactions. A combination of stereotyping, history and experience as well as religious cultural chauvinism blind even the best-intentioned American scholar/policy maker while dealing with the Muslim world.

10
Anti-Americanism in the Muslim World

Anti-Americanism is on the rise around the world. PEW Foundation's latest polls of international attitudes find President Bush and his policies have made America more unpopular in the world now than any other time in post-war history. Public opinion polls have found fairly strong anti-American sentiments throughout the Muslim world. A federal panel investigating American public diplomacy in the Muslim world reported that despite our best efforts to win hearts and minds, hostility towards America has reached shocking proportions. Recent developments have further hardened these attitudes. Increasing number of Muslims surveyed after Iraq war say they see American war on terrorism as a campaign to weaken Muslims. Majorities in 7 out of 8 predominantly Muslim countries say they worry that the US might threaten their countries.

What has the US done to invite this enmity? What does the term anti-Americanism mean? Does it mean that Muslims are anti-jaaz? Or that Muslims are opposed to basic American values? Does it imply that Muslims hate American people? Reasons for loathing the US are easy to point out:

(a) In the first place, Muslim anti-Americanism stems from manifestly unjust consequences of current and past US policies towards the Muslim world. The policies that fuel anti-Americanism include US blind support for Israel in West Asia. US is seen as being directly responsible for Israeli occupation of Palestine through its unwavering support for every Israeli government regardless of its policies.

(b) A very important reason is US backing of illegitimate and discredited regimes across the Muslim world. Significantly, the people did not choose their governments and in any free elections none of them would succeed. The deep level of suspicion for US motive in the region explains the wide suspicion that accompanies any US endeavour to bring reform and democracy to the Arab world. The fact that Washington's closet allies in the region are not particularly known for their democratic governance further supports the widespread view of America's double standards.

(c) Neo liberal economic development strategies-vigorously encouraged by the US-have resulted in widespread economic dislocation, which has, in turn encouraged the growth of radical Islamic movements.

(d) The distorted facts that the western/American media is selling to American people portraying Muslims as the enemy and as a threat is the chief reason behind the widening gulf between the US and Muslim world. US media continues to antagonize the Muslim world, sometimes based on ignorance but more often with malicious designs. Attacks against Islam continue to enrage Muslim sentiments and create bad blood and feeling of animosity.

(e) American political climate is being increasingly hospitable to forces of religious fundamentalism. The nexus between the neo-conservatives who dominate the Bush Administration and the people of right wing Christian evangelists in the south particularly is well known. While Bush Administration is trying to convince the world that its war on terrorism is not a war on Islam, a part of neo-conservative intelligentsia in Washington is doing its best to turn the Bush Administration's war against terrorism as a war against Muslim civilization and Islamic religion. They argue that Islamic religion and civilization are intolerant, hostile to western values, expansionist and violent. Bush Administration cannot succeed in its endeavour if its President speaks of war against rogue states and has general who see the world as a stage on which angles are fighting 'satans'. When an Under Secretary of Defense speaks about a clash between the West and 'Satan', as Lt. General W. Boykin did, it only reinforces the predominant view in the Muslim world that the US war on terrorism is essentially a war against Muslims.

(f) Last but not the least, though people in the Muslim world were long denied free access to information, they developed a critical sense and ability to decipher political realities. People in Muslim world are watching developments in Iraq against the backdrop of another illegal occupation. This action is seen as proof that the US is determined to destroy Islam and Muslim.

On the other hand, Islamist discourse has made anti-Americanism its centerpiece by constructing the idea of an Islamic civilization that is in direct opposition to the west. They blame US for Muslim world's oppressive rulers, stagnant economies and sense of powerlessness. They posit western values as the cause of all Muslim problems. The real and perceived injustices committed by the US and its allies against Muslims, has engendered an extremely vitriolic hatred of America. The Islamists and their discourses are globalizing anti-Americanism.

What can the US do to combat anti-Americanism with Muslim world? Generalizations, libels and stereotypes blunt the kind of awareness that could help the US to play a positive role in the development of Muslim world. Past policies based on erroneous premises need to be re-examined. Only by recognizing errors committed in the past will the US be able to chart out a new course in its foreign policy towards the Muslim world.

Very often, the entire Muslim country is lumped together as a single monolithic group and regarded as a potential threat to the western world. A cohesive, transnational Islamic movement simply does not exist. Thinking of Muslims as a single constituency is unrealistic. Islam encompasses for too many perspectives, which often contend among themselves for recognition and influence. There are clear dangers in the US failing to recognize diversity in the unity of Islam. The various Islamic movements should rather be contextualized and examined against the backdrop of domestic and international events that have helped shape them.

American judgment of Islam has been grossly distorted by taking the extremes to be the norm. it is unwise to judge an entire community on the basis of stray, isolated incidents, which inevitably leads to disastrous and prejudiced conclusions. There is a regrettable tendency to overestimate the influence of the extremist groups in the Muslim world and even more unfortunate tendency to assume that any movement raising the banner of Islam will necessarily be fundamentalist in nature. It is a mistake to assume that a fanatic version of fundamentalist Islam is shared by minority of Muslims. American popular stereotyping of Muslims as terrorists complicate US Administrations efforts to deal with the populist Islam throughout the Muslim world.

Finally, the US should recognize that the problems of Muslims world emanate from the complex factors for some of which former US policies were responsible. The US policy needs to be tailored to meet the needs of local conditions with an imaginative understanding of what can be realistically achieved in each society.

It is worth remembering that most people in the Muslim world are not consumed with hatred towards America but are essentially critical of double standards used in foreign policies by US government. Significantly majority of Muslim governments cooperate with the US government rather than threaten it. For instance Turkey is a member of NATO. Morocco and Jordan have worked with the western governments. So have the rulers of Tunisia, Pakistan, Saudi Arabia and Indonesia. The Saudis have invested so much in the west that their interests are directly tied up with Washington. The picture is hardly of uniform hostility. Not every argued criticism of US policies should be represented as hate. Interestingly, there are many Americans who would be mortified to be associated with their government's policies. In fact, the most scholarly scathing, incisive hilarious critiques of the hypocrisy and contradictions in US policies come from American citizens. Of course there are many in the Muslim world who do express hateful or ignorant views about America. But even among them there are not many who would countenance, let alone do, which the terrorists did on 9/11. Therefore, not every emotional outburst should be equated with a readiness to commit acts of terrorism. The connection between what people say and what they do is often indirect.

Muslims constitute majority in about fifty countries from Africa to South east Asia. And by virtue of its large population and strategic location, that Muslim world is of vital significance to the security of the world. It is unfair to pit such vast and populous areas of the world against the people of US. Historically, the US has played a constructive rule in the development of the Muslim world. There is no reason why the US should not continue to play such a role, which could be mutually beneficial. What binds America and Muslim world is much more powerful that what divides them. The need for better understanding between the US and Muslim world is greater than ever before.

11
Islam and America—Shared Values

The notion that Islam is incompatible with Americanism appears to be preponderant notion among many Americans, especially after 9/11 tragedy. However, Americans as a people share certain human and moral values with Islam. Within the central dogma of Islam, Islamic jurisprudence as well as Islamic history, there are many tenets consistent with and supportive of the founding principles upon which the US is based.

The first and foremost, a deep faith in the one Supreme Being. Islam is monotheistic. Muslims worship the same God as the Jews and Christians. Muslims, Christians and Jews are "Peoples of the Book". They share a monotheistic vision, a belief in divine God, in the transience of earthly life in accountability for actions, and in the assurances of life to come. Muslims also revere the same prophets as Jews and Christians from Abraham, the first monotheist, to Moses, to Jesus-not leaving Noh, Jab or Saiah along the way. The concept of a Judo-Christian tradition which came to the fore in the 1940's in America may turn into a more inclusive 'Abrahamic' view.

The most notable principle, as mentioned in the American Declaration of Independence is a notion of the security of life. This principle is enunciated with forceful clarity in the Quran. This sanctity of life is, in the belief of Muslims, ordained by God as a founding principle for humanity and was enjoined in the earliest revelations to the children of Israel, binding upon all believers in God throughout the ages. This concept is basic, fundamental and unequivocally stated in the Quran. As such it is a central part of Islamic dogma.

The second basic principle upon which the existence of the US is based is the principle of liberty. From the point of view of the founding fathers after securing the right to life, "Liberty was their first principle and also the first goal". This notion just like the sanctity of life is central to the core of Islamic belief. Unlike Christianity, Islam does not believe in the doctrine of original sin. Rather Muslims believe that Adam and Eve sinned and were forgiven. Their descendents are born sin free into this earthly life which serves as a test of their soul. This test the basic purpose for which the human race is created is dependent on the most essential part of the concept of liberty. Without liberty there is no freedom to either sin or believe. Therefore, a system without this basic of God-given human right is not compatible with Islam. This notion of the necessity of human liberty has been there from early Islamic history and intellectual development. Without liberty, the purpose of this life itself becomes null and void. Thus, in Islam, a man is given the freedom of choice to adopt any course of action. It is worth stressing that the central place to the concept of liberty as fundamental within Islamic doctrine is not a post-modern evolution of thought. This understanding has been present since the earliest days of Islam. At the state level, personal liberty, including freedom of religion was seen as a paramount pillar of the early Islamic rule.

If liberty is the main founding principle of the US, then certainly the concept of justice is also a main pillar upon which the American Constitution was founded and framed. The Quran clearly and explicitly states that the purpose of the divine messages to humanity has been the establishment of justice. God says in the Quran: "We send aforetime our apostles with clear signs and sent down with them the book and the balance (of right and wrong) that human beings may establish justice" (57:25). This concept has also been recognized as the chief driving force behind Islamic law. The concept of justice includes equality before law b) due process and c) reasonable laws with reasonable punishments. In the early Islamic state these three pillars were clearly understood and explicitly applied. Even the caliph was not above the process of law-legal contestation, and his citizens understood that if they felt wronged by him, they had the right to sue him in Islam's legal court.

The Declaration of independence also stipulates that one of the inalienable rights of human beings is that of pursuit of happiness. Islam also guarantees the pursuit of happiness within lawful bounds as a right of every human, and does so by a direct inspiration of the Quran itself: "Who is there to forbid the beauty which God has brought forth for his creatures and the good things from among the bounty (which he has provided)" 7.32.

Islam is egalitarian. It is predicated on a level playing field, especially when it comes to standing before God. The pledge of Allegiance (one nations, "Under God") and Lincoln's Gettysburg address (all people are created equal) express themes that are also basic to Islam. The egalitarian streak also lays itself out in relations between the sexes. Prophet Mohammad was a reformer in his times. Following the Quran, he limited the number of wives a man could have and strongly recommended against polygamy. The Quran laid out a set of marriage laws that guarantee married women their own possessions and capital, the right to agree upon whom, they will marry and the right to initiate divorce. In Islam early period, women were professionals and property owners as increasingly they are today. Unfortunately none of these seem obvious to most Americans because of cultural overlys that at time makes Islam appear to be a repressive faith toward women.

Like America, Islam has a history of respecting other religions. During Prophet Mohammad's time, Christians, Sabeans and Jews in Muslim lands retained their own courts and enjoyed considerable autonomy. After capturing Jerusalem during Pious Caliphate period, the first thing the Muslims did was to rescue the Temple Mount, which by then had been turned into a garbage heap.

Islam shares America's new interest in food purity and diet. Muslims observe a month long fast during the holy month of Ramzan, a practice that many Americans admire or even seek to emulate.

Above all, Islam is democratic in spirit. It advocates the right to vote and educate oneself and pursue a profession. The Quran enjoins Muslims to govern themselves by discussion and consensus. There is no priestly hierarchy in Islam. Each individual is responsible for the condition of his or her own soul. Everyone stands equal before God. In this way America is closer in spirit to Islam than so many Arab countries.

All in all, there appears to be a deep resonance between Islam and the US. Although one is world religion and the other is a sovereign nation, both are traditionally strong on individual responsibility. Like New Hampshire's motto, "Live Free or Die", America is wedded in individual liberty and an ethic based on right action. For a Muslim, spiritual salvation depends on these.

Therefore, it is obvious that the pillars of justice, equality before the law, due process, as they are at present at the heart of American

Constitution were cornerstones of Islamic jurisprudence for a millennium, before the framing of US constitution, in nearly identical concepts, and nearly identical words. A Muslim, then feels quite at home and quite comfortable with the American constitution, since it is a familiar echo of the principles which lie at the basis of Islamic law. It is ironical in many ways that misunderstandings between Islam and America persists, for what binds the two together is much more powerful than what divides them.

12
Muslims in America

A quarter of the world's population is Muslim – from Africa to Middle East to Asia and to the United States, where Islam is one of our fastest growing faiths. There are over 1,200 mosques and Islamic Centers in the United States, and the number of rapidly increasing. The Six million Americans who worship there will tell you there is no inherent clash between Islam and America. Americans respect and honour Islam.

Bill Clinton, Former US President

Diversity like freedom has been the hallmark of American Society from the very outset. Many minorities constitute America's multi-ethnic society. US has often been described as a nation of natíons. Religion in America is characterized by its diversity. There are over 220 religious denominations and around 1,200 religious groups in America.

There are 6-8 million Muslims in America and they constitute 3 per cent of the population. America's Muslim community comprises of native American Muslims-both African Americans and whites-as well as immigrants from all parts of the world. African-Americans constitute nearly half of the Muslim population; about 25 per cent of them are of South Asian descent. Arabs represent anther 12 per cent. Majority belongs to Sunni Islam. Nearly all schools of thought such as Hanafi, Shafai Maliki and Hambali are found among Sunni Muslims. Smali groups influenced by sufi ideas complete the Muslim mosaic in US. Muslim population is rapidly increasing on account of immigration, conversion and inter-faith marriages. It is estimated that 14 per cent of all migrants since the 1980s are Muslims. It is set to outstrip its Jewish community by the year 2010, making Islam America's second largest faith after Christianity.

Muslims Immigrants

In the first decades of the twentieth century, the first batches of immigrant muslims came mainly from Syria, Albania, Bosnia - Aerzegonina, Eastern Europe and Russia including Tartar Muslims. Numerically small and of rural background they joined the labour force in the industrializing north-eastern parts of the US. Over a period of time, these Muslims 'melted' away into the broader Christian milieu chiefly because of their own ignorance about Islam. As they were of white racial stock, they got absorbed into the American population easily. The second wave of Muslim immigrants came after the second world war mainly from Turkey and countries of the west, south and south east Asia. Westernized in their outlook, many of them easily assemiliated with the American pluralist culture. These immigrant Muslims insisted on leading an ethical and responsible life according to Islamic tenets, but shed some of Islam's cardinal practices. However, their liberal outlook created the bases of intersect cooperation such as common mosques and collective celebration of Muslim festivals. With the liberalization of immigration laws in the mid 1960's, there started a fresh and larger flow of Muslim immigrants. Coming from societies that are experiencing religious reawakening and ethnic upheavals, religion is of great importance to them because it is a way of maintaining their culture in the host society. The list of Muslim immigrants continued to grow as the cold war created more and more crises around the Muslims world. The post-war revolutions and political upheaval in the Middle East led to an exodus of political refugees from the Arab countries. With the eruption of Islamic revolution in Iran in 1979, Iranians came in droves to the US. A single thread that links all the waves of Muslim immigrants to the larger tapestry of immigrants descending on American shores is their common quest for success in what has always been believed to be the "Land of Opportunities".

How do Muslims live in a non-Muslim world? How do they institute Islamic practices in environments that are alien and even hostile to Islam? How do they establish Islamic institutions which often challenge the way of life and social structures of host societies? How can they integrate in a manner as to be able to influence their own destinies without losing their cultural identity and their basic values? How do they replace Judo-Christian traditions with Islamic-Jude-Christian traditions? Is Islam the primary identity of American Muslims? Are American Muslims evolving into a cohesive community? Do American Muslims have a political agenda? Can Islam be a force in the US political process?

Institution - Building

The rise in the Muslim population has resulted in the development of institutions catering to the needs of the community. Initially, this institution - building essentially meant the establishment of mosques as places for communal worship. The number of mosques in the US has grown threefold since the 1970's. America's 1,500 odd mosques are spread from Alaska to Florida. Muslims pray daily in state department hallways, in white-shoe corporate law firms and in empty boardrooms at Silicon valley companies like oracle and Adaptee. The main factor which led to the growing number of mosques is the increase in conversion and in the growing feeling of self confidence and security among native-born and immigrant Muslims. This psychological feeling is linked to the process of ethnic and regional identity affirmation among the subgroups within the larger Muslims community in the US. As mosques became a visible symbol of Islam in America, they not only drive home the sense that Islam is a part of American society, but they are a source of information on Islam that could be provided to the Muslim, as well as non-Muslim community.

A more recent development has been the Muslim community's awareness of the need to establish centres which are specifically designed to meet the needs of Muslim youth. Numerous schools have opened throughout the country, some of which are associated with a particular mosque, but not necessarily all. The schools provide Quranic and Arabic classes for children as well as adults. While some are essentially Sunday Schools, others hold classes daily, in addition to Friday evenings and Sundays. In addition to schools, the Muslims community is trying to create and maintain institutions of higher learning. The first attempt in this direction is the establishment of the American Islamic college by the late Ismailal-Faruqi and his colleagues from various Muslim backgrounds. The effort received the support of the organization of Islamic Conference in Jeddah, Saudi Arabia. Another institution that has survived and has made some significant progress is the East-West University founded by Dr. Wasiullah Khan. Like the American Islamic college, the East-West University has over the years evolved into a college for inner city Americans into world like to make something out of themselves under a caring and nurturing environment. There are two other efforts at institution-building at the college/University level. The first, in terms of historical chronology is the Muslims Teachers college of Virginia. This college is still in an embryonic state. The second recent attempt to build a college/university for the Muslim population in the US is inspired and financed by the International Institute of Islamic Thought Herndon, Virginia. The leadership of this institution is banking heavily on the intelligence and good-will of the large number of highly trained Muslim scholars and intellectuals around the US who can provide guidance and services to the institutions.

The growing consciousness about the political system and the role and place of American Muslims in American public life has captured the attention of Muslims across the country. The first Muslim efforts in this direction were those of Abdulrahman al-Amandi and two cohorts. Like the Black Rights advocates of the 1950's and 1960's, these Muslims founded the American Muslim council. The AMC has been quite effective in mobilizing Muslims to become involved in the political processes. The AMC has been instrumental in having the White House host an Eid-al-Fitr celebration, and having the US Congress to invite Imam Warith Deen Muhammed, to give the opening prayer. It started pressing Mslim's claims not against any form of institutionalized discrimination of Muslims but against any attempts at the political and social marginalization of Muslims simply because of their religion. The involvement in voter registration and in the cultivation of politicians by individual Muslims and organizations around the country clearly testifies to the growing consciousness that, to be recognized, Muslims must go beyond mosque construction and move toward political mobilisation.

The realization of the danger of social and political marginalization has led to the appearance of another Muslim organiation viz council on American-Islamic Relations (CAIR). Through its chapters and internet facilities, it has created a network of Muslim supporters who monitor local news media for adverse and good reporting on Muslim affairs. Though such network and calls from American Muslims, it has been quite effective in getting grievances redressed all over the country. The

CAIR has shown Muslims how the legal system can be a force for reducing discrimination against Muslims. When a Muslim woman was not hired because she wore a head scarf, CAIR effectively used legal threats to stop the hotel from discriminating her. Indeed, CAIR has emerged, as the equivalent of the Jewish Defense League for the American Muslims.

In addition to AMC and CAIR, there are several other groups working on Muslim issues in the domain of American public policy. The list includes the Muslim Public Affairs Council (MPAC), the American Muslim Caucus (AMC), the American Muslim Alliance (AMA), and the National Council of Islamic Affairs (NCIA). All these groups are striving for greater Muslim political involvement in American life.

Professional Organizations

Many Muslim immigrants after graduating from colleges and universities have become professionals in the larger society. They are the founding fathers of such Muslim organizations as the Islamic society of North America (ISNA), the circle of North America (ICNA), the Association of Muslims Scientists and Engineers (AMSE) and the Islamic Medical Association (IMA). These organizations have created a significant presense among Muslims who are willing to come out of the social and political closet and affirm their faith and their rituals in their workplaces and in those parts of the Public square where they encounter strangers who are committed to their faith as those Muslims willing to do Dawah in America's public fora.

Muslim Publications

There is no reliable accounting of the number of publications coming from different Muslim groups across the country. The most widely read publications among Muslims in the US are the Message International of the Islamic circle of North America, the Islamic Horizons of the Islamic society of North America, the Minaret of the Islamic centre of Southern coralina and the Muslim Journal of Imam Mohammed in Chicago. Other publications circulating among the Muslims are New Trend of the Jamaatal Muslim so on, al-Raya of the Hizbu Tahir, the Muslims magazine of the Naqsbandiyya order, al-Jummah (Friday) of the Islamic Revival Association, the Orange Crescent from the Islamic centre of orange country and the AMC Report of the American Muslim Council.

Beside these better known publications, there are countless regular and irregular publications from local mosques across the country. There are also magazines for women, students and children. In addition to print media, there are numerous websites bearing Islamic and Muslim names. Some of these websites have rich materials for those in search of information about Islamic history and culture.

Halal Food Stores

Another recent significant trend is the opening of halal food stores across the country, especially in the major cities of the US. Halal meat stores have been able to survive in many Muslim communities, mostly because of the Indian and Pakistan Muslims who refuse to eat meat that is not slaughtered by Muslims. Prior to the ubiquity of halal food stores many a Muslim adherent to strict diet found the Kosher food store as a better alternative to the non-halal food stores. Now, as a result of the growing presence of halal food stores, some of the Muslims are beginning to challenge the tradition of other Muslims who buy Kosher food. This trend could eventually call for some ruling from the Muslim jurists in America.

Economic Sphere

On economic front, many Muslim finance companies have been established in the US to help the Muslim community. These companies, like Baitul Mal al-Islam (BMI) provide alternatives to interest based banks financing for buying a car or a home. Although the Muslim community has been slow to respond to such non-interest financing, the positive effects of these companies is growing. Other Muslims Americans are helping the country through financial planning programme. One instance of this is the Income Preservation Policy (also known as life insurance). If the husband dies, the wife receives a sum of money ad a salary based upon how much the family invested in the financial package. This is very important service to the Muslim community, because in the past Muslim widows suffered from poverty, neglect, and humiliation. There are many rich Muslims in America. Safi Qureshi, a Pakistani American is the owner of the fourth largest computer company: AST. Muhammed Hadid, a Palestinian American used to be one of the largest real estate developers in the Washington DC, area. A large number of Muslims have achieved wealth by being medical doctors.

Significantly, most Muslims that become rich in the US are able to do so because of foreign investors like Saudi businessmen, or starting their own businesses.

Challenges

The past decade has been one of unprecedented achievement for Muslim communities around the country. Muslims have proved to be a burgeoning pressure within economic, cultural and political landscape of the US. However, 11 September events were certainly a blow to the image of Islam. What exactly did happen on that day? On that fateful day a group of misguided persons attacked the World Trade Centre and the Pentagon. The perpetrators of the attack— give them any name you like— brought pain and discomfort to the Muslims. Islam is demonized and equated, falsely of course, with terrorism, while the conduct of believers is closely scrutinized. How are the American people, politicians and government acting towards Muslims? While vast majority of people disapproved of terrorism, they are unconcerned with Islam and they are not anti-Muslim. Nearly half of the American Muslims who are native blacks do not appear to have attracted adverse attention of non-Muslim Americans. Of the 3 to 4 million Muslims of foreign origin, a few thousands may have suffered harassment or physical violence at the hands of individual non-Muslim whites. But it cannot be said that any widespread persecution or even discrimination is being visited upon Muslims in America. The official discourse is about what Islam 'is' and what it is not. The going line is that Islam is a religion of peace, which does not advocate killing of innocents and suicides; that what the Osama Bin Laden and terrorists represent is not the real Islam but a distortion of it. For instance during his visit to the mosque at the Islamic Centre of Washington, President Bush reminded the nation that Islam is peace and admonished Americans not to take out their anger on innocent American Arabs and Muslims.

In an appearance before a joint session of the Congress, President Bush denounced the terrorists as traitors to their faith. The preachings of Osama Bin Laden, he said were a grotesque distortion of a great religion. Inspite of provocation, one should appreciate the handling of the situation by the government and public. The President, other high officials and low ranking security and civil services personnel continuously reassured Muslims of their security. Mosques were visited, homes protected and office and business watched. Neighbours and workers sympathized with Muslims and offered them support. And despite several highly publicized incidents of threats and lashing out at people thought to be Muslims, most Americans heeded the President's message, resisting the ugly lure of religious intolerance and hate compared to the degree of anti-German, Italian and Japanese feelings, during the 1940s. During the height of the crisis Muslim Scholars (including the writer who was present in the US in those days) were invited by religious, cultural and academic institutions to explain Islam and its messages. Islamic centres organized open houses, which were well-attended. This was real America in times of national tragedy and social crisis.

On the other hand, there was the contrary position— which borrows from Samuel Huntington's "Clash of Civilizations" thesis as well as from old fashioned racism and ignorance— that Islam is somehow inherently predisposed to fanaticism. Islam and Middle Eastern people represent a cultural totality— a cultural totality other than western and Christian. William Pfaff reported in the International Herald Tribune: "A part of the neo-conservative intelligentsia in Washington is trying to turn Bush's war against terrorism into a war against Muslim coalition and Islamic religion. Such influential figures as Elliat Cohen of John Hopkins School of Advanced International Studies and Kenneth Adelona of the Defense Department Advisory Policy Board, a former Reagan Administration official criticized President Bush to assure Muslims that this war is against terrorism, not against their religion. The Bush critics say Islam itself is America's enemy because Islamic religion and civilization are intolerant, hostile to western values, prosylytising, expansionist and violent". Despite the assurance of protection by President Bush and his Administration, Muslims in America are going through hell. They were harassed and made to feel unwanted. They have become suspects, neither desired nor trusted. The wounds to the community are deeper than any statistics indicate. A big change has come about in the lives of minorities, especially people of South Asian and Middle Eastern descent. For the average Americans, the Muslim community has lost its integrity. Media is largely responsible for the post 11 September biases against the community. A section of the media has managed to establish a link between Islam and terrorism.

On the brighter side, 11 September brought with it a hunger for knowledge about Islam. Americans are woefully ignorant and misinformed about Islam. Muslim scholars have been flooded with requests to deliver talks about Islam. One of the spinfalls of 11 September has been that the average American's understanding of Islam has improved.

Although Muslims have gained momentum in the struggle to gain inclusion in American society the challenges remain immense. Among these, the prominent issues appear to be:

1. overcoming negative stereotypes and images which hamper the abilities of the Muslim community to make its needs heard
2. The maintenance of Islamic way of life in a secular society, and particularly the impact of this society on Muslim children, and
3. Being heard on issues of foreign policy in which Muslim community has particularly strong sentiments

However, the Muslims are not the only community in the US to face these challenges. Earlier in US history, Catholics, Jews, and other groups who were excluded from mainstream society mobilized and organized to make their voices heard. Popular perceptions of who and what belongs to the American mainstream gradually changed to include them. Just as the general public earlier begun to accept Catholics, Jews and other non-whites or non-Protestants as part of the mainstream, it can come to view Muslims as not part of a menacing 'other' but as citizens who are a normal part of Americans society.

The American Muslim community wishes to be considered a part and parcel of America. Yet in voicing their interests and concerns as members of the American community Muslims face a dilemma, which might not be shared by other communities. As they endeavour not only to maintain an identity centred on a strong sense of traditional values and Islamic morality, but also, as a spiritual community, to offer solutions to the problems facing American society as a whole, they must overcome the images of Islam as foreign and menacing. American Muslims should highlight the fact that Islam alongside Christianity and Judaism constitute the trinity of religions which have similar philosophical and politico-cultural roots. They should insist that Islam has to be added to the American 'civic religion' that is the Protestant-Catholic-Judaic tradition of American society. Such inclusion would enable them to enjoy a fuller measure of many positive things which America has to offer. It is worth recalling that with the growth of the Catholic and Jewish population since the 1930's, both religions came to be progressively added to the dominant Protestant ethos of American religion: that is a process whereby

Islam may also enjoin Protestant Catholic Judaic traditions of American society. American Muslims, acting individually or in groups, should engage in broad-based educational campaign to explain Islam, especially the link it shares with Christianity and Judaism, confronting America's false images of Islam, Muslims should take action against these false images. In order to counter the association of Islam and Muslims with terrorism, at every opportunity, Muslims should denounce un-Islamic behaviour by professed Muslims, especially the terrorists, for violating Islamic principles— committing suicides and causing the death of innocent people.

To avoid discrimination, US Muslims must shed their reluctance to enter the political arena. They should join forces with the groups that are seeking amendments to the mis-labeled Patriot Act. The campaign for amendments requires time, energy and money. Muslims should not leave the cause to others.

Happily the greatest change of 11 September has come within the Muslim community itself. It started a process of soul-searching and self-criticism. A healthy view is emerging that the Muslim community's marginalization is self-imposed. This realization within the community is clearly a silver lining. At least a section of the Muslims community has begun to think that change can only occur through an attitude change within themselves.

The boundaries of American pluralism are gradually being redefined in more subtle, yet equally significant manner to include Islam and Muslims as part of the mainstream. For instance, mass market publishers are adding Islamic holidays to calenders, religion pages in newspapers are covering activities at mosques; radio television stations are conveying Ramzan greetings and references to America's Judeo-Christian traditions are being replaced with this more inclusive term 'Abrahamic tradition'. The US President's Eid greetings to American Muslims, Iftar Parties for Muslim servicemen at Pentagon, US Congress invitation to Imama Warith Reen Muhammad to give the opening prayers are indications that Islam has arrived at the religious and political horizon of the country. President Bush's celebration of Eidulfitr with a group of Muslim children at the White House on December 17, 2001, is an affirmation that involvement of Muslims in the American political system has finally succeeded in making Islam and its holy days better known and accepted by the larger American society. Earlier on November 19,

President Bush hosted Iftar party— the first ever by a US President. Rejecting suggestions that Iftar was a symbolic ploy, Bush said, "No, it is real. We are a nation of many faiths."

To sum up, Islam as a culture and a community is slowly becoming a part of the American religious and cultural landscape. The Muslims are becoming more American and more Muslim in their projections of self and group interests. Evidence for this claim rests on the growing success of Muslim advocacy groups. American multi-cultural democracy, with guarantees of religious freedom and speech, makes life easier for Muslims in America than in many so-called Muslim countries.

Unlike other western countries, the US faces less of a problem thanks to its long tradition of immigration and healthy attitude that goes with it. Being an American depends less on ancestry than on shared values. Meritocratic ethics and an open educational system are also important. The remarkable ability of religious and ethnic enclaves to survive in the American pluralistic and cultural Kalediascope is widely recognized. Contrary to popular expectations, American Muslims may as well succeed in retaining and reinforcing their ethno-national and sectarian diversities. The existence of a Muslim public sphere where Muslims can think freely to revive and protect Islam is America's gift to Muslims.

Muslims must value and cherish what America has to offer them. They must engage the system to empower themselves and to strengthen it in return. If the system is still far from Islam then it is because they have failed to influence it. Muslims have a lot to give to America. American Muslims have the least of America's typical problems— crime, drugs, broken families. They can morally and socially stabilize the country.

The future of Islam in America is bright. Despite the travail of this period religious freedom will always be protected and tolerated. If Muslims, at the individual level, resolutely accept their responsibility to defend their faith and participate more meaningfully in politics, Islam will emerge from this period better understood and more warmly welcomed than ever in the past.

13
American Perception on Jihad: Myth and Reality

Introduction

Jihad as a term and practice, has become part of common parlance in the western world. American media is almost daily filled with references-often accompanied by a rising tide of hysteria-to Jihad. The word Jihad has become a disturbing term for Americans who connect it with religious extremism and indiscriminate violence. The outrages perpetrated by organisations like Al-Qaeda, Taliban and others tend to confirm the belief in many that Islam is essentially a violent and intolerant religion that carries the seeds of terrorism[1]. Jihad which is erroneously translated as holy war[2] is integral to its ethos and Muslims cannot live in peace with people of a divergent faith. Jihad widely represents the most familiar and terrifying example of how action can be linked, literally to death. Evident in such representation is an unwitting collusion between those who increasingly claim to act in the name of Jihad and those who discern in creeping Jihad in all things. Jihad is supposed to be synonymous with war and even eminent non-Muslim scholars of Europe and North America have not taken the trouble to refer to the Quran and Hadith to find out the true meaning of the word Jihad. So widespread is the misunderstanding that the well-known scholar A.J. Wensink gives not a single reference under the word Jihad, referring to the concept as "war", as if the two are synonymous terms[3]. Klieg in the "Religion of Islam" makes a similar statement: "Jihad, the fighting against unbelievers with the object of either winning them over to Islam, or subduing or exterminating them in case they refuse to become Muslims, and causing

Islam to spread and triumph over all religions is considered sacred duty of the Muslim nation."[4] Jihad vc. Mc World[5] contains perhaps the best-known discussion on Jihad by an American political theorist. Its author, the distinguished Political Scientist Benjamin Barber posits Jihad as one part of a mutually constitutive dialectic between particularism and globalisation. He transforms Jihad into a kind of shorthand for the atavistic policies of retrabilisation, balkanisation, fanaticism, and tyrannical paternalism- a largely pathological orientation associated with violence, intolerance, and little respect for human life. Barber intends to use Jihad in a generalized way to signify a range of rabid practices. Yet its evocative power rests in Islam. The locus of what Barber calls the "essential Jihad", which is, he concludes despite caveats "relatively inhospitable to democracy and that inhospitability in turn nurtures conditions favourable to parochialism, anti-modernism, exclusiveness and hostility to others-the characteristics that constitute that I have called Jihad." Thus, it is Islamic holy war that Barber mires as a fruitful metaphor for political pathologies rather than the equally evocative language of Christian crusades. Jihad betokens religious struggle on behalf of faith, a kind of Islamic zeal". In its strongest political manifestation it means bloody holy war on behalf of partisan identity i.e., metaphysically defined and fanatically defended. Barber's book exemplifies a broader tendency among American/western analysts, journalists, politicians and scholars to dehistoricize Jihad, to erase the contradictions and ambivalence that have characterized into complex history.

Islamic Concept of Jihad: Theoretical Framework

The word Jihad is derived from the Arabic verb 'Johada', which means "to exert", "to struggle", or "to strive". Jihad literally means "exerting one's utmost power, efforts, endeavours, or ability in contending with an object of disapprobation or "striving towards a worthy goal"[6]. When qualified by the phrase in the path of God (fi sabil Allah), Jihad refers to struggle or striving in the path of God. The word Jihad has nowhere been used in the Quran to imply war in the sense launching an offensive. It is deployed rather to mean struggle. In its primary sense it is a spiritual struggle within one's self to rid one from debased action or inclination. Jihad in Islam requires the believers to do whatever they can towards popularising, defending and keeping alive and flourishing as the best and truest life the way of Islam and servility to God. The

Quran and Hadith (sayings of Prophet) use the word Jihad in several different contexts. It can take several forms depending on the circumstances varying from time to time and place to place. For instance, the Quran delineates the essence of Jihad as follows:

1. Resisting the pressure of non-Muslim parents who try to persuade their children who accept Islam to come back to their old religious belief amounts to Jihad[7].
2. Resisting the pressure of peers, the surroundings and degenerating social milieu in conformity with the Islamic imperatives constitutes Jihad[8].
3. Perseverance to stay on the straight path is Jihad[9].
4. Particularly under adverse conditions in life it requires great Jihad to remain Muslim and persuasively try to advance the Islamic cause[10].
5. To pass the test Allah one needs to struggle (make Jihad) to the utmost of his ability[11].
6. To strive to do the righteous deeds requires Jihad[12].

According to Hadith to carry the divine guidance to those that are ignorant of it and make an earnest effort to persuade them to accept is one form of Jihad. Helping the poor and the distressed could equally be a form of Jihad as could defense of the country from hostile attacks. Then to speak a just word, before a tyrannical ruler be a Muslim or a non-Muslim is again a form of Jihad. According to the Prophet, it has been termed as the best form of Jihad. At another occasion a man asked the Prophet "should I join the Jihad"? He asked: Do you have parents? The man said: Yes. The prophet said: then strive by serving them[13]. In brief, the essence of Jihad as implied in the Quran and the Hadith signifies an all out effort and endeavour to accomplish a comprehensive development of the self and that of society. For instance Syed ahmad Barevi's declaration of Jihad in 1826 was a manifestation of an ideological movement directed against reforming Muslim society by ridding it of an un-Islamic beliefs and practices followed by Muslims. To Maulana Abul Hasan Ali Nadvi, the internationally acclaimed Islamic scholar of present times, the biggest form of Jihad is the reform of Muslim society from within.

Significantly, military action is just a sub-group of Jihad and not its totality. Jihad as war was originally intended as defense of faith and the country in the face of aggression. The armed struggle in the Quranic terminology referred to as quital was forced on Mulsim in response to the aggressive war waged by the enemies of the newly established community who sought to exterminate them. Thus according to Quranic accounts the main objectives for which armed struggle can be reşorted to are:

(i) to stand up against persecution[14]

(ii) to repeal the open aggression[15]

(iii) to dismantle oppressive and tyrannical system if they cannot be rectified and removed otherwise[16].

According to Hadith, Prophet made a distinction between armed fighting against unbelievers and the struggle against one's own desires and temptations of Satan. On returning from a battle he is reported to have said, "we have returned from the lesser Jihad to the greater Jihad." When asked which is the greater endeavour, he reportedly replied, "it is the struggle against one's self.[17] It is thus the internal straggle that is termed the greater Jiḥad (Jihad-al-Akbar) and is incumbent on all individuals, whereas the Jihad of the sword is the lesser (Jihad-al-Asghar). This authenticated Hadith of Prophet alone suffices to dispel the utterly false impression among Muslims, no lesser than the rest, that Jihad is synonymous with warfare. Thus, in this way references to Jihad in the Quran and Hadith are made, Jihad appears less a fixed doctrine about warfare than a recurrent and flexible motif with multiple interpretations.

Gradual Transformation

However, as the Muslim community expanded outside the narrow confines of Arabian desert the notion of Jihad underwent radical transformation. The doctrine of Jihad, as it is now known, was codified in legal scholarship undertaken in the second half of 8th century, the period that coincided with the greatest Muslim conquests. While Jihad had been regarded but one of the many duties in the Quran, the Arab conquests "gave a psychological twist to Islamic thought, as a result of which the duty of Jihad was exalted in the Hadith.[18] The result was that a doctrine in which Jihad came to be equated with the Jihad of the sword or the lesser Jihad. It was primarily meant to apply to the relations among Muslims and non-Muslims-or what is also referred to as Dar-al-Islam (Abode of Islam) and Dar-al-Harb (Abode of war)[19]. In its most general formulation, this doctrine came to be understood as "any act of warring authorised by legitimate Muslim authorities on behalf of the religious community and determined to contribute to the greater good of Islam or community of Muslims, either in part or as a whole. Some Muslim rulers employed this concept to legitimize their internal conquests, blessing their attacks on non-Muslim lands as holy wars. Then some misguided groups within the Muslim community raising the banner of revolt against what they believed as corrupt ruling Muslim elites, saw themselves as engaging in Jihad. The earliest of these were Khwaraj. They called for killing of all those who disagreed with them. The wars launched by the imperial Muslims dynasties the Ummiayyads, the Abbasides, the Fatimides and the Ottomans were not exercise in Jihad still less the campaigns which Muslim extremist advocate or commit in the name of Islam today. Following the disintegration of the initial ummah and the remarkable expansion of Islam between 1000 and 1500 AD, Jihad as it was classically conceived was less frequently invoked because it was not taken to apply to relations among Muslim states. Despite the relative elasticity of the practice of Jihad, the idea of active Jihad as formulated by classical jurists "assumed a dormant status[20].

Recent Interpretation of Jihad

In recent years influential radical thinkers like Syed Qutub and Maulana Maududi have insisted that Muslims must go beyond the spiritual Jihad (the struggle to be good Muslim). They urge Muslims to actively assert their faith and their values even with violence. The single most important contribution to radical activism especially in the Arab world is the writing of Syed Qutub. He urges activism. It is not enough to pursue the 'greater Jihad' (Jihad Akbar), the continual individual struggle of all muslims to perfect their observance of God's law and overcome carnal other mundane temptations. Instead, Muslims must act. The founder of Jamat-I-Islami Maulana Abul-Ala Maududi draws explicitly on Ibn Taymiyyah the 13th century scholar who counseled action against oppression (in contrast to the traditional view, traced to Al-Ghazali), that one night of fitna, or chaos, is worse than ten years of dictatorship. Both Maududi and Qutub argued that Jihad is an urgent imperative. They mark a significant departure from antecedent doctrine and prevalent practice regarding the scope and purpose of Jihad. Their formulation of Jihad also entails and explicit repudiation of the argument that Jihad is primarily defensive. If the focus of Qutub and Maududi were their own countries, men like Osama Bin Laden have broadened the scope of action by concluding that Jahiliya regimes are kept in power by the west in general and by the US in particular. However, the notion that Jihad is neither expansive nor offensive has been embraced by majority of contemporary Muslim thinkers.

Rigorous Conditions

Islam imposes strict conditions for waging a Jihad:

1. Individuals and organizations cannot declare a Jihad
2. Owing allegiance to an Ameer, political ruler is a necessary condition for carrying out a Jihad for the sake of God
3. There should be some persons, who by their character and outward appearance look life true slaves of God.
4. Such a step must not be motivated by any personal or national self-interest, or greed or enmity.
5. It should be taken solely to carry out the command of God to serve the cause of his faith.
6. One cannot kill innocent when conducting a Jihad.
7. One cannot kill women, children and elderly in a Jihad.
8. One cannot kill Muslims in a Jihad.
9. One cannot fight against a country in which Muslims can freely practice their faith.
10. At the end of every type of Jihad, the noble cause of Islam should be strengthened. This is the only criterion to judge different types of Jihad.

The Quran declares noble motive as the condition for appring armed struggle as a Jihad. "March forth whether you are light or heavy and strive and struggle with your wealth and your person in the cause of Allah. That is the best for you. Explaining Jihad in the cause of Allah, the Prophet declared that Jihad is free from any taint of personal gain, i.e., intention to loot, kill and terrify people that motivated by noble ideal to serve Allah by following his commandments to fight injustice, oppression and to work for the collective good of mankind". On another occasion he said that any struggle which is made in the name of Islam but with the intent of surging in popularity or gaining political mileage and dividends has no validity in Islam. The Prophet defined the mujahid (one who carried out Jihad) is one who strives against himself for the sake of obeying Allah. Thus, the use of force by way of Jihad, permitted by the Quran, is a highly regulated and disciplined exercise. It has to fulfill both the internal and external requirements of validity set by Islam. The traditions of Prophet lay down some rules of warfare for the conduct of Jihad:

(i) Be advised to treat prisoners well.

(ii) Looting is no more lawful than carrion.

(iii) God has forbidden the killing of women and children.

(iv) Muslims are bound by their agreements, provided that they are lawful.

The Quran and the Hadith provide strict code of ethics to be achieved by a fighter who engages in Jihad as in the Islamic paradigm, means is equally important as the end. Jihad has to be carried out by those who have passed the test of inner Jihad because the inner Jihad, is a basic prerequisite for the combative Jihad. Secondly Islam does not permit any brutalities such as ethnic cleansing, genocide and atrocities that are committed in the course of modem day warfare. The Prophet as part of his implementation of divine instruction forbade the killing of civilian population, women and children and those who live in peace with Muslims, as he said: "Fight in the cause of Allah, make Jihad; do not embezzle the spoils, do not break your pledge, do not multilate the dead bodies, do not kill the children and women. Do good and show kindness because God loves that who do good to others[21]. Abu Bakr, the first caliph, summarized the ethics of war in the Islamic view as: "O people that I may give you these rules to keep by heart. Do not commit treachery. You must not multilate, either kill a child or an aged man or woman. Do not destroy a palm tree, nor burn it with fire and do not cut any fruitful tree.[22]

In view of the above the normative rules sanctioning the recourse to armed struggle and the binding ethical standards with which it has to conform, there is hardly any room for identifying Jihad with the carnage, committed by misguided zealots with self righteous pathological motivation to achieve political ends. Therefore, the Jihad in the sense of armed struggle excludes from its ambit much of today's anarchic fighting that are unleashed to advance the cause of exclusivist, radical and segmental political views in the name of Islam.

Not a Holy War

Jihad is supposed to be synonymous with 'holy war', a usage that the western media has popularized. However, the term 'holy war' is alien language in Islamic literature. It does not have a counterpart in Islamic glossary and Jihad is certainly not its translation. According to Islamic teachings it is unholy to start a war. As a matter of fact the term 'holy war' was coined in Europe during the crusades, meaning the war against Muslims. The concept of religious wars has been in all religions and wars on religious grounds were fought by the followers of all religions. For instance, Judaism imposes war on its adherents to protect their existence and to spread their rule and conquests in the earth even it leads to public massacres and the extermination of the people in the conquered countries. Christianity made a complete prohibition of war and some Christians even sacrificed their lives in the cause of prohibiting war, rather say the prohibition of military profession itself. However, tremendous efforts were made to reconcile Biblical teachings and the necessities of the state and such efforts resulted in a differentiation between permissible war and prohibited war. In the fourth century, that is after having established a state under the leadership of Constantine the Roman emperor, Christianity had to use force in order to uproot paganism from the Roman empire. Even in India, Ramchanderji waged a war against Ravana and Pandavas against Kauravas. Lord Krishna persuaded Arjun to fight a war against his own cousins for the sake of truth.

Jihad not Against Non-Muslims Alone

Jihad is not a declaration of war against other religious and certainly not against Christians and Jews as some western media and political circles want it to be perceived. Significantly, Christians and Jews are regarded as fellow inheritors of the Abrahamic traditions by Muslims, worshiping the same God and following the traditions of Prophet Abraham. Islam does not fight other religions. Jihad is struggle against oppression, against the people who suppress the fundamental rights, who are tyrants and unjust. It is waged against perpetrators of 'torture, murder, rape and injustice, in a peaceful manner. But if required, it can be with arms too. Jihad is not a war against non-Muslims only. Take the case of Battle of Kerbala in which Imam Hussain, the grandson of Prophet fought against Yazid who was also a Muslim. The objective of Jihad is to fight the aggression and mischief of the adversaries and not to eliminate them because of their belief. Because the normative rule governing the relationship between Muslims and others is one of the peaceful coexistence, mutual intimacy and shared security as all humans constitute a single brotherhood by virtue of origin from one parentage, namely Adam and Eve. History bears testimony to the fact that Prophet Mohammad as the true implementer of Islamic Jihad never practiced and pursued any kind of unprovoked and indiscriminate Jihad against non-Muslims but instead lived in alliance with them unless they betrayed him. The objective of Jihad is not to convert others to Islam or to fight others people purely on accent of a different faith they profess but to repeal war of aggression against Muslims. The spread of divine guidance has to be carried out by peaceful means and not by force as Quran says, "Invite all to the way of the Lord with wisdom, beautiful preaching and argue with them, in way that are best and most gracious chastisement. It declared that overriding principle to be, 'Let there be no compulsion in religion." And since this verse was revealed after the injunction to war of self-defence had been given, thus combative Jihad has no connection with the mission of propagating Islam. Prophet said to Ali, "Never be the aggressor who starts a war. First invite our enemy to the true God. If God leads one person through you to enter the life of faith, that will be of greater benefit for you than if you owned all that the sun shines upon." To assume that Islam enjoins permanent hostility against people of other faiths is a misstatement of the fact. Islam acknowledges all the apostles that came before Prophet Mohammed, beginning with Adam. It believes in the tenets received from God by Moses on the mountain, in the virgin Mary and the Holy Ghost, in the healing power of the Messiah, and much else that the Christians, the Jews and the followers of other prophets before Mohammed believe. Even in the process of invitation, the Quran lays stress on the commonalities between one religion and the other rather than differences thereof. Especially, when followers of earlier revealations are to be addressed by the Muslims, they should start with common prepositions are 'tenets' rather than difference. In other words similarities need to be highlighted rather than dissimilarities. Quran says: "O' followers of earlier revealation! Come into that tenet which me and you hold in common: that we shall worship none but God, and that we shall not ascribe divinity to ought, beside, Him, and that we shall no take human beings for our Lords beside God."

Jihad is not Terrorism

Those who do not understand Islam and who have a vested interest in distorting truth about the religion of Islam, have been trying to make the word terrorism and terrorist synonymous to Jihad. A distinction must be made between Jihad and terrorism. In fact they are antithesis of each other.

While terrorism is a violent act that violates international law and intends to intimidate civilians, and influence government policies through coercion. On the other hand, Islam condemns killing of civilians for political purposes. Terrorism is a secret act by a group of politically motivated individuals but Jihad is an announced strategy that calls upon armed battalions to conduct a war.

Inward and outward peace is the goal of Jihad, while terrorism seeks only more conflict and chaos. Islam never allows an individual or group to take other persons' life without ample justification. Murder is so much detested in the cyes of Allah that murder of one innocent person has been held as equal to the murder of entire humanity.[23] Indeed no condemnation of a killer could be stronger than of holding him guilty of having killed all mankind. When a single such killing is regarded as serious as this, one can imagine how heinous will be the killing of large number of people. Islam awards death penalty for such a crime, intending to act as a deterrent. On the other hand terrorism means indiscriminate killing. Islam forbids violence against innocent civilians, women, children, elderly and environment in Jihad. Terrorists do not believe in sparing anybody. In the light of outright condemnation of the shedding of blood of innocent, Islam cannot and does not support acts of terrorism in any form. Similarly there is no Quranic support for suicidal bombing. Significantly, suicide as such is strictly prohibited in Islam and whoever commits suicide will be denied a place in heavens. Islam is very clear on the subject of suicide. It is a major sin and is punished by eternal damnation in the form of endless repetition of the act by which suicide killed himself. The following passages from Hadith make the point clear: "Whoever kills himself with a blade will be tormented into that blade in the fires of Hell". He also said: "He who strangles himself will strangles himself in Hell, and he who stabs himself will stab himself in Hell. He who throws himself off a mountain and kills himself will throw himself drowned into the fires of Hell forever and ever. Whoever kills himself in any way in the world will be tormented with it on the day of resurrection. A clear distinction is made between certain death at the hands of enemy and dying by one's own hand. According to tradition, Prophet refused to say prayers over the body of a man who had died by his own hand. Significantly, two features mark the 9/11 attack and other such actions: the willingness of the perpetrators to commit suicide and the lack of concern at the slaughter of innocent bystanders. For instance in order to kill 12 US diplomats in Africa, the terrorists were willing to slaughter more than 200 Africans, many of them were Muslims, who happened to be in the vicinity. Similarly, in the case of TWC, the victims included thousands of innocents including some Muslims from Muslim countries. Can these in any sense be justified in terms of Islam? The answer is a categorical no. Such acts have no justification in Islamic doctrine or law and no precedent in Islamic history. These are not just crimes against humanity but they are also acts from a Muslim point of view of blasphemy, when those who perpetrate are Muslims. Therefore, acts of terrorism performed by Muslim terrorists will have to be viewed in the historical and political context and not as licenced by Islam. Muslims can never indulge in terrorism if they are true Islamists. How can they go against the Quranic verse, which says that murder of one innocent person is the murder of whole mankind? How can they go against the tolerant teachings of prophet? How can they go against Islam which not only means total surrender to the Creator but also means peace? How can a religion, a few teachings of which are discussed above be associated with terrorism and warfare?

However, the outrages perpetrated by the organisations like Al-Qaeda, Taliban and others tend to confirm the belief in many that Islam is essentially a violent and intolerant religion that carries the seeds of terrorism. Jihad or holy war is integral to its ethos and Muslims cannot live in peace with people of a divergent faith. But Islam has nothing to do with any of these organisations. Jihad is not a pillar of Islam. It does not necessarily mean war. Jihad stands for dedicated effort on all fronts-military, political, economic intellectual, social and ethical. The ethics of war in Islam and relations with people of the faith have been for too long overlooked. One may cite the Islamic traditions and guidelines in dealing with non-Muslims. "God forbids you not, with regard to those who fight you not for your faith nor drive you out of your homes, from dealing kindly and justly with them. For God loves those who are just".

Misquoted Verses

The so-called experts on Islam have been repeatedly distorting Quranic verses. People like Falwell, Graham, Swaggart, Robertson and others in the US keep spewing poison against Islam with their fabrications and double talk. They are found quoting verses which were revealed within specific historical contexts as well as those verses which are frequently taken out of context. These include "And kill them whenever you find them and drive them out of the places where they drive you out". Quoting this, Robertson emphasised to his TV audience that this teaches Muslims to kill the Christians. The verse Robertson read is not about the Christians but about the pagan Arabs of Mecca, who had for 13 years persecuted, killed and driven Muslims out of their homes. This verse has to be read with another verse from the some surah that identifies the enemy as, "who broke their oath and aimed at the exclusion of the Prophet and they attacked you first." Obviously it implies to fight a war of self-defence against those who attacked and waged a war of aggression against Muslims because they were invaders and not on account of them being idolaters. He also kept things out of context by not reading the verse that follows the one he read. It says: "If one amongst the pagans asks you for asylum, grant it to him, so that he may hear the word of God Almighty, and then exert him to where he can be secure. Unfortunately, Pat Robertson's misuse and misinterpretation of the above mentioned Quranic verse to malign Islam and preacher Jerry Falwell's blind support of him is not an isolated incident. The basic reason for misunderstanding about Quran's teachings and commands is that no effort is made to understand the specific background and circumstances under which some of the verses and commands were revealed. It is worth remembering that Quran was revealed in gradual process over a period of twenty-three years. During this period, the Muslims had to undergo different circumstances, problems and hostilities. They had to take up arms in order to defend themselves and their faith against aggressive designs and policies of their enemies. They also entered into agreements with their enemies for peace. All verses and commands of the Quran which speak of Jihad and killing of others were revealed during these periods and circumstances when the followers of Islam were engaged in do or die wars against their enemies. The basic reason for misunderstanding about Quran's teachings and commands is that no effort is made to understand the specific backgrounds and circumstances under which some of the verses and commands were revealed. It must be remembered that the complete Quran was revealed in gradual processes over a period of 23 years. During this period, the followers of Islam had to undergo different circumstances. They had to take up arms in order to defend themselves and their faith against aggressive designs and policies of their enemies. They also entered into agreements with their enemies for peace. All verses and commands of the Quran which speak about Jihad and killing of atheists were revealed during these periods and circumstances when the followers of Islam were engaged in 'do or die' wars against the enemies. In normal circumstances, however, Quran preaches and commands its followers to treat nor Muslims in a spirit of friendship, love, peace and solidarity. Every verse of the Quran must be read and interpreted against the background of the Quran as a whole. A totally false impression can be created by isolating a single verse and by quoting it out of context.

Fallacious Argument

It is argued that Islam does not at all tolerate other religions and their followers and that it wants to introduce and practice its own beliefs and teachings in the world. Thus, the terms like Jihad is explained and defined in this sense only. However, such arguments are totally false and injustice to Quran because Quran clearly states that there is no force or compulsion with regard to religion. It says "O, Mohammad you tell the atheists: to you your religion and to me my religion." In fact one of the unique features of Islam is its insistence on respect for other religions. It maintains that God sent his messengers to every country in every age for bringing back people to the path of righteousness and good conduct. The Prophet enjoined respect for all divine messengers, which is a precondition for peaceful coexistence between diverse communities.

Prophets' Example

Prophet was born at a time when an atmosphere of militancy prevailed in the Arab society. But Prophet never initiated a military move himself. He always opted for avoidance of conflict when his opponents wanted to embroil him in war he would on all occasions apply some strategy to avoid war and fought only when there was no other way left out. For instance, in the campaign of Ahzab, Prophet ordered his companions to dig a trench between them and the enemies, thus prevented a head-on-clash. Another well-known instance of Prophets' dislike for hostilities is the Hudaibiyah peace treaty when he accepted unilaterally all the conditions of enemy.

Jihad is a term that has been corrupted and misinterpreted both by those who do and do not claim to be Muslims. The worst enemy of every religion is the fanatic who professes to follow it and tries to impose his views of his faith on others. People do not judge religions by what the prophets preached or how they lived but by the way their followers practice them. The problem is that some Muslim activists are carrying out their militant campaign in the name of Jihad and people perceive their movements as acts approved by Islamic tenets. Islam has to be assessed on the basis of principles enunciated and values as promoted in the Quran and the traditions of Prophet who is regarded as the harbinger of kindness and mercy for the entire universe. Islam is definitely opposed to the culture of bullets and bombs. It teaches peace compassion and forgiveness. Unfortunately, the label of Jihad is put on every conflict. This is simply misuse of holy word of Jihad in the path of God. Literally every struggle is Jihad. But Jihad in the path of God is something else and its terms and conditions are different. Jihad in the path of God can take the form of battle only if certain conditions are fulfilled. It is therefore pertinent that a clear distinction should be made between what the faith teaches and what the adherent practices. If a person or group claims to be Muslim, but their behaviour is not Islamic, then one must note the difference and not call this persons' wrong doing Islam. No true Muslim will commit evil in the name of religion.

Jihad and Fatwa

Over the years Islamic jurists became the primary authorities for the meaning of Jihad, when to declare and when to restrict Jihad. While Muslim rulers declared and conducted Jihad, legal experts, known as muftis provided fatwas (legal opinion) that could be used to legitimize or to challenge the legalising of a Jihad, a practice that continues upto the present day. However, the fatwa is not an edit. It is a mere legal opinion. The shorter Encyclopaedia of Islam defines fatwa as a formal legal opinion given by a mufti, or canon lawyer of standing in answer to a question submitted to him either by a judge or by a private individual. It is politics, not religion which inspires cries of Jihad and declaration of fatwas, exposing both to ridicule and Islam to misunderstanding and misrepresentation. The concept of Jihad is bound with so many restrictions and conditions that fatwa of Jihad is hardly needed. The condition of being Amirul-momenin is most significant out of other conditions. Amirul-momenin (Islamic ruler) only is entitled to issue a fatwa.

Why Contradictions between Principles and Practice

In the light of ongoing conflict, one must ask why so great a contradiction has arisen between the principles of Islam and the practices of Muslims. Why horrifying acts have been committed in the name of Islam? How religion could be used to justify slaughter of innocents? The so-called contemporary Jihadism must be seen as a reaction to complex interaction of internal as well as external circumstances and does not necessarily flow from a simple reading of Quran itself. The so-called fundamentalist Islamic terrorism is not an inevitable outcome of the teachings of Quran. It is the result of several factors-failure to remove the corrupt, oppressive and anti-democratic regimes of the Islamic world and to evil Israeli rule in Palestine, hatred towards the US for its support to these regimes and Israel. Muslim societies are the outgrowth of their own history and regional culture and have deviated from the prescribed Islamic values and norms. Significantly, terrorism was introduced to the Muslim world by Zionists who founded the state of Israel. The very term terrorism unleashed by the state of Israel has become the role model for the outbreak of Arab and some other Muslim terrorism. The volatility of that part of the world is not necessarily caused by Islamic activity as such. It is much less a manifestation of religious fervour than of political and economic justifications.

To sum up, Jihad happens to be one of the most misunderstood and misinterpreted terms. Western media and the so-called champions of Islam are responsible for the distortion of its meaning. Jihad in its truest and purest form is the determination to do right, to do justice even against one's own interests. For from being archaic remnants of some tribal era as maintained by Benjamin Barber, action in the name of Jihad has always been, in the service of a universalist and universalizing political and social order. The shifting understanding of the scope and meaning of Jihad as evident in the Quran, the Hadith and in the various juristic responses to the early Arab conquests, the invasion of the Muslim heartland by foreign converts and the experiences of colonialism and imperialism all suggest that Jihad is less a fixed set of rules for violent, fanatical conquest than a category that refracts changing understanding about the scope and meaning of wordly action given radical political and social change. Jihad is a war for just cause and not against innocent civilians. Jihad essentially means struggle with one's own self to remain on the path of truth, to remain away from evil, from lust, from devil or devilish thoughts or actions, struggle for survival, struggle against evil forces, struggle for the path of Allah, with all efforts, with one's belongings and even with one's life. Last can be in the shape of war against evildoers and oppressors. This is the greatest sacrifice in the path of God provided it is done with sincerity (without a desire for name, fame or booty and not against innocent, women, children, old people and not against people who do not come to battlefield, without a single case of rape, without destruction of fields, civilian property etc) only then the reward is Heavens. Jihad in Islam does not include striking for individual or national power, glory, wealth, prestige or pride. Islam forbids the killing of people merely because they embrace a different faith, nor does it allow Muslims to fight against those who disagree with them on religious grounds. The fact that must be kept in mind is that Muslim history and Islamic teachings and commands are not synonymous things. If there are some objectionable examples or acts by some Muslim individuals, groups or organisations these are exceptional cases and represent individual acts only. That a few Muslim countries have produced a highly perverted group like the Taliban has an exclusively political origin. The terrorist groups that have latterly surfaced in the world of Islam consist of men driven to desperation. Their actions which result in deaths of innocent people and destruction of property are reprehensible. But they stem from the widespread belief among Muslims that Christianity and Judaism are waging a global war against Islam. However, a Jihad can only be waged by an Islamic state not by Muslim state or the interested groups. For instance Mahmood Ghaznavi's attack on India could not be treated as a Jihad. Neither the Al-Qaeda outfit could be, in Islamic jurisprudential terms, can wage a Jihad whatever be their motives. To regard these cases as practical results of Quranic teachings is unfair. It is worth pointing out that out of 6666 verses in the Quran, a mere 40 are related to Jihad which Islam permits only in self defence. Jihad as a concept is an umbrella term that connotes striving to one's utmost ability to bring his entire behaviour in conforming with requirements of Islam. A Mujahid is a very special type of individual. All his action is in the name of Allah and for the preservation of Islamic State. His will is totally obedient. One of the most famous Hadith of Prophet says, "a mujahid is one who wages Jihad against his self (nafs), i.e., suppressing his wild and evil filled passions and whims. Therefore to equate Jihad squarely with armed struggle or legalistic Jihad is a narrow, incomplete and limited notion, which is susceptible to polemics, and even misunderstanding. It is worth emphasising that there are several words in Arabic language denoting armed combat such as herb (war), sira (combat), maarka (battle) and qital (Killing) which the Quran could have easily used if war had been the Muslims' principal way of engaging in this effort. Instead the Quran chooses a richer word with a wide range of connotations. This implies that the above armed struggle related terms lose much of their significance once the war is over, while Jihad continues to be a significant notion. Islamic Jihad is a positive and continuous process. Jihad has a relevance in contemporary society provided it is shorn of the connotation of violence and is informed by a moral purpose-justice for the underprivileged. Significantly, in Islam the concept of Jihad is inextricably linked to the concept of oppression. The Quran is replete with references to the problems of oppressed and to forbearance from aggression. Jihad according to Quran and Hadith demands a perpetual self-reexamination in term of one's potential to fight tyranny and oppression-a continued reassessment of the means for achieving peace and inculcating moral responsibility. Jihad stands for dedicated effort on all fronts-military, political, economic, intellectual, social and ethical. Warfare is a part of string but not a major preoccupation. A Jihad is to be fought against ignorance, economic deprivation, social justice and political wrongs. In this battle Muslims should not only accept but seek the help and cooperation of all, irrespective of their faith.

References

1. Far instance Norman Podhartez, the former editor of 'commentary' argued in the magazine (February 2002) that Islam has become an especially fertile breeding ground of terrorism in our time. This can only mean that there is something in the religion itself that legitimizes the likes of Osama Bin Laden, and indeed there is the obligation imposed in the Koran to wage the holy war.
2. As eminent historian Bernard Lewis points out, there is no word corresponding to holy war in classical Arabic usage. See The Political Language of Islam, Chicago: Chicago Press, 1988, p.17.
3. Jihad Vs Terrorism", Minaret, Vol.24, No.2, February 2002, Los Angeles, p.20.
4. *Ibid.*
5. Barber Benjamin, Jihad Vs Mc World: How Globalism and Tribalism are Reshaping the world, New York, Ballantine Books, 1996.
6. Edward Lane, An Arabic English Lexicon, Book 16 London 1865, p.473.
7. We have enjoined on people kindness to parents; but if they strive to

make you ascribe partners with Me that of which you have no knowledge, then obey them not" 28:8.

8. "So obey not the rejecters of faith, but strive against them by it (the Quran) with a great endeavour" 25:52.
9. "And strive for Allah with the endeavour which is His right. He has chosen you and has not laid upon you in the din (religion) any hardship".
10. "The true believers are only those who believe in Allah and his messenger and afterward doubt not, but strive with their wealth and their selves for the cause of Allah". 49:15.
11. "Did you think that you would enter paradise while yet Allah knows those of you who really strive, nor knows those of you who are steadfast". 3:142.
12. "As far those who strive in our way. We surely guide them to our paths, and lo! Allah is with the good doers". 29:69.
13. Fazlul Karim, Mishkat al-Masabih, Islamic Book service, New Delhi 1994, vol. 2, p. 353.
14. "To those against whom war is made, permission is given to defend themselves, because they are wronged and verily, Allah is most powerful to give them victory, they are those into have been expelled from their homes in defiance of right." 22:39.
15. "Fight in the cause of Allah against those who fight against you, but do not transgress limits. Lo! Allah loves not oppressors". 2:190.
16. "And why you not fight in the cause of Allah and those who being weak are ill treated and oppressed men, women and children" 4:75.
17. AH B. Uthman al-Jullabi al Hajwiri, the Kashif al Mahijub, trans. Reynold A. Nickolson, London, 1976, p.200
18. A Nineteenth Century view of Jihad, Stadia Islamica 32, 1970, p. 181.
19. "DiJihad" in AAR Gibbal and J.H. Kramers, eds. The shorter Encyclopaedea of Islam, Leiden 1974. However, there have always been jurists into argued that as the Quran states "there is no compulsion in religion" (2:256) such an interpretation and the division of the world into warring opposites it presupposes is incorrect.
20. Majid Khadduri, War and Peace in the Law of Islam, John Hapkins University Press, 1955, pp. 65-66
21. Fazlul Karim, op.cit, p.388.
22. Majid Khadduri, op.cit, p. 102.
23. We did ordain into the children of Israel that if anyone slays a human being unless it be (in punishment) for murder or for spreading corruption earth-it shall be as though he had slain all mankind; whereas, if anyone saves a life it shall be as though he saved the lives of all mankind" 5:32

14

USA and International Terrorism

Terrorism is a multi-faceted and dynamic phenomenon, which defies description. It employs extreme physical violence to shock the targeted audience, but the psychological impact upon the people at large matters more to them than the physical attack on victims. Terrorism appears to have increased markedly in recent years. It poses a serious challenge to democratic societies by putting their liberal systems under stress. The freedom of action of the common citizen is restricted under terrorist threats. This may result in militarization of certain countries and in the weakening of democratic processes in others.

The Americans of late have worked themselves in to a tizzy over terrorism. Like nuclear winter, Islamic fundamentalism and global warming before it, terrorism in the later 1990's has lodged itself in the national psyche as a seemingly existential threat. Incidents like the World Trade Centre (1993), Oklahoma City (1995), Atlanta's Centennial Park (1996), Khabar Towers (1996), US embassies in Kenya and Tanzania (1998) attack on World Trade Centre and Pentagon (2001) are cited as evidence that terrorism is on the rise and becoming ever more deadly. According to a report of the congressional research services, "the next great challenge for the US is to combat international terrorism". Terror, in the words of the former Secretary of State, M. Albright, is "the war of the future". The State Department defines terrorism as 'premeditated, politically motivated violence perpetrated against non-combatant targets by sub-national groups or clandestine state agents, usually intended to influence an audience". Washington' newest nightmare is the threat of a massive terrorist attack with chemical, biological, or nuclear weapons. The recent events appear to have convinced the policymakers elite and the general public that a disaster is imminent. Former Defense Secretary, William Cohen, summed up well the prevailing mood surrounding mass destruction terrorism: "The question is no longer if this will happen, but when."

Since the Clinton Administration issued its Presidential Directive on terrorism in June 1995, the US federal, state and local governments have heightened their efforts to prevent or respond to a terrorist attack, involving weapons of mass destruction. In his 1998 state of the Nation Address, President Clinton promised to address the dangers of biological weapons obtained by outlaw states, terrorists and aggrieved criminals. Indeed the President's budget for the years 1999, denotes hundreds of millions of dollars to super-terrorism response and recovery programmes, including large decontamination units, stock-piles of vaccines and antibiotics, improved means of detecting chemical and biological disease outbreaks, and training for special intervention force. To fight terrorism, the US Administration has jettisoned traditional US policy that categorized terrorists as criminals and defined terror as a law enforcement issue. In its place, President Clinton instituted a new comprehensive strategy, global in scope, proactive in approach, and tapping the resources of agencies across the federal government. The aim of this strategy is not simply defensive. It aims to pre-empt terrorist action to identify and dismantle terrorist networks, and ultimately to eradicate the threat altogether. Rather than reactive, the strategy plans to seize the initiative. Seizing the initiative implies a great reliance on military power. In President Clinton's war against terror, the Pentagon plays a leading role, employing its high-tech arsenal not only to exact retribution but also to take the offensive. This new stress on the use of US military power does not imply that waging war on terrorism is exclusively the government's affair. According to President, Clinton, a full-fledged national mobilization is in order. In the fight against terror, "every American counts".

From the above, it is evident that the US is engaged in a long-term struggle against international terrorism. It uses a variety of foreign policy tools, from military force when necessary, to vigorous diplomacy, law enforcement, improvement in US security and the development of new technology. Two Presidential Directives were issued in 1998 to coordinate efforts to prevent and respond to unconventional attacks, and to shield information and transportation facilities. In July 1999, President signed an Executive Order imposing financial and other commercial sanctions on the Afghan Taliban for its support for Osama Bin Laden and his terrorist network. In addition the State Department designated thirty foreign terrorist organizations, making it illegal for US citizens and institutions to provide funds or other forms of material support to such groups. The US is engaged in vigorous campaign to promote by the year 2000 the universal adoption and ratification of all eleven existing international terrorist conventions.

The terrorist threat to the US and its interests is real. The post-cold war world swarms with shadowy extremist groups, religious fanatics and assorted crazies eager to launch a major attack on US territory. Walter Laqueur, terrorism's leading historian, recently wrote that "scanning the contemporary scene, one encounters a bewildering multiplicity terrorist and potentially terrorist groups and sects". Senator, Richard Lugar, argues: fanatics, small disaffected groups and sub-national factions who hold various grievances against governments, or against society, all have increasing access to, and knowledge about the construction of weapons of mass destruction... Such individuals are not likely to be deterred by the classical threat of overwhelming retaliation". Many of the counter measures taken by the US government are likely to be ineffective because the level of rhetoric and funding devoted to fighting terrorism may actually advance a potential terrorist broader goals: sapping the resources of the state and creating a climate of panic and fear that can amplify the impact of any terrorist act. President Clinton, his secretaries, officials and journalists must tone down the rhetoric feeding today's super-terrorism frenzy. All terrorists benefit from such heightened attention and fear. The Americans fail to distinguish among four different types of terrorism; mass casualty terrorism, state-sponsored chemical or biological weapons terrorism, small-scale chemical or biological terrorist attacks, and super-terrorism. Today's prophets of doom blur the levies of these four distinct categories of terrorism. As a matter of fact these four types of terrorism are unrelated. The threat of conventional chemical biological terrorism requires neither massive preparations nor large intervention forces. It calls for neither costly new techniques, nor a growing number of insurgency coordinating tactics. The decision to form and train joint response teams in major US cities, prompted by 1995 Presidential Directive, will be productive if the teams are kept within proper preparations. The ideal team should be streamlined so as to minimize the interagency rivalry that has tended to make these teams grown in size and complexity. The intelligence community should assume the most significant role in any productive campaign to prevent chemical and biological terrorism. New early warning indicators that focus on radical group behaviour are urgently needed. The most neglected means of countering chemical biological terrorism is psychological research. Terrorism scholars and US intelligence agencies have so far failed to discern the psychological mechanisms that compels terrorists to contemplate seriously the use of weapons of mass destruction. The US response to terrorism should distinguish between threats demanding military action and those of which an alternative approach may make more sense. American military power may be less effective against terrorists themselves than against states that sponsor terror or offer terrorists sanctuary.

The US campaign against terrorism rests on a flawed conception of international politics, of America's role in the international system and of the consequences that derive from that role. As a matter of fact Bush Administration's growing preoccupation with terrorism reveals less about an actual threat than about the premises of American foreign policy in the Bush era. The essence of the President Bush's views on international politics can be summarized briefly. In the aftermath of the cold war, the inexorable logic of globalization is transforming the international order. Democracy and free market principles are on the march. The worldwide embrace of political values and economic policies favoured by Americans is both inevitable and irreversible. There emerges as a result an international order whose abiding characteristic is openness, with trade, capital, people and ideas all moving freely across borders. This openness will yield a world that is both peaceful and prosperous and in which old notions of politics as a competitive quest for power lose their salience. The result, predicts President Bush, will be a new era of interdependence where nations work together – not simply for peace and security, but also for better schools and health care, broader prosperity, and a cleaner environment". However, terrorism represents the continuation of politics by other means. The survival of terrorism in the era of globalisation illustrates the persistence of politics beyond the end of the cold war. The matters of fundamental importance and concern remain unresolved. Prominent among them are disputes over the sanctity of life, the meaning of freedom, and the definition of justice. The survival of politics implies that an effective strategy against threats manifesting themselves as terror must itself be broadly political. Most terrorists possess political objectives, whether Basque independence, Kashmiri separatism or Palestinian nationalism. Terrorists strive to gain sympathy from a large audience and wish to live after carrying out any terrorist act to benefit from it politically. As terrorism expert Brian Jenkins, has remarked: "terrorists want lots of people watching, not lost of people dead". Terrorists who threaten to kill thousands of civilians are aware that their chances for political and physical survival are exceedingly slim. Their prospects for winning public sympathy are even slimmer. Then, terrorists take time to become dangerous, particularly to harden themselves sufficiently to use weapons of mass destruction. Groups such as Hamas, Hizbullah, and Islamic Jehad, which so many Americans love to revile and fear do not make the list of potential super terrorists. These organizations and their state sponsors may loathe the Great Satan, but they also wish to survive and prosper. Their leaders understand that a Hiroshima like disaster would effectively mean the end of their movements. Insisting that terrorism is irrational and atavistic, the Bush Administration robs it of political context. The possibility of terrorists using weapons of mass destruction exists and cannot be ignored. Yet an effective response to terror should entail not all out war in a pursuit of utopia, but a differentiated strategy that tailors a particular response to a specific threat. Such a strategy should recognize that the underlying problem is not terror as such, but the grievances, ambitions, and apprehensions that propel groups or individuals to violence. An effective strategy may well entail the unilateral use of force to deflect a challenge to American interests and ideals emanating from a particular quarter. It may also mean a response that relies on other methods: contemptuous disregard, containment, mutual concession, contracting third parties to do the dirty work, or even appeasement.

The US, in its legitimate concern about terrorism worldwide, and particularly in West Asia, should realize that terrorism as we know it today was introduced to the Arab and Muslim worlds by the Zionists who founded the State of Israel. The 1947 dispatch of letter bombs to British cabinet ministers, the bomb attacks of December 11, 1947 in Haifa, terrorizing Palestinian civilians, the blowing up of the Arab-owned Semiramis Hotel in Jerusalem, killing innocent civilians including viscount de Tapia, the Spanish counsel, the famous April 9, 1948 massacre of Palestinian old men, women and children at the Palestinian village of Deir Yassin near Jerusalem, the assassination on September 17, 1948 of UN Palestine mediator count Folke Bernadette and his aide, Col. Andre

Pierre Serat, the series of bombs in Baghdad in 1950 by Israeli agents to terrorize Iraqi Jews into immigrating to Israel are some of the innumerable instances. The irony is lost on Americans that the very terrorism unleashed by the state of Israel has become the "role model" for outbreaks of Arab and Iranian terrorism. If Americans are really concerned about terrorism, they by all means should be concerned about curbing Israeli State terrorism, whether it is against Palestinians in the West Bank and Gaza, Lebanese in Southern Lebanon, or Syrians in the Golan Heights.

The US national interests require that it should remain engaged in global affairs, not as the world's policeman but as the major catalyst for an emerging new international order. The US must adopt a more transparent policy towards international terrorism, if it is to enlist the cooperation of other countries of Asia and Africa in this effort. The US had been concentrating on Iran, Libya and Syria on the issue of international terrorism. Now the time has come for the US decision-makers to make a more objective assessment of the terrorist campaign through out the world including Kashmir and Palestine.

Washington needs a complete reappraisal of the geopolitical strategies that it had followed since the end of the cold war. If Washington is serious of fighting international terrorism it must abandon obsolete shibboleths. President Bush is not wrong in sensing that terrorism poses a grave danger but campaign against terror is the wrong war against the wrong enemy. Given an ample investment of American energy, know-how and technology, the war on terror may produce the share of tactical successes but in the ultimate analysis, tactical dexterity will not compensate for the faulty premises on which the war is based.

15

Human Rights in US Domestic and Foreign Policies

In 1948, the US took the lead in drawing up the Universal Declaration of Human Rights. The thinking was that despite permissible differences in culture, certain human rights were basic, including proscriptions against cruel, inhuman, or degrading punishment, equality before the law; protection against arbitrary arrest, detention, or exile; the right to fair court trial and the right of free movement and asylum. The bottomline was the basic right to live.

After the Second World War, tackling domestic racism in US was as much a foreign policy decision as anything else. A Civil Rights Committee appointed by President Harry S. Truman concluded: "We cannot escape the fact that our civil rights record has been an issue in world politics. They have tried to prove our democracy an empty fraud and our nation a consistent oppressor of underprivileged people". However, in the decade following Universal Declaration of Human Rights, the US frustrated international efforts to create an enforceable standard on the basis that its own violations of the rights of minorities, particularly Native Americans and African-Americans might be called into question. During the early cold war years, human rights concerns in US foreign policy were generally thought to be worth sacrificing for the greater goal of containing communism. In fact, throughout history, balancing civil liberties with the national security has always been a delicate task. Civil liberties have been a target of government restrictions throughout history, especially in times of crises— foreign and domestic.

Post 9/11 and Human Rights

The post 9/11 era has been one of tumultuous change in US foreign and domestic policies. Ironically, the greatest source of negative effects (on civil liberties) has come from US Administration's pursuit of war on terrorism at home against the backdrop of heightened terrorist threats. Civil Rights advocates in US have expressed outrage at the Justice Department's callous disregard of the Bill of Rights and at the refusal of the US to look at the root causes of the nation's problems, preferring instead, what appears to be the pursuit of blind vengeance.

Civil Libertarian organizations such as American Civil Liberties Union (ACLU) described the government's penchant towards attaining new powers after 9/11 as an insatiable appetite, characterized by government secrecy, lack of transparency, rejection of equality under the law, and disdain for and outright removal of checks and balances. A full-page newspaper advertisement by the ACLU tells that the Patriot Act, the Administration's major security initiative goes 'far beyond fighting terrorism', and has allowed government agents to violate civil liberties tapping deep into the private lives of innocent Americans.

From the Libertarian Left Anthony Lewis in the New York Times Magazine charged President Bush with undermining safeguards for the accused in a way that Lewis did not believe "was possible in our country", while from the Libertarian, Right, William Safire protested the Administration's effort "to realize the super snoop's dream of spying on all Americans". Articles in popular press expressed similar sentiments. For instance writing in American Prospect, Wendy Kaminer expressed the apprehension that "Give the FBI unchecked domestic spying powers and instead of focusing on preventing terrorism, it will revert to doing what it does best-monitoring, harassing and intimidating political dissidents and thousands of harmless immigrants". In brief, it has been argued that in order to protect Americans from terrorists, democracy may be jeopardized, if not lost and America is well on the way to become a 'police state'.

Unlike many other countries, in the US, an independent judiciary and powerful Congress ensure that the appropriate balance between security and human rights is achieved. However, America has, in the past over-reacted to perceived security threats; the Palmer raids after first world war and the treatment of Japanese-Americans during second world war are the most glaring instances of such over-reaction from US establishment.

Civil libertarians now condemn the indignities of security checks at the airports, the tracking of Muslim visitors to the US, detention of suspects for indefinite periods without trial and when criminal charges are brought, the government's attempt to limit the access of the accused to important evidence. Still worse in their view is Administration's evident intention of using military tribunals to try suspected terrorists. Last but not the least and most frightening of all to critics, the government's proposed Terrorist Information Awareness (TIA) programme, which would employ computers to gather and assess unknowing American citizens.

According to Ibrahim Hoofer, a spokesperson for the Council on American-Islamic Relations, American Muslims have already lost many of their civil rights. The most salient outward sign of this is said to be ethnic profiling that occurs routinely in America—a form of discrimination widely considered to be self-evidently evil. Ethnic profiling, it is alleged, is also responsible for the unjustified harassment and occasional detention of Arab and Muslim visitors to the US. This is said to be an egregious violation not only of the rights of such persons but of America's traditional hospitality toward foreign visitors.

According to civil libertarians, the constitutional safeguards that normally protect individuals suspected of criminal activity have been destroyed in case of persons suspected of links with terrorism. Undoubtedly since 9/11, civil liberties have been curtailed in the US and its officials have been accused of resorting to violence during interrogation of captured Al-Qaeda operatives.

The Justice Department's harsh approach has thus sent a painful negative signal around the world emboldening governments as diverse as those of Belarus, Cuba and India to crush democratic liberties, supposedly in aid of their own struggle against terrorism. In brief, recent information about detainees, racial profiling and infringements on academic free-dom caused many people to question the future of personal freedoms in the US.

US Foreign Policy and Human Rights

The US has been a leading, if inconsistent, proponent of the idea that foreign policy should involve attention to the Human Rights record of other countries. From the early 1990's the idea that 'security' and 'protection of human rights' are complementary rather than mutually exclusive has taken hold. The events of 9/11 served as a catalyst for a new era of democracy promotion in the world. Significantly, two months after the attacks, Under Secretary for Global Affairs, Paula Dabriasky declared: "The advancement of human rights and democracy is.. the bedrock of our war on terrorism". The 2002 National Security strategy reiterated the importance of democracy to US foreign policy objectives. The document proclaimed that "the national security strategy of US must look outward for possibilities to expand liberty" and stated that the United States will use its foreign aid to promote freedom and support those who struggle nonviolently for it, ensuring that nations moving towards democracy are rewarded for the steps they take.

The Administration has since taken a number of significant measures. For instance the Millennium Challenge Account (MCA) announced in March 2002 initiative, will provide up to 5 billion dollars annually to countries that "rule justly, invest their own people and encourage economic freedom". The Departments of State's Bureau for Democracy, Human Rights and Labour (DRL) set aside an enhanced part of its worldwide units for promising democracy-building projects in West Asia. Moreover, DRL has collaborated with the Bureau of Near Eastern Affairs to undertake a comprehensive review of assistance efforts in Egypt— strategically an important US partner in the ongoing war against terrorism. The Middle East Partnership Initiative (MEPI) announced by then Secretary of State, Colin Powell, in December 2002, was designed to address the political, economic, and educational underdevelopment of the Middle East. The programme provided 29 million dollars in the fiscal year 2003 to promote civil society, educational reform, equal status for women, economic reform and promote sector development. The Administration also launched initiatives beyond the Middle East, including new and comprehensive assistance programmes in Afghanistan and Pakistan. Democracy programmes in several Central Asian countries have been significantly increased in recent years as well.

American Sincerity in Doubt

However, an emphasis on democracy and human rights is in question in US policy, with regard to a host of countries including Pakistan, Afghanistan, Egypt, Saudi Arabia, Indonesia, Russia, China and many others. Skeptics doubt whether policies aimed at. democratization can even be pursued fully, given the reliance in the war on terrorism on non-democratic partners. US policies and assistance in Pakistan and Afghanistan have raised doubts about how much the Bush Administration may be willing to back democratization as part of an anti-terrorist strategy.

The US resumed a large-scale assistance programme in Pakistan after 9/11 but the programme doesnot have democracy-building as centerpiece of its agenda, despite the evident need for political reform. The US government has also been remarkably quiet on the face of a number of decidedly undemocratic actions taken by President Musharraf. Despite its promising new rhetoric on the importance of democratization, the Administration has largely ignored the promotion of democracy and has given General Musharraf blanket support in exchange for his cooperation with US objectives. It is on and around the frontlines of the campaign against Al-Qaida that the tensions between America's prevailing security concerns and its democracy interests are clearly visible. Afghanistan is a living example of this dilemma. The initial post 9/11 action by the US certainly reflected its concerns for democracy. But the conduct of US military operations undermined the Administration's promises of a durable, deep commitment to democratic reconstruction.

The tensions posed by the war on terrorism for US support of democracy abroad have spread out beyond the immediate frontlines. South East Asia is one such affected region. In this region, Indonesia has become an important theatre in the US anti-terrorist campaign. As a setback to human rights policy, the Administration has resumed aid to the Indonesian military in recent months. The willingness of the US government to enter into a partnership with a security force that just a few years ago was involved in a horrendous campaign of slaughter and destruction against civilians has sent a powerful negative signal throughout region and beyond. In the case of Malaysia, Washington's earlier critical stance has been reversed in response to Malaysian Prime Minister Mahathir Mahmmad's useful cooperation.

Central Asia also presents a mosaic of dilemmas relating to the tradeoff between democracy and security in US foreign policy. The US need for military bases and other forms of security cooperation in the region has moved Washington much closer to the autocratic leaders of Uzbekistan, Kazakhstan and Kyrgyztan. The tensions between America's pressing new security concerns and its democracy interests are evident in US policy toward Russia and China as well. President Bush regards Russian President Putin very favourably and has not pressed the Russian leader about his shortcomings on democracy and human rights (such as in the case of Chechnya) or with regard to monitoring a free press.

So far as China is concerned the current relatively positive state of relations— with mild US pressures on human rights, greatly overweighed by an ample mutually beneficial economic relationship— is not especially different from the overall pattern of the past decade. So far as Middle East is concerned, during the initial period after 9/11, the US turned to its traditional autocratic allies in the Arab world, especially Egypt and Saudi Arabia. However, a growing chorus of voices within and around the Administration has started questioning the value of America's friendly tyrants in the region. These individuals, invoking what they believe to be the true spirit of President Reagan's foreign policy, call for a change toward promoting freedom in US Middle East policy.

Attracted by this idea, President Bush's last summer declarations on the Middle East shifted noticeably in tone and content, setting out a vision of democratic change there. According to this vision, the US will first provide democracy in Palestinian territories by linking American support for a Palestinian state with the achievement of new, more democratic Palestinian leadership.

But the expansive vision of a sudden, US led democratization of the Middle East rests on questionable assumptions. It is worth noting that Middle East happens to be the least democratic region in the world. The region has been dominated by a range of authoritarian, political systems, including military regimes, monorchies, theocracies and one-party statist regimes. In his new book The Failure of Freedom, noted columnist Fareed Zakaria describes the situation as "an almost unthinkable reversal of a global pattern in which almost every Arab country is less free than it was forty years ago. There are few places in the world about which one can say that". Throughout Middle East, the secular opposition lacks dynamism and broad-based political support. Civil society is weak as a result of severe legal restrictions and coercive methods that the region's regimes adopt to stifle political expression. Independent media are largely non-existent.

Promoting democratization in lands without a tradition of democracy, of course, carries certain risks. Democratization assistance is not something that could solve the region's problems. That is why people like Fareed Zakaria argue that the US should not support democracy— by which they mean elections— in the Middle East but should instead gradually encourage reform of authoritarian regimes by working towards constitutional liberalism, rather than try to establish systems which make the state electorally accountable to its own people. In short, supporting democratization carries risks that must be taken into account while designing US strategies for the Middle East.

The current political situation in the Middle East is primarily driven by internal realities, but it also is a reflection of past US policy choices not to support democratic reforms within the region. Although the war on terrorism has greatly raised the profile of democracy as a policy matter, it has hardly clarified the issue. On the one hand, the fight against Al-Qaeda tempts Washington to put aside its democratic scruples and seek closer ties with autocracies throughout the Middle East and Asia. On the other hand, US policymakers have increasingly come to realize that it is precisely the tide of democracy in many of these countries that helps breed Islamic extremism.

Conclusion

To conclude, the events of 9/11 proved to be both a catalyst and watershed in US history. There is no doubt that the law enforcement agencies are keen to ensure that terrorist acts like 9/11 are not repeated. They are looking at potential terrorist within Muslim community as all 19 hijackers reportedly were Muslims. To Muslims, it sounds like religious and ethnic profiling and to law officials, it is simply part of their job. How can the two reconcile their position in a manner that can secure the security of the nation as well as civil rights of people? It is a delicate issue, which warrants serious thought. Muslim Americans are an integral part of American citizenry. They are as committed to the security of the country as the FBI and other law enforcement agencies are. They are as much keen to root out terrorism from their ranks as is the case with law enforcement agencies. A partnership is possible between the two. The law enforcement agencies have to create the impression through their actions that they are not after the 'Muslim Community' and that the Justice Department is not promoting a secret agenda against Islam. This is possible only when more and more Muslims are involved in open debate and policy discussions in the Justice Department.

It is a tribute to the US democratic traditions and freedom of expression that even after 9/11 the general public is not losing sight of larger cause of US foreign policy and human rights. Having witnessed and faced the brutality of 9/11, the US public opinion remains steadfast to its commitments, which is widely indicated by an outcry on the treatment of Al-Qaeda and Taliban prisoners as reflected in American press. The American media has been impressing upon the US Administration that it should respect Geneva Convention on Human Rights in its handling of all its detainees.

By and large the US public opinion wants the US Admin-istration to make it clear that it upholds the individual human rights laws. The Wilsonian stress on democracy and human rights can definitely make US policies attractive to others when these values appear genuine and are pursued in a fair-minded manner. America is the most powerful nation on the face of the planet because it has combined raw power with American ideals such as freedom, justice and dignity. These ideals are admired around the world and are more important to its position of global strength than its ability to shoot a missile down a chimney. The creation of a world based on fair play and justice and in which America takes its global responsibilities more seriously reflects the US's deepest values. The globalization of the economy must be paralleled by the globalization of American morality and reflected in domestic and foreign policies of the US in days to come to endear them to the rest of the world.

16
US India Relations

The collapse of the erstwhile Soviet Union and the reunification of Germany indicate the demise of the old world order and the birth of a new world order. Old world order implied the international system that had emerged after the Second World War. The atmosphere was surcharged with Cold War rivalry and bipolarity. The Cold War has been defined as "a situation in which each side continuously envisages war with an acknowledged rival, it is a state of continuous preparation for war, a continuous war alert... compatible with all forms of organised violence short of direct encounters between the armed forces o' the two super powers.'' In the military sphere, there was a real balance between the two poles maintained by the ability of both sides to annihilate each other. The sudden disappearance of one pole in an ideologically and strategically bipolar world transformed almost everything. As the international situation has undergone overall and profound change, the new world order is bound to be different from the earlier one in terms of formation, content and purpose. Recent happenings have basically altered the power structure in international politics, world economy and world security system. Old alignments, supportive alliances and treaty obligations have been rendered redundant by the emerging order. The collapse of the old order is final. It is definite because in the first place, one pillar of it, i.e., the Soviet power with all its ideological, political and military characteristics already belongs to the past and there is no sign of its resurrection. Secondly, because the Yalta system created an equilibrium which suppressed the processes that burst to the surface during the recent years. These markedly manifest processes constitute the emerging elements of the new world order. The emerging world order is as much a redefinition of what is important as it is the discovery of new forces at work.

Fundamental changes in the international order have made it obligatory for every nation to review its foreign policy postures. Each country, super power or regional power has to adapt its policy to the new agenda of the impending era, with its special economic, social and environmental challenges. Recent developments have not only paved the way for significant geostrategic changes in general and South Asia in particular. In the past few years, the events around South Asia have brought about a major change in global politics. A change in US-Soviet ties is sure to affect South Asian power balance. Any bilateral relationship is bound to be affected and influenced by the changing global scenario. Indo-US ties cannot be an exception. This relationship has to be adjusted in the light of spectacular transformation of international relations. As the ground realities that determined Indo-US relations have changed, bilateral relations between the two have to be restructured. With the end of the Cold War, the American and Indian policy-makers are called upon to reevaluate their bilateral relations in view of rapidly changing world situation. What are the implications of changes in the international environment to Indo-US relations? How is the demise of the Soviet Union going to affect Indo-American relations. How have the two nations adjusted their relations in a changing world? The crucial question is: How do India and the US view each other after the Cold War? Together with this question comes an equally important question: How India and the US see themselves without the Cold War?

In the past, Indo-US relations were shaped less by bilateral issues in disputes between them than by the threat each other perceived from other's international alignment. The tension between the two countries were not because of any conflict of basic national interest but a side effect of the Cold War. Most of the conflicts in Indo-US relations have arisen due to perceptional variations between the US as a global power and India as a regional power in their mutual security considerations. The world's most powerful democracy and the most populous democracy have a long record of public conflict and confrontation, than a record of cooperation. It is this lasting perception of the conflict in Indo-US relations that has led analysts to characterise India and the US as unfriendly friends[2] and their relationship as one of love and hate.

Two factors had played crucial role in determining Indo-US relations. One was the Soviet factor and the other was Pakistan. The Soviet Factor: During the Cold War period, the Soviet Union was regarded as enemy number one by the US and given the close and friendly Indo-Soviet relations, the Cold War politics also extended to create difficulties in the path of Indo-US relations. The 1970s clearly saw operation of what Professor Cohen described as system of balance of power[3] between the US-Pakistan-China on one side and India and the Soviet Union on the other. India needed the Soviet Union to act as a counterweight to China, to block any resolution in the UN Security Council inimical to India's interests on the Kashmir issue, to provide seemingly inexhaustible arms assistance at highly concessional rates, and to serve as a market for Indian consumer goods. The Soviets, in turn, relied on India for help in meeting equally specific needs. The Indo-Soviet friendship could indeed be best described as "a coincidence of interests."[4] But this relationship could not be simply renewed with the Soviet Union's successor state. With the collapse of communism and dissolution of the Soviet Union, the Soviet factor ceases to be an impediment in Indo-US relations. The crucial difference between them and now is the absence of the Soviet Union. In fact, the dissolution of the Indo-Soviet nexus has forced India to reconsider several central assumptions that used to underline its foreign policy. The Soviet-Indian alignment has ceased to have any meaning. That is the profound factor. The disintegration of the Soviet Union has taken out one corner of the Pentagon itself and the end of the Cold War has set in motion new thinking in the remaining four corners of the power alignment. The demise of the Soviet Union has had a profound impact on foreign policies of the two countries and relations with each other. While for Washington, the collapse of its enemy has had far more critical implications than its impact on relations with New Delhi, for the latter it has had direct and important implications for ties with Washington. Since a major determinant of Indo-US discord has been divergences regarding the Cold War, its end is bound to have a beneficial impact on bilateral relations. Indeed, a number of issues flowing from the very existence of the Soviet Union and Cold War, and which seriously hampered Indo-US relations during the past four decades, are no longer as relevant. For India, the loss of Soviet Union has removed a critical counterbalance to China and Pakistan. Hence, the US is viewed as potentially useful in helping restrain India's main antagonists. The US too has reasons to regard India more important geopolitically in the post-Cold War period. Under the existing circumstances, India has little option but to turn to the US. On the other hand, for the US, the imperatives of the Cold War are missing. The US is poised to consider relations with India on its own merit than as a derivative of US-Soviet relations. Thus, the possibility of even Indo-US cooperation becomes manifestly possible.

The Pakistan Factor

US's decision in the mid-fifties to build Pakistan militarily, extensively to "contain" the Soviet threat to the free world had a formative impact on Indo-US relations. American military assistance to Pakistan not only seriously undermined India's role in the sub-continent but also created a major security threat for India, a threat that was clearly visible in 1965, when Pakistan actually used American weaponry against India. Later in 1971, US openly tilted towards Pakistan. With the Soviet threat evaporating, the US has now few compelling reasons than loyalty to an old friend to stand by or in the words of Kissinger, "tilt" towards Pakistan. The US need to protect Pakistan against Soviet might has essentially vanished. Since the Soviet withdrawal from Afghanistan, the US simply does not need Pakistan's cooperation. Simultaneously neither side can meaningfully invoke the Cold War and anti-communist considerations as the basis for a continuing relationship. Since the US policy towards Pakistan has always affected Indo-US relations, the US policy towards Pakistan in the post-Cold War period is bound to affect Indo-US relations. In a report to the US Congress on National Security Strategy, President Bush pulling his Administration's approach towards the subcontinent had said in 1990: In South Asia, Pakistan and India are both friends of the US... The US will try to steadily improve relations with India and encourage both India and Pakistan rapprochement and a halt to nuclear proliferation.[5] In the post-Cold War period, Pakistan is suddenly looked upon in US, less as a traditional ally and more as a troublesome, bomb-in-the-basement, Islamic power. Sensing the popular mood in Congress in 1990, the Administration decided not to seek a waiver under the terms of Pressler Amendment, to the Foreign Assistance Act, which requires the President to certify that a nation is not actively acquiring nuclear weapons before it gets US aid.[6] Until such a waiver is sought or appropriate clarification provided, Congress will not continue foreign assistance to Pakistan which relies heavily on US assistance to modernise its armed forces. The US largely overlooked Pakistan's clandestine nuclear weapons programme for the better part of a decade, primarily because of the exigencies of the Afghan conflict. The suspension of US aid to Pakistan clearly reflects the diminishing strategic significance of Pakistan. The most important thing from the Indian view point for the long-term is the gradual tilt away from Pakistan. While Washington is unlikely to entirely abandon Islamabad, the latter's utility has certainly diminished.

Kashmir Issue

Concern is also growing in the US about Pakistan's involvement in Kashmir. While the US still regards Kashmir a disputed territory but now it adopts the public stand that the dispute should be settled under the terms of Simla Agreement. The testimony to changing American perception came in March 1990, when the Bush Administration gave up its support to Pakistan's demand for a plebiscite in Kashmir.[7] When the Indian Ambassador Abid Husain presented his credentials to George Bush, the President reiterated American support for the Simla Agreement as a framework for resolution of the dispute.[8] What was new in US stance was its blunt warning to Pakistan that if Pakistan started a war with India, the US would remain neutral. Robert Gates, Deputy Assistant Secretary during the course of his visit to the subcontinent told Pakistan leaders that "aid and spare parts would not be forthcoming for the US supplied weapons."[9] The US has also taken the strong position that aid to terrorists and separatists should be totally unacceptable and what is more significant, it has made it known that sentiment to Pakistan. For instance, the US Ambassador to Pakistan Robert Oakley in a letter to the President of Pakistan occupied Kashmir, Sardar Qayyum Khan, wrote in 1990 that "such support is a violation of the UN Charter and makes a political solution more difficult.[10] The Clinton Administration was not bugging for any particular option for Kashmir, a point that has been made clear through diplomatic channels. It wanted the bloody civil war to stop and the issue resolved between India, Pakistan and the people of Kashmir. The American official and unofficial minds believe that a united, fully autonomous federal or confederal state of Kashmir, with its security guaranteed by India and Pakistan will be the best solution. It would be worthwhile to mention about Gary Ackerman Sub-Committee of House of Representatives on Asia and Pacific. The sub-committee's report is enormously significant as this is the first time that a section of US Congressmen have challenged the traditional American opinion on the issue. The sub-committee rejected the plebiscite option as "overtaken by history," and therefore, irrelevant to present circumstances.[11] What is significantly new among the US Congressmen is the growing perception that the Kashmir dispute demands a fresh approach - away from the traditionally persistent demands for a plebiscite, for international invention and for a trilateral solution.[12] In other words, with the end of the Cold War, the US appears moving away from the traditional US-Pak alliance of the Cold War days when a UN plebiscite on Kashmir was urged. The US is now adopting an even handed approach in dealing with the two countries. It seems that America's approach to the nations of South Asia will now be bereft of Cold War hangovers and much more principled. Though there is an understandable weariness among the Americans to get involved in the sub-continental disputes; but greater involvement of the US appears inevitable. The US remains the only country which is in a position to ensure that internal problems do not jeopardize the South Asian region. It would be worthwhile for the US to help the besieged elites in the two countries to get out of the ethnic tensions. Kashmir has become the metaphor of both internal paralysis and external vulnerability. The US has to realize, as Stephen Cohen put it, "there is a failure of imagination in New Delhi and Islamabad concerning this mid 20th century issue.[13]

With the removal of these irritants, the contemporary international context and the immediate future seem particularly opportune for the betterment of Indo-US relations. Scope for cooperation with the US has broadened with the dismantling of the old power structure. Several important areas of cooperation between the two democracies may be identified.

Defence Cooperation

Freed from the Indo-Soviet nexus and the concomitant Cold War constraints, India and the US can envision ways of expanding their military cooperation. The turning point in Indo-US military cooperation came in April 1991, when the Commanding General of the US Pacific Command, Lt. General Clande Kickleighter visited India. After his visit, he made a set of proposals for increased service to service contacts between the two countries. These proposals are now commonly referred to as "Kickleighter Proposals." Their objective was "to pursue a common policy of gradually strengthening ties towards expanded cooperation and partnership by the end of this decade."[14] The Indian Army chief General Rodrigues visited the US Pacific Command in August 1991. Admiral C. Larson, commander of the US Pacific Fleet visited India in

December 1991. Besides visits, the first meeting of the Indo-US Army Steering Committee was held in New Delhi in January 1992. The meeting resulted in far-reaching decisions being taken which would expand Indo-US Army Cooperation.[15] Some of the decisions taken include substantial increase in funds for India under the US's International Military Exchange Training Programme, exchange of officers between the US Army Training Command and the Indian Army's newly created equivalent, the Army Training Command ARTRAC. A decision to establish a similar steering committee for Navy to Navy cooperation had also been taken. In June 1992, for the first time since 1964, India and the US completed a joint naval exercise off the Western Coast of India. All these activities envisage a level of military cooperation that India never had even with the Red Army in the heyday of the Soviet Union. Similar cooperation is envisaged between the air forces of two countries. These contacts are growing at all levels of the defence forces. Such military cooperation is taking place only because both sides consider it mutually beneficial. This cooperation cannot be regarded as aimed at any other country, but in the interest of regional peace. The US as a super power sees India as a growing middle power. This is not merely a "self identification"[16] by India but recognised by the US. In the absence of the Cold War and a rival power, US would increasingly see India as a regional power to maintain peace and stability in South Asia. India alone among the Indian Ocean littoral nations have a blue-water navy which can play a major role in maintaining freedom of seas in cooperation with the US and other interested nations.[17] There is definitely a qualitative change in the Indo-US defence cooperation in the post-Cold War period.

Economic Cooperation

The US has emerged as India's largest trading partner. Currently, India exports as much as 3 billion dollars worth of goods annually to the US. Encouraged by the recent economic liberalisation, the US has also emerged as one of the principal investors in India. The US seems genuinely interested in taking advantage of the economic potential released by India's programme of economic reform and liberalisation and is pursuing investment and collaborative plans for mutual benefit. The Americans are immensely interested in the huge Indian market which remains unpenetrated by any great power that the US regards as a rival.

India's attempt to reform and open its economy and woo foreign investment to join the global capitalist system have obviously enhanced India's attractiveness to the US. The Secretary of State Warren Christopner, in his confirmation hearing before the Senate Foreign Relations Committee made it clear that "economic competition is eclipsing ideological rivalry. We will not be bashful about linking our high diplomatic goals with our economic goals." In this context, if pursued to their logical end, have the potential of lending a cutting edge to India's diplomatic initiatives, not just in South Asia, but in the wider world as a whole. Indeed the card of economic reforms offers India the ability to exploit to its advantage the contradictions between the regional trading blocs or spheres of economic influence. The Carnegie Endowment Report provides the right clue to India's foreign policy establishment. It exhorts the US to forge closer ties with India because in seeking to counter Japanese economic dominance in Asia, the US will have relatively limited opportunities to compete in areas where the Japanese grip is already strong such as South East Asia. By contrast, India with a middle class population totaling about 175 million and the world's third largest pool of trained manpower, is emerging as an important manufacturing centre and will offer more significant commercial and investment opportunities. If the liberalisation process is sustained, two important and mutually desirable consequences could follow. The US would have growing access to India's middle class and given its size and resources on India firmly integrated into the world financial markets would be a big boost to international capitalism. India requires American capital and the US could exploit infrastructural well-poised to take off to speed. In brief, India's efforts to fundamentally reform its economy along free market lines have buttressed New Delhi's need to seek American assistance, especially through the IMF and World Bank, trade and investment.[18]

Technological Cooperation

The major catalytic agent propelling Indo-US relations into a more positive phase has been the easing of American restrictions on the supply of dual-use technology (technology that can be used for civilian and military purposes. In October 1986, President Reagan has signed a secret directive instructing all US Government agencies to seek improved relationship with India and accommodate Indian requests for dual-use technology.[19] The prospects for cooperation under the Memorandum of understanding signed between New Delhi and Washington grew much brighter during the Rajiv Gandhi regime (1985-89), getting an additional boost from the beginning of the end of the Cold War. Earlier main obstacle was the American perception of a close relationship between India and the Soviet Union; hence the fear of transferred technology falling the Soviet hands.[20] Now, no such fear on ideological grounds exists, though the US may still like to safeguard its scientific inventions on commercial grounds.

Common Threat

The end of the Cold War has added another dimension to Indo-US relations. This is the growth of Islamic fundamentalism. The world peace is threatened by the explosion of religious fundamentalism all over the world. Its fall out has affected not only the Muslim countries, but also secular democracies like India and the US. Religious territorism and attempts to set the clock back are producing a backlash in the concerned countries and even outside when they are supported by the state. With the end of the Cold War, it is possible to put this growing threat of state terrorism and religious fundamentalism in its time perspective and not assess in the Cold War context of foster years. The time has come when secular democracies like India and the US should work together to meet this growing menace to peace and stability, democracy and development. Countries such as India and the US could set an example in this regard. One effect of the collapse of the Soviet Union has been the creation of a number of Central Asian Republics which are susceptible to Islamic fundamentalism. The emergence of Central Asia as a new political entity, with five states adjacent to other Muslim nations further South is significant. Any such Islamic grouping specifically for security cooperation, could be a security threat to a secular India and a potential threat to the US as a global power. This has been anticipated by some American observers as Senator Larry Pressler, when he said, "I foresee a possible new coalition of states there, probably eight or nine countries, that would be a new strategic force in the world. There is also a danger that such a coalition could be dominated by Islamic fundamentalism."[21] India and the US have a common interest in serving as a bulwork against such potential radicalism. In the aftermath of the disintegration of the former Soviet bloc, the US is redefining its security concerns in the region. To secure stability in what has emerged as a geopolitical vacuum in the Central Asian

Republics, it would like to prevent the rise of hostile Islamic fundamentalism. That India has to be preferred option in this context is obvious. Against, this backdrop, the Carnegie Endowment Study Group on Indo-US relations has identified India as "one of the world's major battle grounds for the struggle between secularism and religious fundamentalism. At the same time, the growth of militant Islamic fundamentalism in areas adjacent to India underlines the possibility that New Delhi and Washington will share common security concerns in the region.

Israel Factor

India's decision to upgrade diplomatic relations with Israel is for obvious reasons going to be a positive step in maintaining upward trend in Indo-American relations as well. Apart from economic cooperation two areas where India is likely to benefit from Israeli connection, are defehce and combination of terrorism. After India's new friendly stance towards Israel, even on the very stubborn Middle East issue, India does not any longer quarrel with the peace plans in this region and is full agreement with the recent Israel-PLO agreement brought about at the initiative of President Clinton. This also has another positive influence on Indo-US relations.

China Factor

Washington's interest in ties with India relates to its own troubles with China. Sino-US relations have been foundering since 1989 as a result of disputes over human rights, weapons export and economic matters. Under the changed international environment, the US has no relevance for the China Card and US-Indian relations are likely to be more durable in essence, the altered global scenario has also provided a strategic impetus to improved ties between India and the US.

From the above it becomes evident that the end of the Cold War, the demise of the Soviet Union, and the downgrading of Pakistan's strategic-cum-political importance to the US transformed the basis of the relationship between India and the US. In turn the US reversed to perception of India's role in South Asia, helped by policies of economic liberalisation pursued by New Delhi and by a reassessment of India as a force for stability in a troubled subcontinent.

The mid eighties had already witnessed an improvement in the political climate between India and the US. The reinterpretation of India's role in South Asia was helped by US perception of Rajiv Gandhi as being more liberal in his economic policy, and by a reassessment of India as an independent power that could be a force for stability in a troubled region. Thus, the US openly approved India's role in Sri Lanka when in July 1987, India sent its troops to Sri Lanka to stabilize peace in that country, similarly, India's role in crushing the coupled by mercenary forces against the government of President Abdul Gayoom of Maladives was also seen favourably by the US. The US endorsement was in fact a tacit acceptance of India's meaningful role in South Asia. The factors which facilitated and motivated the pursuit of accommodation in Indo-US relations during the eighties included a reappraisal of perceptions, the evolution of respective foreign policies, emerging regional and global changes, and developing domestic priorities especially on India's part. While their specific manifestations have changed since the end of that decade, these general compulsions underlying Indo-US reapproachment remain valid today. Indeed, as a result of developments in the nineties, many of them have become even more powerful forces for improved ties. The end of the Cold War has reduced the strategic significance of South Asia in US perceptions. This has had a beneficial effect for India because US perceptions of Pakistan's role in Cold War politics had invariably come in the way of closer Indo-US ties especially in areas of strategic and security interests in the past. Earlier India and the US permitted irritants to undermine an underlying harmony of interests between the two great democracies. However, in a new world order there could be a reciprocal underpinning of a global order centred on America and a South Asian balance based on India.

In the past, a strategic friendship with the former Soviet Union that did not incur a strategic enmity with the US gave India the best of both worlds. Now, New Delhi has to deal with the break-up of the Soviet Union and the resulting emergence of an essentially new world order. India has to ensure its security in the wake of its being surrounded by nuclear weapon states like China, Pakistan and now Kazakhstan and the development of nuclear weapons in the Indian Ocean. The disappearance of the Soviet Union destroyed India's most important source of defence supplies, took away a major export market, left India more vulnerable in the northern neighbourhood and brought about new competitions for foreign aid. It is in this context of changed international scenario that India has to recast its foreign policy priorities in international politics, economy and world security system. At present, India is striving to reorder its domestic economy to enable to take an increasing part in the emerging world order in a part that is consistent with its size and capabilities. This requires enhancing and building partnerships based on mutuality of interests with all countries, particularly the major powers. In this context, the current leadership of the US needs to be understood in its overall perspective. Under the existing conditions India has little option but to turn to the US. As matters stand today, India needs a good understanding with the 5 veto-holding permanent members of the Security Council. Given the world as it is today, such an understanding has to be achieved primarily with the US. On the other hand, for the US, the imperatives of the Cold War are now missing. The US is poised to consider relations with India and Pakistan on their own merits rather than as a derivative of the US-Soviet relations. It is in India's interests to adjust its foreign policy to emerging post-Cold War order. It is worth recalling that Jawaharlal Nehru in 1949 had proposed to do exactly this to forge closer economic and scientific cooperation with the US without surrendering independence on political and strategic initiatives on global issues.[22] It is hoped that India, if it adopts such a stance now, may be better understood by the US policy-makers.

The new revolutionary international scene offers India with a stork choice. It has to choose between the comforting familiarity of the old order or the challenge of exploiting the opportunities opening up in the new world order. The age of the Cold War is over. The identity of the "Second World" has vanished and the former Soviet Union, the super power of yesterday is reduced to the status of a European power. India should not remain a prisoner of the past. A perpetual transformation about India surfaced in Washington as a result of disappearance of the Soviet Union as a major threat to US security. It is upto India to recognise this process. The US is looking afresh at India and no longer regards it to be of marginal importance. The US perception on the Indian sub-continent is undergoing a change. Not to take advantage of it would be a grievous error. A prime consideration of India's new policy should be to strike a mature, mutually respectable relationship with the US.

The end of the Cold War may even give a boost to middle powers such as India. The Cold War had artificially held them back and turned them into under performers. Now, they have the opportunity to enhance their influence in international arena. The end of the Cold War and the emergence of the US as the only super power with global military and political reach have reduced the significance of India's antagonists- China and Pakistan - in Washington's strategic calculations and have created opportunities for India to augment its position in South Asia. Indian aspirations in the region often ran counter to US policy in the past because of the strategic imperatives of the Cold War. During the Cold War period, Pakistan was in the Western alliance and in the American eyes India was a client state of the Soviet Union. American calculations made in the context of the Cold War led to military and political support for China and Pakistan, which actively opposed Soviet power. With the global framework transformed, there is no valid reason for Indian and American interests and policies to conflict seriously. The international changes that have relieved India of the often agonizing choice between the US and the Soviet Union, and that have reduced the significance of Pakistan in US strategy, provide India opportunity to play a regional and international role commensurate with its size and potential. With the Cold War over, Washington has no reason to oppose such Indian aspirations. In fact, give the coincidence of political values between India and the US and the absence of major conflict of interests between the two countries, a regional security structure that reflects Indian power and strength should be appealing in the US.

In the post-Cold War world, India's problems with the US relate mostly to bilateral or trilateral issues confined to the South Asian geopolitical region. The negative issues remain on the road ahead. Non-proliferation is one. Trade relations is another, especially the question of whether India protects patents and other intellectual property rights adequately. However, controversies about patents and access to markets for specific products are not serious enough to strain the bilateral relationship. Such rough patches cannot be removed from Indo-American relations. They can only be transcended by reinforcing positive trends. Such patches can be expected to come in the way of any bilateral relationship, all the more when both nations happen to be democracies. But they are not unbridgeable canyons. The divergences in respective perceptions of two countries are not likely to affect confluence of interests between the two countries. And to that matter no two nations are devoid of a degree of divergence in their perceptions.

To sum up, the new world situation, while posing fresh challenges for Indo-US relations, also presents it with tremendous opportunities. The US could help India more in right direction by offering discreet encouragement to secular and democratic forces in India, permitting the speedy transfer of dual-use technology and supporting Indian requests for assistance from IMF and World Bank. Such US actions would herald a new era of Indo-US relations in which policy-makers in New Delhi and Washington could overcome a legacy of mutual suspicions. These suspicions are likely to have little life of their own in the absence of super power confrontation. The ties that bind the two democracies should dictate a much higher level of Indo-US cooperation than was in the past. Such cooperation will serve the long-term interests of both countries especially the international agenda begins to emphasize the developmental and environmental issues neglected during the Cold War. In this new world, India and the US both are required to come to terms with the new reality of a multi-polar world. It is worth remembering that there is no clash or conflict of national interests between the two, on the other hand, there is much that is common. The values, goals and ideals of democracy and secularism that unite them are far more lasting and important than what appears to divide them from time to time. The great potential of America could be harnessed with the potential of other democracies like India and used for creating a better, more peaceful world where human rights, individual liberty and equality of opportunity are ensured on the basis of mutual respect and understanding.

References

1. Peter Lyon, "Neutralism," Oxford, 1963, p. 18.
2. See for instance, T. V. Kunhikrishnan, "Unfriendly Friends : India and America," New Delhi, 1974.
3. See his paper, "South Asian Security Issues : An American Perspective," presented at the US-India Bilateral Conference at New Delhi, February 2-4, 1988.
4. S. Kidwai, "Indo-Soviet Relations," New Delhi, 1985, p. 115.
5. 'The Times of India,' March 21, 1990.
6. Sumit Ganguly, "South Asia After the Cold War," 'The Washington Quarterly,' Autumn 1992, p. 181.
7. Times of India,' New Delhi, March 8, 1990.
8. *Ibid.*, May 31, 1990.

9. B. K. Shrivastave, "Prospects of Indo-US Relations," in 'Yearbook on India's Foreign Policy,' edited by Satish Kumar, New Delhi, 1990, p. 32.
10. "US Enuay Wants Pak to Stop Backing Terrorism," 'India West,1 December 11 -28,1990, p. 20.
11. "Times of India", New Delhi, June 12, 1993.
12. M. Saleem Kidwai, "American perspectives on Kashmir", Journal of Peace Studies, New Delhi, Vol. 1, November-December, 1993, p. 56.
13. Stephen Cohen "Kashmir" The Road ahead", Journal of Peace Studies, New Delhi, Vol. 1, November-December, 1993, p. 56.
14. Arun Katoch, "Closer Defence Towards Indo-US Military Cooperation", The Statesman, New Delhi, April 23, 1992.
15. *Ibid.*
16. See Leo E. Rose, "India's Regions Policy: Non-Military Dimension," In Stephen P. Cohen (ed.), 'The Security of South Asia American and Asian Perspective, New Delhi, 1983, p. 3.
17. P.M. Kamath, "The End of the Colone Implications for Indian-American Relations, India Quarterly, New Delhi, January-June, 1993, p. 62
18. Edward A. Gargan, India seems a changing world; New York Times; January 2, 1992.
19. N. Chanda, "A New Indian Summer Far Eastern Economic Review", February 25, 1988, p. 34.
20. J.N. Parimoo, "Pentagon Does not Trust India With Hitech", Vol. 3, "The Times of India, February 5, 1986.
21. "Pressler Warms of Islamic Force, January 1, 1992.
22. Gopal S., "Jawaharlal Nehru: A Biography", New Delhi, Vol. 2, pp. 58-59.

17
US and Kashmir Issue

Introduction

The role of the United States in the developments leading upto and resulting in the partition of India was minimal. The American policy was that the subcontinent was still a British preserve and consequently the US appeared to have no desire to actively involve itself in an area about which it knew little and seemed to care-less. Therefore, in the immediate aftermath of independence, the US treated India and Pakistan as back waters of the tense post-war world. However, the Indo-Pak dispute over Kashmir which was a consequence of tribal attack from Pakistan on Kashmir, which ultimately erupted into a war in 1948, soon brought America into the fray. Soon after the outbreak of war, India brought the Kashmir case before the UN Security Council[1].

Ever since the Kashmir problem was tabled in the UN, the US has been actively involved in it. The US interest in Kashmir primarily arose in part from Kashmir's strategic location being close to the Soviet Union and bordering on Afghanistan, Sinkiang, Tibet, India and Pakistan[2]. The immediate US concern apparently centered on the possibility that the dispute would lead to a general war between India and Pakistan; or in case there was no general war but if high tensions continued, both countries would be greatly weakened by their exhausting military budgets. Evidence of this American concern is found in the statement of Ambassador Grady in New York that Kashmir was one great problem which might cause the downfall of two dominions[3]. The majority in the UN Security Council led by the US tended to adopt a pro-Pakistan line. By refusing to discriminate between parties on an extended principle of jurisprudence, the US delegate very subtly brushed aside India's contention that the Security Council should call upon Pakistan to stop its aggressive activities. While agreeing with the majority in the Security Council, the US delegate stressed the importance of the assurances given by Lord Mountbatten and Jawaharlal Nehru for holding a plebiscite in Kashmir[4]. The US representative refrained from commenting on the role of Pakistan in the aggression on Kashmir. In the resumed meeting of the Security Council, the US delegate made a scathing and satirical attack on the Indian delegate exhibiting an unprecedented sense of intolerance and ignorance[5].

The US media on the Kashmir issue reacted more or less on the official line. It showed no inclination to appreciate India's version. Instead, it was inclined to give consideration to Pakistan's position on the issue. For instance, the New York Times commented: "The Indian delegation wished to limit the discussion to the actual armed invasion of Kashmir and the question of Pakistan's participation or responsibility in that are aspects of the problem. But the invasion in itself reflected some deeper differences, some other questions that had not been answered" [6].

It is evident that the US government took a position on Kashmir issue from the very outset that did not concede India's point that Pakistan had committed aggression on her soil and that the aggression must be vacated. This basic position was an important concession to Pakistan's stand on the issue. The US had, by and large accepted the view following the UN resolution of 1948 that:

(a) Accession was incomplete and Kashmir was a disputed territory;

(b) The finality of accession was to be determined by a plebiscite;

(c) Though the questions of this plebiscite were not determined, the basic question was to determine whether the people wanted to join India or Pakistan.

India felt offended by what it regarded as unsympathetic and even hostile American attitude towards its position on the Kashmir question from the time the question was raised in the Security Council. It felt that the US was siding with Pakistan, the aggressor, against India, the victim of aggression. India was particularly irritated by what it considered as selective and biased views of the US on the plebiscite issue, a highly sensitive and emotionally charged issue with the Indians[7].

The question arises why the US had adopted such an attitude? What were the reasons behind it? What was the rationale of the US Kashmir policy?

In the first place, the US view of the problem can be comprehended from the cold war perspective and attempts at containing international communism. The US chief concern was to prevent the problem from escalating into a general war between India and Pakistan as this would adversely affect US policies and strategies in Asia generally and might push either or both of the belligerents into the communist camp[8]. Coincidentally, the Kashmir problem emerged at the peak of communist "expansionism". Hence, the US predicament was based on the fragility of the general situation. In general, the US desire was to bridge the gap between the views of the belligerents so as to reduce the incentive for war. The US regarded the origin of the problem to be complex. For the US, the basic task was the disposition of the problem. It believed that the plebiscite would be the final step in resolving the problem. The plebiscite would enable the people to choose without coercion from either side. The other important reason was that the US wanted to back Pakistan in order to make India amenable to her broad policies. Last but not the least, America knew that it had no hope of getting military base in Kashmir, a territory of great strategic significance if it remained a part of India. In this respect only Pakistan could oblige her. Whatever be the reasons, in the early phase of Kashmir dispute, the US attitude was more acceptable to Pakistan than to India. The US view appeared to be that while India's legal position was strong due to the use of Pakistan territory for invasion of Kashmir, the dispute had a communal or religious aspect which was denied by India.

On 27 July 1949, an agreement was reached on a cease-fire line, which was ratified by India and Pakistan. The peace attained in Kashmir through case-fire was certainly an achievement on the part of Security Council. The influence of the US in the Security Council had obviously been a factor that contributed to this accomplishment. However, the political aspects of the truce agreement remained insurmountable. While commenting on the appointment of Fleet Admiral C.W. Nimitz of the US as Plebiscite Administrator in 1949, the US Secretary of State, Dean Acheson, made for the first time certain remarks on the responsibility of Pakistan in the invasion of Kashmir. Significantly he took care not to condemn Pakistan for her action in Kashmir. He merely concluded with the non-committed announcement that Admintal Nimitz would take over the difficult task of organizing the plebiscite[9]. This was a belated admission by the US of Pakistan's aggression in Kashmir, but the subsequent behaviour of the US belied Indian hopes of any change of heart on the part of the US.

During the period when UN Commission was busy negotiating with the Governments of India and Pakistan, the US became keenly interested in the solution of the Kashmir dispute. Thus, in August 1949, the US President, Truman took the unusual step of appealing to the Governments of India and Pakistan to accept the arbitration proposals made by the Commission. The US was guided in this by the triumph of communists in China. The proposal evoked sharp reactions in India. In November 1952, Graham submitted his fourth report to the Security Council. After the acrimonious debate on the Graham Report, the US and British delegates jointly sponsored a resolution, giving, Graham another opportunity to do the mediating effort to resolve the issue. The Soviet delegate accused the sponsors of the resolution of having imperialist designs in Kashmir[10]. The debate witnessed one of the most important developments in the four year old history of Kashmir issue. The unstinted Soviet support for India appears to have hardened the American attitude towards Kashmir. Pakistan's overtures to the US and its involvement in US military pacts had brought her closer to the US. On14 February 1957, the Western powers sponsored a resolution in the Security Council which envisaged the induction of foreign troops in Kashmir and authorize the Security Council President to proceed to the sub-continent and offer his mediation[11]. The Soviet veto prevented India's isolation at the hands of Pakistan and her allies. The Soviet Union again came to India's rescue when at its autumn session, the Security Council again debated the issue, and a draft resolution was prepared by the western powers which referred to the need for demilitarization as a step towards plebiscite determining the future status of Kashmir[12].

Pakistan President Ayub Khan's visit to the US in 1961 failed to elicit American assurances on Kashmir. In the joint communique issued after Ayub's visit, the US President Kennedy "expressed" the hope that progress towards a settlement of Kashmir issue would be possible on an early date[13]. Thus, the Kennedy Administration declined to take an active role in settling Pakistan's dispute with India over Kashmir. Kennedy favoured bilateral talks between India and Pakistan to resolve Kashmir issue and made a similar suggestion to Nehru during latter's visit to Washington in November 1961[14]. In January 1962, Kennedy suggested to Governments of India and Pakistan that the good offices of Eugene R Black, President of International Bank for Reconstruction and Development(IBRD), be used by them in a fresh bid to resolve Kashmir issue through direct negotiations[15]. India rejected Kennedy's offer on the ground that it did not favour any third party arbitration on an issue of this kind[16]. However, despite Kennedy's open preference for bilateral negotiations, when Pakistan raised Kashmir issue in the Security Council in 1962, the US supported Pakistan and voted against India[17]. During the Sino-Indian conflict of 1962, the US attitude towards Kashmir problem became more compromising. The US was convinced, after the Sino-Indian conflict, that any successful long-term regional defence against China would be through joint Indo-Pak endeavours. And Kashmir settlement was regarded by Americans as a pre-requisite to a joint sub-continental defence system. While providing military aid to India, the US also attempted to pressurize both sides, especially India towards a final settlement of Kashmir peacefully and bilaterally. Thus, between December 1962 to May 1963, India and Pakistan had six rounds of talks but no agreement was reached. The failure, according to Pakistan, was due to lukewarm US pressure on India. In 1965, Kashmir issue once again resulted in a war between India and Pakistan. Despite the US sympathy for Pakistan on Kashmir problem, Washington blamed Pakistan for provoking the crisis. To make the UN ceasefire effective, the US placed an arms embargo on both the "belligerents" [18]. The next day, US declared its neutrality in the conflict. Ostensibly, Pakistan's filtration with China from 1963 onwards caused a shift in the US Kashmir policy[19]. Thus, by the time of 1971 Bangladesh crisis, the US had ceased to be pro-Pakistan on Kashmir; rather she stressed bilateral talks on Kashmir.

A careful analysis of the US role during the cold war period reveals that the US had placed herself on record as stressing for a peaceful settlement of the Kashmir dispute by negotiations between the two parties and through mediation, if necessary. In trying to carry out this policy, the US, however, adopted certain measures that hindered the solution of the problem. It also left the impression that despite public expression to the contrary, the US had a soft corner for Pakistan. While the US desired to secure an early and peaceful settlement of the dispute, it wanted it to be achieved under its own leadership and in accordance with her wishes. The US hoped for a solution of the problem through the assistances of Security Council where it occupied an influential position. Yet the fact remains that the US approach on various occasions tended to favour Pakistan's case against India's. This neither improved US-India relations nor brought the Kashmir issue nearer to any solution. The US policy encouraged Pakistan to adopt an increasingly hostile posture towards India, creating several problems. Obviously, the US had failed to appreciate India's viewpoint.

Post Cold War Era

A radical change brought about by the end of cold war resulted in a major shift in US policy towards Kashmir issue. A testimony of the changed perception came in early nineties when the Bush Administration adopted the public posture that the dispute should be settled under the terms of Shimla Agreement. For instance, at the time of credentials presentation ceremony of the then Indian ambassador Abid Hussain, President George Bush declared America's support for Shimla Agreement as a framework for resolution of the conflict[20]. Then, the US Assistant Secretary of State for the Near East and South Asia, John Kelly, testified, at a congressional hearing that the US was no longer urging a plebiscite for Kashmir and would leave it to India and Pakistan to settle their dispute bilaterally[21]. Later on, a State Department advisory note repeated Kelly's observations in clarification of its stand on Kashmir issue. At the same time, the US permanent representative, Thomas Pickering, stated that the US belief in the Shimla Agreement remained "strong and abiding" and the US was opposed to a UN role in settling the Kashmir issue[22].

The US also showed concern about Pakistan's involvement in Kashmir. It had taken a strong position against aid given by Pakistan to terrorists and separatists. Significantly, it had made this sentiment known to Pakistan. For example, the US ambassador to Pakistan Robert Okley, in a letter to the then President of Pakistan occupied Kashmir, Sardar Abdul Qayyum Khan wrote in 1990 that, "Such support is a violation of the UN Charter and makes a political solution more difficult[23]."

During Bush Administration, there was a strong move to declare Pakistan a terrorist state. In the waning days of Bush Administration, the acting Secretary of State, Lawrence Eagleburgar, had in a letter to the US Congress specified that the Administration should take 120 to

160 days to decide on the issue of listing Pakistan as a terrorist State[24].

In the wake of high tensions in Kashmir as a result of intense cross border firing, the US Under Secretary of State for Political Affairs, Robert Kimmett, publicly called upon the two countries to avoid steps which could lead events to spin dangerously out of control[25]. When India-Pakistan tensions over Kashmir rose to the highest level, President Bush sent his deputy National Security Advisor, Robert Gates to urge caution on India and Pakistan. Gates warned leaders of both countries that their relations with the United States would suffer badly if they went to war. What was new in the US stance was its blunt warning to Pakistan that if Pakistan started a war with India, US would remain neutral. Gates told Pakistan leaders that "aid and spare parts would not be forthcoming for the US supplied weapons[26]." He also made it clear that Washington no longer backed a UN plebiscite as the preferred way to solve the Kashmir dispute but instead supported bilateral India-Pakistan talks in accordance with the Shimla Agreement[27].

The US Kashmir policy under Bush Administration thus corresponded with India's own strongly held preference for bilateral negotiations and was at odds with Pakistan's desire to involve outsiders in settling the dispute. As rightly pointed out by the former Indian ambassador to the US, Abid Hussain: "The US had come much closer to the Indian point of view by clearly stating that the plebiscite proposal had been overtaken by time and the intervening events and that the matter should be settled within the parameters of the Shimla Agreement[28]."

This significant transformation of US Kashmir policy occurred because with the end of cold war, US started looking militant Islam as one of the biggest threat. Under the changed circumstances, Pakistan could not be a credible ally against militant Islam. Indeed Pakistan appeared to be aiding militant Islam by arming terrorists in Kashmir, and had therefore drawn a sharp rebuke from the US. With the Soviet threat evaporating, US need to protect Pakistan against Soviet power vanished. Simultaneously, neither side could invoke the cold war and anti-Communist considerations as the basis for a continuing relationship. Pakistan was suddenly looked upon in the US less as a traditional ally and more as a troublesome bomb-in-the basement Islamic power. The US global concern about the threat to nation states from sub-nationalism, which often manifested itself as religious fundamentalism in Kashmir, was no doubt another reason for the change in the US stance on Kashmir. Needless to say, Bush's policies caused satisfaction in India.

Clinton Administration

However, with the taking over of Bill Clinton as President of the US, the American position on Kashmir started hardening. The first visit by a senior State Department official to New Delhi was marked by public criticisms of India's human rights record in Kashmir. In May 1993, the then interim Director of Bureau of South Asian Affairs, John Malott, openly criticized the role of India's Security forces in Kashmir[29]. Malott minced no words while describing American apprehensions about the situation in Kashmir. He declared that there were three basic principles governing the US position in Kashmir. They were one, the US considers whole of Kashmir to be a disputed territory, two, the dispute should be settled peacefully between India and Pakistan and three, the US is prepared to push, prod, cajole and encourage both countries, to move beyond rhetoric to détente[30]. This was followed by President Clinton's reference to Kashmir in his address to the UN General Assembly. Clinton's reference to Kashmir came early in his speech, which had, as its overall theme, the adjustment of the world to the post-cold war situation. He said: "Thus as we marvel at the era's promise of new peace, we must also recognize the serious small threats that remain. Bloody ethnic, religious and civil wars range from Angola to the Caucasus to Kashmir"[31]

Significantly, none of Clinton's predecessors had made such a reference in any international fora. The first such mention by an American president was phrased so as to link it clearly to the question of non-proliferation of nuclear and missile technologies. Responding to a question on why President Clinton in his UN speech had mentioned Kashmir, Robin Raphael, the US Assistant Secretary of State for South Asian Affairs said: "It was meant to say we see Kashmir on the radar screen along with Yugoslavia and Somalia and lots of other places in the former Soviet Union, Georgia, where there is civil conflict going on. We cannot easily overlook it and there is a message in that" [32].

It is worth noting that Clinton's reference to Kashmir in his UN address came after the Indo-US bilateral talks had reached a dead end, with the then India's Foreign Secretary J. N. Dixit making it clear that New Delhi would not compromise on certain bottomlines on technology for nuclear or missile-cum-space programmes.

Change in US policy

Later on, certain pronouncements made by Clinton Administration officials strengthened the doubts in India about the change in the US's Kashmir policy from that of its predecessor, Republican regime. These utterances by officials indicated a change in the earlier American policy of supporting Shimla Agreement and ruling out the plebiscite formula.

For instance, Robin Raphel during a "background briefing" questioned the 1947 Instrument of Accession, the then ruler of Jammu and Kashmir had signed with the then Governor General of India merging his princely state with India. She also raised doubts about the efficacy of the Shimla Agreement which binds India and Pakistan to settle their disputes bilaterally free from third party intervention. She declared that the entire Kashmir was a disputed territory and there were three parties to it, India, Pakistan and Kashmir. She added that any solution to Kashmir must be acceptable to Kashmiris who were unhappy with the existing set up[33]. The real shock among Raphel's revelations was her repudiation of Kashmir's accession to India as a depiction of US policy. So far no US Administration had disputed the Instrument of Accession or the Independence of India Act under which 500 odd princely states had acceded to India. The second important aspect of Raphel's statement was to downgrade the meaning and substance of Shimla Agreement of 1972 between India and Pakistan. Last but not the least, Raphel injected a new element in the conflict by saying that the people of Kashmir should be an active participants in the ultimate peace negotiations for the future of Jammu and Kashmir. Significantly, this statement was made during the height of Hazratbal crisis. The timing was important. As rightly pointed out by the then External Affairs Minister of India, Dinesh Singh, the remarks had come just as it appeared that militants inside the Hazratbal shrine were about to release their hostages[34]. Raphel's statement offered great succour to the militants entrenched in the shrine and their mentors across the border. Expression of doubt on the finality of Kashmir's accession to India served as morale booster to the secessionist movement in the state. The militants in the valley felt convinced that the US, the lone super power, would secure Azadi (Independence) for them eventually provided they continue their fight against India.

The Government of India, while lodging a strong protest, accused Washington of questioning the unity and integrity of India[35]. The charge was promptly refuted by the US State Department which maintained that there was no change in the US stand on Kashmir. Clarifying the US stand, the State Department spokesman, Mike McCury, said: "There is nothing that was said by any senior official of Administration indicating a change in the US policy on Kashmir" [36].

However, doubts that Raphel's remarks might signify a change in the US policy were reinforced by this clarification. The official spokesman did not characterize the Assistant Secretary's remarks as a "misspeak", the diplomatic term it uses to disassociate itself from embarrassing remarks made by officials or politicians. In this case, the clarification reaffirmed the original remarks. The spokesman said that Raphael was only reiterating the stated policy. Raphael's statement was interpreted in the Indian media as encouraging the secessionists in Kashmir, strengthening the forces of fundamentalism and emboldening Pakistan to wage its low intensify war against India with greater impunity. The Indian ambassador in the US, S S Ray asked for a formal letter setting out the US policy on Kashmir. Sensing the violent reaction in India, the Clinton Administration felt constrained to calm the storm by obliging the Indian envoy. The carefully worded letter signed by Peter Turnoff, Under Secretary for Political Affairs repudiated several of Raphael's formulations and gave the assurance that the Clinton Administration placed considerable value on Indo-Us relations[37]. However, the letter did not in any way change Raphael's assertion that Kashmir is a disputed territory." While invoking the authority of Shimla Agreement, Turnoff's letter demanded that India and Pakistan should not only solve the Kashmir problem but also do so in accordance with the wishes of Kashmiri people. Regarding the most objectionable part of Raphael's statement questioning the legality of the 1947 Instrument of Accession, it was stated that Kashmir being a disputed issue, it followed that the Instrument of Accession and other documents were widely disputed too[38].

After Raphael's controversial remarks, President Clinton in his reply to a Kashmiri-American, Dr. Ghulam Nabi Fai, assured, "to work with you and others to bring peace to Kashmir" [39]. Indian press and government reacted vehemently to this letter from White House. It was interpreted as signalling major shift in US policy towards Kashmir in keeping with the alleged ground strategy of balkanizing India. Selig Harrison, South Asia expert at the Carnegie Endowment for International Peace found the Clinton letter episode very tragic" and said: "After

Raphael's unfortunate remarks Clinton would have been careful not to pour oil on troubled waters[40].

A little later, President Clinton rubbed salt to injury by sharing Pakistan's concern about alleged human rights abuses in Kashmir[41]. This was no off-the-cuff remark. It was a statement on the US policy on the occasion of the presentation of credentials by Pakistan's ambassador to US, Maleeha Lodi, who had not only embarked on an anti-India tirade but also invited the US President to use his good offices on the front burner of world attention[42]. President Clinton's remarks indicated a reluctance on Washington's part to view Kashmir problem in all its complexity and to endorse the patently motivated Pakistani propaganda on human rights violations in Kashmir. At the same time, Robin Raphael, in her speech to Asia Society, equated the situation in Kashmir with the civil war in Afghanistan[43]. Raphael told all concerned that this was not her personal view but had the full backing of the President. In essence, the US was bent upon describing what was happening in the valley as an intensifying civil war in which the Indian security forces were supposedly acting like an occupation army. Such statements not only threatened to rupture relations between India and the US but also encouraged Kashmir terrorists and their supporters from across the border.

As part of an effort to undo the damage caused to Indo-US relations by the Raphael affair, the US Secretary of State, Warrren Christopher wrote a letter to Indian Prime Minister congratulating him on the successful prosecution of the Hazratbal affair. But even this letter conveyed a more meaningful message. Warren Christopher did not really disassociate himself from the basic thrust of his subordinate's remarks. By referring to "all parties" in Jammu and Kashmir, the US persisted with its newly articulated view that the Kashmiris in the valley were a party to the dispute[44].

Human Right Factor

The US soon came to view the Kashmir issue in the light of human rights issue rather than in terms of transborder terrorism in which India found itself to be embroiled. Throughout the year 1993, the US urged India to improve human rights situation in Kashmir Ostensibly pressure from domestic human rights groups forced the Clinton Administration to take a tough stand on Kashmir. The stress on human rights was coupled with the realization that the Kashmir problem involved a much larger issue, i.e. the right of self-determination of the people of Kashmir. The most significant aspect of US Kashmir policy under President Clinton was that it questioned the legality of Kashmir's accession to India and denounced India for alleged human right violations in the state in very specific terms. This policy caused a furore in New Delhi and an euphoria in Pakistan. However, at the international foras like UNHRC, the US maintained silence when Pakistan moved a resolution censuring India for the human rights violations in the valley.

Kashmir Elections and US diplomatic Initiative

Towards the end of Clinton Administration's first term, the US policy towards Kashmir issue changed again. The American response to elections in Indian part of Kashmir epitomized the fluctuating policy of Clinton Administration over Kashmir issue. It seemed to acquire a more realistic tone. For instance, before the Indian parliamentary elections, the US Assistant Secretary of State, Robin Raphael said: "If the Kashmiri people participated in India's Lok Sabha polls, the verdict would be acceptable to the US Administration"[45].

She stressed that it would not be fair to denounce the election process from which positive results could be expected. Subsequently, the US ambassador to India, Frank Wisner, in a speech to Pakistani Command and Staff College at Quetta observed: "I submit that there are compelling reasons why the time is right to look again at the issue of Kashmir. A political process that enjoys broad participation is the single best antidote to the violence that plauges the valley. It will rejuvenate a weary people and revitalize a moribund economy[46]."

The developments in Afghanistan made it imperative for the US as the sole super power to ensure peace and stability in the region. In order to achieve the objective, the American ambassadors accredited to New Delhi and Islamabad were asked to do the necessary spadework. The US invested quite a bit of political capital in creating the right atmosphere for a peace process to be started. The then US ambassador to India, Wisner, along with a team of specialists visited Pakistan. In Pakistan, the US ambassadors accredited to India and Pakistan acted in tandem and met all the key personnel. Commenting on Wisner's Mission, President Clinton observed: "Our embassy in New Delhi is in frequent touch with major Kashmiri political groups and with Indian officials involved in Kashmir. Through these channels, we are working to reduce human rights violations, allow greater access by international organizations and encourage political dialogue in Kashmir that would lead to a credible democratic process[47]".

By urging India and Pakistan once again to initiate a dialogue over Kashmir, the Clinton Administration apparently endorsed what had been termed as the beginning of a political process in the state. While commenting on the state elections, the US Ambassador to India, Wisner observed: "They (elections) are not an end in themselves; indeed many Kashmiris will not participate. But to the degree that the elections have been preceded by political dialogue and one followed by further dialogue between Kashmiris and between the State and the Central government over a fresh constitutional definitions, then a process is underway that offers promise to India, to the region and to the world[48]."

Elaborating further, the Ambassador said: "The US will continue to express its support for a political process in Kashmir and a resumption of dialogue between India and Pakistan, as we have done for over the 40 years[49]".

While talking to a high level delegation from the Pakistan occupied Kashmir (POK), Robin Raphael reportedly asserted that the just concluded elections in Kashmir were free and fair[50]. More importantly, Raphael came out openly against the Pakistan Government's proposal for a Nine Nations Conference on Kashmir and regional disarmament and squarely blamed Islamabad for the inability of any Indo-Pak dialogue to get off the ground. She was quoted as saying that in the US opinion, it is Pakistan that is reluctant to hold a dialogue with India on Kashmir. She further stated: that the US has been urging Pakistan not to meddle in Kashmir[51]. Earlier in an important speech, the US Ambassador to Pakistan, Thomas Simons, reiterated the centrality of the Shimla Agreement and called for a less cenfrontationist approach to the Kashmir problem[52].

The above-cited extracts reflected the changing American perceptions on the desirability of encouraging separatist activities in Kashmir. This discrepancy in the US policy which on the one hand regards Kashmir as a disputed territory and on the other supports Indian attempts to keep the state within its fold deserves thorough explanations. Whether Washington had taken a pro-India line over Kashmir or whether it wanted to take out the US-India relationship from the ambit of the issues involving the relations between India and

Pakistan is not clear. There appears to have been an implicit change in the US approach towards the end of first Clinton Administration. The US looked at the electoral exercise with a certain degree of approval. The battomline is that the political process in Kashmir could lead to some kind of solution. The reason why the US made such a demonstrative effort was related to the need for creating a comprehensive bilateral framework in which not only Kashmir and Indo-Pak cold war could be tackled, but several other issues including a non-nuclear regime for South Asia to be endorsed by India and Pakistan in association with other states in the region, could be handled.

Third Option

There is nothing new in the US perception of Kashmir being a disputed territory but what has now been injected by the US is that the parties to the disputed territory are not what they were at the time when Instrument of Accession was signed, or when the Shimla Agreement was arrived at. A third party, i.e., the people of Kashmir have been projected as a party to the dispute. As a Political Counselor in New Delhi, it was Robin Raphael who coordinated the US interaction with the Kashmir activists and reported back to the US Government on the happenings. She travelled to the state as well as maintained personal links with various leaders of the secessionist movement in Kashmir. In the face of India's inept handling of the situation according to her perceptions convinced her that India had in fact lost the game. At the same time she became aware that the majority opinion in the valley opposed joining Pakistan. So the "third option" of independence was given shape. During his visit to New Delhi in May 1993 John Mallott spoke of the "Kashmiri people" and declared that the US now recognized the people of Kashmir as a third party to the dispute[53]. This 'creative interpretation' was taken one step further by Raphael's assertion. In fact her October 28 statement was a logical progression. Her formulation of the American position on Kashmir simply represented the manner in which policies get defined. In this context, President Clinton's reference to Kashmir in his UN address could not be dismissed as a mere rhetoric. It is worth pointing out that President Clinton while sharing Congressman Rahall's view, that the Kashmir dispute if left unresolved, posed a threat to peace and stability in South Asia, observed: "I believe the only way to obtain a solution is through direct negotiations between India and

Pakistan, negotiations that take into account the views of the people of Kashmir[54]". The US ambassador to India Frank Wisner said: "The US would like India and Pakistan to settle the Kashmir dispute through bilateral negotiations, negotiations that take into account the attitude and wishes of all the people of Jammu and Kashmir".[55] George Pickart, a senior advisor to the South Asian Bureau of the State Department repeated such a view in August 1997 by stating that the US: "believes that Jammu and Kashmir is a disputed territory and is an issue to be resolved between India and Pakistan, taking the desires of Kashmiri people into account".[56]

These utterances appeared to indicate a change in the earlier American policy of supporting the Shimla Agreement and ruling out the plebiscite formula. The Clinton Administration added a third element to the Kashmiri dispute: the will of Kashmiri people and pleaded for a trilateral solution of the Kashmir problem.

US opinion Makers on Kashmir

There is no unanimity of views among American opinion-makers on the nature of Kashmir dispute, the relevance of Shimla Agreement in the present context, how the dispute ought to be resolved or the role of US Administration in resolving the dispute. On the one hand, there are people like Tom Thornton, a former staffer of National Security Council and now with the John Hopkins University who feels that there is no role for US in the Kashmir dispute.[57] On the other hand, there are people like professor Stephen Cohen who plead that even when the US has no vital interests in South Asia, it must sustain its presence and advance new South Asian Regional Initiative (S.A.R.I) and for this it must keep pressing India regarding Kashmir.[58] At the Carnegie Endowment , Selig Harrison and James Clad, have been supportive of the Trieste-Type settlement where the Line of Control separating the two Kashmirs would serve as a porous border. This would be done to facilitate the intermingling of populations from the India and Pak-held Kashmir. The proposal calls for the integration of Jammu and Ladakh with India with a special autonomous status to a new entity in the Kashmir valley.[59] According to the Independent Task Force Report, sponsored by the Council on Foreign Relations, the US Government does not have a great deal of leverage in regard to Kashmir dispute and the time is not ripe for Washington to launch a major new initiative[60].

While individual members of the Task Force favour alternative US stances-including active support for the Indian position toward Kashmir, absolute neutrality, or support for a solution based on some form of self-determination, the majority of the group believes that US interests in both India and Pakistan are best served at this time by working with their respective governments on a step-by-step approach toward a series of practical and interim objectives[61]. At the most benign Americans appear to be stating that the settlement of the Kashmir dispute involves the Indians, the Pakistanis and the Kashmiris. But this approach does not even pretend to outline a solution within the parameters acceptable to all the three parties. While recognizing Kashmir as a third party to the bitter dispute between India and Pakistan, opinion-makers in the US are simply unable to conceive a settlement that would be acceptable to all three. This is the complexity of the crisis and the unwillingness of India and Pakistan to budge an inch from their respective positions.

Fresh Approach

It appears that, the US has moved away from the traditional US-Pak alliance of the cold war days, when a UN plebiscite on Kashmir was urged. It would be worthwhile to refer to Gary Ackerman Sub-committee of the House of Representatives on Asia and the Pacific report. The report is enormously significant as this is the first time that a section of US Congressmen challenged the traditional American opinion on the subject. The report rejected the plebiscite option as "overtaken by history", and therefore irrelevant to present circumstances. The UN resolutions calling for a plebiscite were no longer relevant as they did not provide Kashmiris with a choice other than accession to India or Pakistan. Since majority of Kashmiris would probably reject both of these countries in favour of independence, the sub-committee termed plebiscite as doomed to failure".[62] What is significantly new among the US congressmen is a growing perception that the Kashmir dispute demands a fresh approach away from the traditionally persistent demands for a plebiscite. Although the US is yet to come out openly with a solution to the Kashmir crisis, nevertheless, a covert process is on to end the strife in the Valley. The US is looking for a fresh and a pragmatic approach to the problem. And this is going to be something outside the framework of UN resolutions on Kashmir. According to this view, the US would like India and Pakistan to maintain the status quo on Kashmir and go in for a Camp David-like agreement. After that the two-countries could sign an Oslo-type agreement, under which the people of Kashmir would have the right of self-governance with some constitutional as well as international guarantees. The substantive American demand is that India and Pakistan should seek American good offices for improving their bilateral ties. This could hopefully be pushed to the point where a bilateral framework for solution-seeking is created in which the present tensions in Kashmir are progressively reduced and both the countries are enabled to gradually take various measures on mutual and balanced forces reduction, defence budget and other confidence building measures.

After Nuclear Tests

It has become fashionable in the American academic as well as policy making circles to speak of a nuclear danger in the Indian sub-continent. The Kashmir issue has been linked with the nuclear issue. It has been suggested that the next nuclear holocaust may occur in the Indian sub-continent where India and Pakistan may resort to war over the Kashmir issue. For instance, the annual report of the US Arms Control and Disarmament (ACDA) for the year 1996 mentioned: "While the likelihood of a fourth war between India and Pakistan is small, the possibility of a war in the region going nuclear is perhaps higher than anywhere else in the world. We continue to believe that both nations could assemble nuclear weapons within a short time; and that both have tested missiles and acquired aircraft capable of delivering such weapons. In addition, the past year has witnessed a significant decline in Indo-Pak relations.. Regional instability, and, therefore, proliferation, continue to be driven by Indo-Pakistani tensions, particularly over Kashmir".[63] Earlier in early 1995, the US Secretary of Defence, William Perry, in his speech at Washington's Foreign Policy Association said: "I'd start off by observing that India and Pakistan have long standing ethnic, religious and territorial differences dating back to their partition in 1947. These differences have caused them to fight three wars since partition. Today, each of them has the capability to build nuclear weapons. Because of this nuclear capability, a fourth India/Pakistan war would not just be a tragedy, it could be a catastrophe – so we care a lot about what happens there".[64]

In order to counter the challenge of nuclearization in South Asia, the US has adopted a strategy which includes internationalization of Kashmir issue. Spelling out the American policy on Kashmir after the

India-Pakistan blast for blast diplomacy, the Deputy Secretary of state S. Talbott in an interview to the Far Eastern Economic Review said: "The US would urge the UN to play a constructive role in resolving the issue which has been on its agenda since the birth of India, the birth of Pakistan and the birth of the UN".[65]

After the detonation of nuclear devices by India and Pakistan, the US has been chiefly instrumental in bringing back Kashmir on the international agenda. The references to the Kashmir in the statements of the P-5, G-8 and the UN Security Council bear testimony to this. The permanent members of the Security Council led by the US argued that the risk of conflict over Kashmir has multiplied manifold by the acquisition of nuclear weapons. The Geneva initiative could be called the beginning of international involvement in the Indian sub-continent and the internationalization of Kashmir issue. Until now New Delhi had successfully shielded Kashmir from third party interference especially after the Shimla Agreement with Pakistan. For eight years, Pakistan tried to focus international attention on the valley by promoting insurgency but failed. However, Pokhran II and the belligerent speeches made by the members of the BJP government that followed have reversed the gains made by assembly elections in Kashmir and the reinstallation of an elected government. For instance, the then Home Minister, L K. Advani virtually threatened a nuclear attack on Pakistan if the latter continued to wage a low intensity war in Kashmir. Some others have been even more blunt. Such irresponsible statements gave the American hawks, who feel that India's decision to disregard the US warnings and hold the tests has directly challenged American's global dominance, a chance to get into the game. Writing in the Washington Post, Columnist Stephen Rosenfield revived the specter of an imminent nuclear war in South Asia, which would start with India exercising the right of 'hot pursuit' and chasing terrorists into the Pak-occupied Kashmir. The fact that the CIA revived the scenario of nuclear war in South Asia that it would begin in exactly the same way has lent further credibility to such projections. The Clinton Administration, taking strong exceptions to Advani's remarks, said, it appeared to indicate that India is foolishly increasing tensions with its neighbours and it is indifferent to world opinion. "It is disturbing to see Indian officials using nuclear rhetoric when talking about Kashmir", a senior US official told later.

The US is trying to convince the world that India and Pakistan would be less responsible with their nuclear weapons than the other five nuclear weapon states have been with them. The risk of disaster is high in South Asia, after the nuclear Tests by India and Pakistan, warned the Secretary of State Madeline Albright speaking at the Stimson Centre. Conjuring up an apocalyptic picture of the impending doom over South Asia, the Secretary of State portrayed a nuclear scenario where even a limited exchange could obliterate matters in the sub-centurit. The South Asian strategic reality is truly alarming. The tests have resulted in the nuclearization of the region, which has degraded security in numerous ways. But the internationalization of Kashmir issue is not going to help in creating a more tranquil situation in the sub-continent. From the Indian viewpoint, an old pressure point has been reopened by the Clinton Administration. No Indian government is in a position to accept third party involvement in Kashmir. There is a clear consensus among India's political parties that Kashmir is not open to third party intervention. On the contrary, Pakistan has always wanted to internationalize the Kashmir issue. America's efforts to internationalize Kashmir issue only added to the negative perceptions about US policies on Kashmir in the Indian public. They are being perceived as a tilt towards Pakistan, regardless of the justification and rationale given by the US; Washington, instead of trying to temper Pakistan's aggressiveness, appears to be interested in using the Kashmir issue to browbeat India.

Kargil and After

There is no denying the fact that Washington exerted pressure on Pakistan right from the start of the Kargil crisis, both at the bilateral and multilateral levels. President Clinton's telephonic admonitions to Nawaz Sharif, the then Pakistani Prime Minister, the G-8 communique and raising of the issue at the South Asia Task Force meeting in Kiev were reflective of this effort. It culminated in the visit of Nawaz Sharif to Washington and his promise to ensure the withdrawal of all Pakistani and Pakistan supported forces from the Indian side of the line of control. However, the US did not act out of love for India or India's Kashmir policy. The US is hardly driven by altruism in the matters of international relations. A paradigm shift in the US policies has clearly not occurred. The US had its own reasons to take tough stand against its traditionally Pakistan. In the first place, the phenomenon of the crumbling of the Pakistan state and its coming under the domination of various extremist groups might have led the US to take a realistic view on the Kargil based on its own national security interests. President Clinton's announcement of the Sanctions on the Taliban rulers of Afghanistan pointed to the seriousness with which the western world led by the US is taking the threat of Islamic militancy. Significantly, President Clinton acted within two days of his talks with Nawaz Sharif on the Kargil conflict. The twin developments should relieve the Indians of any notion that the US and the G-8 nations had acted out of any love for Indians or India's Kashmir viewpoint. The joint statement issued by Nawaz Sharif and President Clinton in Washington on July 5, 1999 was a manifestation of the increasingly significant role that the US thinks itself destined to play in what it regards to be potential areas of conflict. Significantly, President Clinton called the Indian Prime Minister while Nawaz Sharif was talking to him. What was said is not known but what is evident is that the US has been persuading India all along by projecting itself as a broker of peace. The joint statement only confirmed the personal interest that President Clinton has been evoking in the affairs of the sub-continent. The real significance of the joint statement was President Clinton's statement that he would take a personal interest in encouraging an expeditious resumption and intensification of bilateral efforts between India and Pakistan to resolve all issues dividing the countries, including Kashmir, which has the potentiality of being internationalized in the long run. Pakistan has long sought to drag the US into the Kashmir conflict as an international mediator, as a strategic ploy to enhance its position in the conflict. From Pakistan's standpoint, it would be delighted if the US persuades India not deal with Kashmir on its own terms. It is in this context that the joint statement which talked of President Clinton's personal interest in the matter assume significance. The US intervention in Kargil when it asked Pakistan to withdraw was seen as the opening of a new chapter in Indo-US relations. Since the US was on India's side for the first time, the fact that its inspiring role could be interpreted as interference was glossed over. Does that sudden support for India's restraint have strings attached? Does it give Washington a handle on India vis-à-vis the CTBT? Has President Clinton decided what he and America want to do to resolve the one active dispute in this would that could escape the laws of conventional warfare and turn nuclear? The semitic jugglery is necessitated by the phrase "personal interest" which leaves room for ambiguity in interpretation. After the coup in Pakistan, it raises a few questions: Whether General Pervez Musharraf has indicated to the US his commitment to the Clinton-Nawaz Sharif statement of July 5? Whether the military regime has expressed its willingness to respect the sanctity of the line of control and whether the Agreement will be honoured? In brief, the conglomeration in Kargil provided the perfect opening for Washington. The route from Kargil leads to Kashmir. The US appears convinced that Kashmir is a potential nuclear flashpoint. Things did get out of hand in Kargil and they do not want that repeated.

New Delhi's endeavour to drive home the point that Kashmir issue had to be seen in the backdrop of rising Islamic extremism failed to receive adequate political support from the US. Several US intelligence reports on the Pakistani involvement in militancy in Kashmir and several US official statements on the Pakistani involvement in Kashmir terrorism failed to brand Pakistan as a state sponsoring terrorism. For instance an influential US Think Tank, The National Defence University (NDU) stated that Pakistan has provided funds, arms and training for young Kashmiris in Pakistan controlled areas and also helped raise radical Islamic resistance groups modeled after Afghanistan resistance. Islamic volunteers from Afghanistan, Pakistan and other Muslim countries joined these groups. The Clinton Administrations' top counter-terrorism official Ambassador Michael A Sheehan rejected Pakistan's claim that it was providing only moral and diplomatic support for some of these militants. He stated this before testifying before a Senate sub-committee. Significantly this is the first time any top US official has bluntly accused Pakistan of aiding terrorism in Kashmir. After the hearing in the sub-committee headed by Sam Brounback, Sheehan told reporters that "within Pakistan, there are numerous Kashmiri separatists groups and sectarian groups involved in terrorism, which use Pakistan as a base. Pakistan has frequently acknowledged what it calls moral and diplomatic support for terrorist training in Afghanistan. The US, he declared has urged Islamabad to close down Islamic schools. He said: "We have repeatedly asked Islamabad to end support for terrorist training in Afghanistan, to indirect travel of militants to and from camps in Afghanistan, to prevent militant groups from acquiring weapons and to block financial and logistical support to camps in Afghanistan. We have also urged Islamabad to close down certain madarsahs, or Islamic schools that serve as conduits for terrorism".[66]

The American obsession to portray Pakistan as a moderate Islamic state, in glaring contradiction to Pakistan's involvement in subversion and terrorist activities is part of the new American strategic containment design for Central and South Asia. The mid 1995 American appraisal of the Hank Brown military package to Pakistan by side-stepping the Pressler amendment, was a means to that end. In the post-cold war era, the US hopes that Islamabad would help containing and controlling the Islamic fundamentalist forces who spawn the bulk of international terrorism. Apart from being the gateway to gas rich Central Asia, Pakistan has convinced Washington of its indispensability in dealing with the Taliban. Interestingly the US has not taken an ideological stand on the rise of General Pervez Musharraf and is happy to do business with him. Significantly, during his days in Afghanistan as trainer of Mujahideen, General Musharaff developed close contacts with people like Osama Bin Laden. Perhaps, the US wants to retain its little leverage and also see how far the military regime will go in cooperating with America in restraining the Taliban forces now openly threatening the US interests in the name of religion. The US has been concentrating on Iran, Libya and Syria on the issue of international terrorism, and playing down the extremist activities directed from Afghanistan and Pakistan in view of its own past association with these extremist groups. In fact, the US has been far too permissive of international terrorism centred in and directed from this region. It is worth pointing out that these terrorist activities are a fallout of CIA operations in Afghanistan during the period the Mujahideen campaign against the Soviet forces in that country. Mercenaries all over Islamic world were brought in, the enormous quantities of small arms were distributed and training imparted in the sophisticated use of explosives. Most of these were handled by the Pakistani inter-services intelligence wing under the overall guidance of the Central Intelligence Agency. After the withdrawal of Soviet forces from Afghanistan, these militants fanned out all across the globe. These mercenaries have been killed in large numbers in Kashmir. Training camps for many of these organisations are in Afghanistan and Pakistan, and one of them Harkatul Ansar, has been recognized as an international terrorist outfit by the US State Department. If Washington is serious about fighting international terrorism it has to refrain from compartmentalizing terrorism as domestic and international. The US State Department's annual report on terrorism, "Patterns of Global Terrorism 1996, regards terrorism in India, Algeria, Sri Lanka and Pakistan as domestic terrorism. It says, "Domestic terrorism is probably a more widespread phenomenon than international terrorism. Because internationalism has a direct impact on US interests, it is the primary focus of this report". The US must adopt a more transparent policy towards international terrorism, if it is to enlist the cooperation of other countries of Asia and Africa in this effort. In the past, Washington has tended to view India's rising terrorism problem largely as a domestic issue, related only to the unrest in different parts of the country, especially Kashmir, while discounting the outside forces that sustain the scourge. Although the US is still circumspect about discussing Pakistan's complicity in fomenting terrorism, there appears to be an increasing recognition in Washington that encouraged by certain maverick elements in the ISI, the country has become a fertile ground for terrorism. The recent Indian Airlines hijacking crisis has brought the US and India closer on the issue of combating terrorism with Washington providing high level of cooperation and interaction to end the horrible episode. However, inspite of credible evidence from its own intelligence services and that provided by India, the US has failed to brand Pakistan as a state sponsoring terrorism. After the hijacking incident, the US State Department in response to Indian Prime Minister's request to the US to declare Pakistan a terrorist state refused to do so. The US Administration said that there is no clear-cut evidence yet that Pakistan is a state sponsor of international terrorism. Terrorist threat to the US and its interests is real. Washington needs a complete reappraisal of the geopolitical strategies that it had followed since the end of the cold war. Now, the time has come for the US decision-makers to make a more realistic and objective assessment of the terrorist campaign through out the world including Kashmir. The US must break the Pakistan-Afghanistan axis and should coopt a number of states including India in the near vicinity of Afghanistan and Pakistan to deal with this problem.

Conclusion

To sum up, the Kashmir issue has been one of the focal points of America's policy in the sub-continent. It has changed from time to time. From its initial reaction in the UN Security Council, it could be inferred that the US gave scant consideration to the Indian complaint and pursued a policy which could be termed as pro-Pakistan. The strategic significance of Kashmir in the context of cold war was responsible for the traditional US-Pakistan alliance of the cold war days when a UN plebiscite was urged. During the cold war period the US views on Kashmir were dominated by the Indo-Soviet friendship. In the post-cold war era, the US has to view the Kashmir problem in the context of its overall strategy in South Asia. After the end of cold war, the Bush Administration had come round to the view that Shimla Agreement provided the best means of solving the Kashmir dispute. The Clinton Administration initially went along with this stance but gradually changed, adding a third element to the dispute: the will of the Kashmiri people. Clearly, the official American perceptions of the solution in Kashmir has come a long way from what the eminent American historian from Columbia, A. T. Embrey, once characterized as US blindness to India's sensibilities.[67]

Though the US has adopted a restrained posture on Kashmir, its greater involvement appears inevitable in the coming years. There is an understandable weariness among Americans to get involved in the sub-continental affairs; but it is obvious that all other American strategic goals in South Asia will remain hostage to an improvement in Indo-Pak relationship. This does not necessarily mean that the US should choose between India and Pakistan, as the Independent Task Force Report rightly points out. The US remains the only country which is in a position to ensure that domestic problems do not jeopardize the South Asian besieged elites in the two countries to get out of the ethnic tensions. Kashmir has become the metaphor of both internal praralysis and external vulnerability. The US has to realize, as Stephen Cohen put it: "There is a failure of imagination in New Delhi and Islamabad concerning this mid 20th century issue".

Kashmir' grievances need to be addressed sympathetically but to recognize Kashmir's right of self-determination is to challenge the very concept of India. If Washington should press India to grant self-determination to Kashmir, India's efforts to maintain a secular state could be terminated, secessionist movements in other Indian states would be strengthened, and India could experience intensifying civil strife. A contagious effect could sweep across neighbouring countries, including Pakistan, which has secessionist troubles of its own. None of these would be to Washington's liking. So the US should refrain from encouraging sub-national forces who proclaim the right to nationhood on the basis of religion or ethnicity.

Washington has to redesign its stand on the Kashmir issue in the light of recent developments rather than harp on the obsolete theories and assumptions. The Kashmir dispute has zero-sum characteristics and will be difficult to resolve by diplomatic means. Still, the US Administration can play a constructive role in certain respects. Being as significant partner in the politics of the sub-continent and being the lone super power, the US is in a position to contribute positively in conflict resolution. Considering the leverage on Pakistan as amply demonstrated during the Kargil crisis and the strong ties between them, it is not beyond Washington's limit to prevail on Islamabad with the logic of improving overall relations with New Delhi putting Kashmir issue in the back burner for the moment. The US policy to encourage bilateral negotiations involves a neutral position. Kashmir happens to be an extremely sensitive issue. Therefore, the US needs a new cautious approach. Lest its actions or remarks complicate the already tense situation. In its attitude towards this sensitive and complex problem Washington needs to be as circumspect in dispelling that it has ulterior designs of intervening in Kashmir and thereby in South Asia. It should refrain from actions that could exacerbate tension and kindle warfare between India and Pakistan. American officials need to recall from their own country's historical experience and from recent happenings in Africa and Eurasia that civil conflicts do not have easy, tidy solutions. The answer to separatist strife will rarely be found in secession but more constructively in devising ways to satisfy the aspirations of insurgents, within the constitutional and economic structures of the existing state. The American officials should try to convince Islamabad to face the reality that neither internationalization of the Kashmir issue, nor support to Kashmir insurgency will convince India to hold a plebiscite and that the conflict cannot be solved by war. Pakistan should be urged to accept the best deal on the table, which is turning the current line of control into a permanent boundary and greater autonomy for Kashmir. Any meddling by the US in Kashmir can only be counter productive. The US should view militancy in Kashmir in its proper perspective rather than as a case of mere violations of human rights by the state security forces.

References

1. *Security Council Official Records*, 3rd Year, Supplement for November 1948 p. 139.
2. L.K. Rosinger, *India and United States*, Macmillan 1951 p. 105.
3. *New York Times*, January 7, 1948.

4. *Security Council Officials Records*, 3rd year, 4 February 1948, p. 371.
5. *Ibid.*, p. 376.
6. *New York Times*, 17 February 1948.
7. N. D.Palmar, *The United States And India: The Dimensions of Influence*, New York, 1984, pp. 121-22.
8. *US Department of State Bulletin*, Vol. LVI, April 25, 1966, p. 669.
9. *US Department of State Press Release* No. 177, 23 March 1949.
10. *Security Council Official Records*, 7th Year, Mtg. 611.
11. *Security Council Official Records*, 12th Year, Mtg. 768.
12. *Ibid.*, Mtg. 806.
13. *New York Times*, 14 July.
14. *New York Times*, 15 November 1961.
15. *New York Times*, 7 January 1962.
16. J.K.Galbraith, *Ambassador's Journal: A Personal Account of the Kennedy Years*, London, 1969, p. 299.
17. *Security Council Official Records*, 17th Year, Mtg. 1015.
18. *Ibid.*
19. S.M. Burke, *Pakistan's Foreign Policy, A Historical Analysis*, Oxford, 1973, p. 341.
20. *The Times of India*, New Delhi, May 31, 1990.
21. *Ibid.*, June 25, 1991.
22. *Ibid.* August 18, 1991.
23. *India West*, December 21-28, 1990, p. 20.
24. *The Pioneer*, New Delhi, September 10, 1991.
25. *The Pioneer*, New Delhi, July 10, 1991.
26. B. K. Strivastava, "Prospects of Indo-US Relations" in *Year book on India's Foreign Policy*, Edited by Satish Kumar, New Delhi, 1990-91, p. 32.
27. *Ibid.*
28. *New York Times*, May 16, 1990.
29. *The Times of India*, May 20, 1993.
30. *Ibid.*
31. *Times of India*, September 28, 1993.
32. *Times of India,* October 7, 1993.
33. *Times of India,* October 28, 1993.
34. *Ibid.*
35. *Times of India*, November 6, 1993.
36. *Times of India*. November 7, 1993.

37. *Ibid.*
38. *Ibid.*
39. *Sunday Times*, January 30, 1994.
40. *Ibid.*, *The Times of India*, February 11, 1994.
41. *Times of India*, November 17, 1994.
42. *Ibid.*
43. *Times of India*. November 24, 1994.
44. Farzana Shakoor, "The State Elections in India held Kashmir", *Pakistan Horizon*, Vol. 1, No. 4, October, October 1996, p. 96.
45. Saleem Kidwai, "US and Kashmir: Changing Perceptions"; *Strategic Bulletin*, New Delhi, Vol. 1, No. 2, September-October 1996, p. 3.
46. *The Hindu*, September 11, 1996.
47. *Times of India*, September 12, 1996.
48. *Ibid.*
49. *Dawn*, Karachi, October 6, 1996.
50. *Dawn*(Karachi), September 26, 1996.
51. *Dawn*(Karachi), September 26, 1996.
52. Saleem Kidwai, op.cit, p. 4.
53. *Times of India*, 7 November, 1996.
54. *Times of India*, 7 November, 1996.
55. *The Hindustan Times*, August 12, 1997.
56. Inder Malhotra, "Worsening, Widening", *Times of India*, November, 1993.
57. *Indian Express*, New Delhi, November 7, 1993.
58. *Ibid.*
59. A New US Policy Towards India and Pakistan, Report of an Independent Task Force, sponsored by the Council on Foreign Relations, New York, 1997.
60. Ackerman Sub-committee Report.
61. *Ibid.*
62. Arms control and Disarmament Agency Annual Report, 1966, Excerpt on South Asia, USIS, New Delhi, February 3, 1995.
63. Official Text, USIS, New Delhi, February 3, 1995, *Far Eastern Economic Review.*
64. *Far Eastern Economic Review* quoted in *Indian Express*, New Delhi, July 3, 1996.
65. *Indian Express*, New Delhi, July 3, 1996.
66. Saleem Kidwai, "American Perspectives on Kashmir", *Journal of Peace Studies*, New Delhi, vol. 1, November-December 1993.
67. *Ibid.*

18

US Role in Indo-Pak Relations

Introduction

While the end of cold war has yielded peace dividends in Europe and elsewhere, the conflict situation in South Asia has exacerbated. While the rest of the world is undergoing fundamental changes, only South Asia is not learning the obvious lessons[1]. The South Asian situation is almost totally centered on the unrelenting hostility between India and Pakistan, ever since the two countries attained independence in 1947. Due to Indo-Pak antagonism, South Asia remains locked in an unstable situation of neither war nor peace. The two countries have fought three wars. The Kargil crisis is referred to as a fourth war. Since 1989, they have been engaged in a log-intensity conflict in Kashmir. This conflict aggravates an already precarious situation in which international and domestic politics interwine with ethnic and religious passions. Nuclearization has worsened matters further. The Indian sub-continent is far likelier to witness a nuclear attack/exchange than NATO/ Warsaw Pact ever did. This is because after half a century after independence, Indo-Pak relations are less extensive than were those of the US and the former Soviet Union at the height of cold war. Temporary positive action, followed by a reversion to enemity as has repeatedly been the case, in the past, has became too dangerous to be repeated in the new, nuclear environment. The strategic reality in the sub-continent is truly alarming. Recent events particularly Kargil crisis have only strengthened the belief that bilateral arrangements like the Shimla agreement and other confidence building measures between India and Pakistan are inadequate by themselves to ensure either stability or continuity of meaningful bilateral dialogue. The present 'no war-no peace' situation along the line of control, the daily mortar and artillery firing, attempts to infiltration, the strong retaliation and bodybags coming home every day have made peace prospects a distant dream. The deep distrust between New Delhi and Islamabad is also rejected in the formal deployment of conventional forces by both sides along their entire border, leading to every present fears of surprise attack.

New Peace Paradigm

India and Pakistan are in dire need of a new peace paradigm because contemporary forms of insecurity are incompatible with conventional paradigms of international relations and especially with the military security system. Peace has to be achieved through extra systemic ways. The two countries could achieve agreement on vexed questions only through greater understanding of each other which leads to greater trust. Such understanding can be fostered by individuals, groups, chambers of commerce, professional bodies, films, education and environmental activists and others. The end of cold war had led to a renewed focus on non-conventional notions of international and regional security. A variety of social, economic and environmental crises are emerging that go beyond the purview of military security paradigm. These include non-military threats to security. They call for alternative security systems. The development of a non-military security paradigm for India and Pakistan would be a far more superior strategy to address the new realities of security.

Need for Confidence-building

Since the near war situation between India and Pakistan in 1990, mind-searching on confidence-building measures suitable to South Asian conditions has started. As a noted defence analyst put it, there was need to:

(a) Focus primarily on CBMS rather than searching for more problematic arms control measures (Mutual Balanced Force Reduction/MBFR).

(b) An institutionalized political discourse on how to establish bilateral and multilateral CBMS on framework and process of arms control in the region, and on commitments by extra-regional powers to strengthen cooperative security in the region;

(c) A reaffirmed commitment to peaceful resolution of disputes, respect for borders and lines of control, and non-use of force;

(d) A greater transparency in military postures and power;

(e) Shifting strategic (politico-military) doctrines towards a 'non-offensive defence',

(f) The peace-time deployment of strike forces to provide time and space against surprise attack/pre-emption;

(g) Bilateral and multilateral agreements on conventional forces reduction (CFRS);

(h) The development of technical means of verification (open skies) extending upto 100 KM from international borders and lines of control;

(i) Bilateral and multilateral agreements on a nuclear 'no first use', and

(j) Extending the Indo-Pakistani agreement on Non-attack on Nuclear Installations to population centres and economic targets[2].

A noted Pakistani scholar, however, emphasized the need for:

(a) concerted honest efforts to resolve the outstanding Kashmir conflict;

(b) evolving a common security framework to ensure stability in the South Asian arms race, including a political process within a comprehensive security concept;

(c) introducing arms control measures, e.g., serious considerations regarding MBFR;

(d) strengthening economic linkages in the region;

(e) India and Pakistan to seriously address the problem of using extremism in their countries;

(f) Encouraging CBMS e.g., various steps to increase communication between the military personnel in India and Pakistan; and

(g) Evolving a regional conflict central mechanism[3].

Although the establishment of military CBMS may help prevent an immediate out break of hostilities between India and Pakistan in the short run, but in the long run, both of them must establish non-military CBMS in the economic, technical, cultural diplomatic, social fields in order to end the existing hostilities between India and Pakistan. The functionalist and neo-functional theories of international relations provide further rationale for the adoption of non-military CBMS between otherwise hostiie nations. These theories posit that cooperation between adversary nations on 'low politics' issues such as environmental and economic issues, may facilitate cooperation on the contentious issues of 'high politics, such as war and diplomacy[4]. These arguments are perfectly valid for India and Pakistan. Only the CBMs can give operational substance to the concept of security by generating confidence among the people of hostile nations. The CBMS must be properly established and implemented to build mutual trust between India and Pakistan. They can expedite the process of normalization of relations.

United States Stake in South Asia

The US has long standing enduring and broad gange interests in the region. It has a stake in keeping regional tensions from boiling over, lowering them where possible, and developing its bilateral relationships[5]. In dealing with the Indian sub-continent, the US is faced in one place with all the key post-cold war foreign policy concerns - regional instability, preventive diplomacy, prevention of war, promotion of democracy and human rights, countering terrorism and the smuggling of narcotics, encouraging economic reforms, free trade and open markets. Thus, the US policy towards the region is shaped by its overreaching global concerns. The end of cold war has enhanced opportunities for accomplishing these tasks. But seizing this opportunities require creative thinking and skillful diplomacy. Being the only super power, what the US thinks and wants vis-à-vis this region is important. The US has influence, power and opportunity motivation to make an impact on the sub-continent. The US's role in South Asia in comparison with its presense and importance in East or West Asia is minor. Nevertheless, in the South Asian Security context, it remains a vitally important player. US interests in South Asia, although not vital, are important and increasing for too long and it is time to regard it as a new frontier for US diplomacy. The region's strategic, economic and human significance demands greater attention and a revised approach. More than one fifth of the world population resides there. South Asia is important geographically, bordering on China and the former Soviet Union, lying adjacent to shipping routes of three important bodies of water, and serving as a land and air bridge between southwest and South East Asia. The time has come to rethink the US approach to Indo-Pak rivalry. It is easy to stress the inevitability of Indo-Pak conflict. However, no conflict is inevitable. It is worth recalling that France and Germany and earlier Britain and France were once as hostile, as filled with hatred as one encounters among the worst Indian baiters in Islamabad and Pak haters in New Delhi. Its continuation at very high level for the indefinite future is not inevitable. The US should take an objective measure of two states clash. Friendship is a rare commodity in international relations. There is always an upper limit to relations. The one finds an extremely sincere phobia in the US of a war between India and Pakistan. Some benefit of doubt based on logic and reality should be awarded to two countries, who would not necessarily jump on to a nuclear especially in the light of their present struggle to stabilize their economy and policy. It is argued that whereas India and Pakistan have fought three wars the Russians and Americans never fought a direct war. It is worth remembering that a US-USSR confrontation was risky and dangerous precisely because the two were not neighbour. To argue that passion of both by India and Pakistan would lead to war is not necessarily true. If both the US and the former Soviet Union could resort to deterrence and cooperation, then it an also be expected from India and Pakistan. A starting point of new US diplomacy should be that India and Pakistan have the right to determine what it necessary to attain their security.

Need to End Balancing Act

In the new environment the US will have to end the balancing act that successive US Administrations have been practising in South Asia. To equate the two countries in all matters would be unjustified. Both nations have their own separate identities, separate strengths and differences. It is time that the US judged New Delhi and Islamabad on merits. Under the existing circumstances, the US is not playing a zero-sum game where it sees that what is good for Pakistan is bad for India. Similarly, whereas earlier India might have responded to the economic depression in Pakistan by saying it serves them right, it now sees negative consequences for India as well. It is a part of maturing process. It is high time that the US should end the twining of it policies towards India and Pakistan. Even with US's current engagement with the sub-continent, the main discussion is undoubtedly with India. Pakistan's responses have became merely reflexive. Until that reality is factored into its policy making, America's endeavours in South Asia will continue to be flawed. The current US policy is a legacy of cold war competition when the size and significance of a nation were viewed both in

Washington and Moscow, as less important than the ideological affinity. The US should realize that two nations demand differentiated policies. It is illogical to bracket Pakistan with India.

Structural Flaw in US Approach

The US believes that it can successfully fit the model of other peace and arms reduction talks to South Asia. However, there is a structural flaw in such simplification. Deterrence and capability were first nurtured among the protagonists whether it was during the East-West confrontation or the Egypt-Israel breakthrough. Such a priori environment permitted the breaking of proposals and confidence-building measures. None of these conditions prevail in South Asia. Thus for Washington to impose a pre-conceived solution that would only address its own security interests at the expense of trampling over other interests and sensitivities is a case of putting the American cart before unwilling South Asian horses. Resolution of regional tensions in South Asia will come from decisions and actions of the regional parties themselves[6]

US and Kashmir

The heart of the Indo-Pak conflict, the Kashmir dispute has zero-sum characteristics. The US does not have a great deal of leverage in regard to this complex issue. Kashmir happens to be an extremely sensitive issue. Therefore, the US needs a cautious approach. Lest, its actions or remarks complicate the already tense situation[7]. In its attitude towards this thorny problem Washington needs to be circumspect in dispelling that it has ulterior designs of intervening in Kashmir. It should refrain from actions that could exacerbate tension and kindle warfare between India and Pakistan. Any meddling by the US in Kashmir can only be counterproductive. The US Government should not became actively involved in efforts to resolve the dispute. History and current dynamic provide no reason to think that US involvement would improve the prospects for resolving the dispute or depending relations with both India and Pakistan. The US should pursue mainly quiet diplomacy, in regard to Kashmir, promoting modest but incremental steps to ease tensions and reduce friction between the pratagonists with the help of other countries. It is concert with other members of international community should seek to lower tension and violence, reduce military forces and restore political normalcy in Kashmir. Civil conflict do not have easy, tidy solutions. Instead of ambitious diplomacy which had failed in recent past and is bound to fail again, the US should encourage India and Pakistan to start bilateral talks devoted to discuss ways of classing the situation in Kashmir. Resumption of dialogue is essential. The US can continuously try to contribute to a Kashmir solution in a low key manner.

US and Indo-Pak Talks

As India and Pakistan argue about the shape of structure of their future negotiations, the US being the lone super power can play a limited but significant role in pushing the peace process forward. Thanks to the recent exchange of state visits, the US is no longer seen in India as tilting towards Pakistan. The US role during the Kargil crisis and the perception of neutrality over Kashmir leaves Washington in a good position to encourage political solutions to the long-standing disputes between India and Pakistan. While the American role in promoting a peace process is limited at this stage, Washington will always have a significant impact on the evolution of Indo-Pak negotiations once they commence. The US has to see that these talks are substantive, and not merely rhetorical, because there is a tendency to meet and reject each other's point of view, and then go away. If India and Pakistan agree to formally talk to each other, and these talks are properly orchestered, there will be some change on the ground in what is happening in Kashmir. The first and foremost thing the US should do is to encourage India and Pakistan to adopt policies that will help stabilize situation in the region. It should call upon both India and Pakistan to implement fully and unconditionally existing bilateral CBMs including regular use of hotlines and provision of advance notification of military exercises. It should urge the two countries to negotiate and implement additional CBMs including regular high-level bilateral meetings, increased trade and other exchanges. The two countries should be advised to reach agreements about less contentious issues like Sichen Glacier and about mutual interests like trade expansion. The US should offer to provide technical means to verify troop movements or withdrawals, the location or activity of nuclear or missile installation and to demarcate complete border area. American diplomats should subtly remind the Indian and Pakistani officials about the serious consequences of their prolonged conflict, including the risk of devastating war, the waste of scarce financial resources on military expenditure, the barriers to South Asian cooperation and the loss of global repute.

Greater US Engagement with South Asia

The US should expand its economic, Political and military relations India and Pakistan simultaneously, seeking positive improvements in relations with both countries as opposed to either/or approach that characterized past US effort to deal with the rivalry. The US has to establish a more constructive relationship with these two countries. The US can assists the sub-continent in overcoming its numerous economic challenges. Washington's most effective course would be to raise region's profile in corporate community and to direct greater resources for commercial programmes in the region. The US should strongly support economic reforms in both countries. The US has provided support and encouragement for the process of liberalization, but it should step up its efforts in this regard even further by sharing relevant technical, administrative and financial expertise; by working in conjunction with other national governments and international financial institutions; by working with representatives of governments in India and Pakistan to develop optimum legal fiscal, financial and bureaucratic arrangements for efficient growth and development, and perhaps even by providing direct economic incentives (including US assistance and support for India and Pakistan in international financial institutions) in response to further progress in liberalization[8]. The US should encourage an international effort to promote greater economic cooperation between India and Pakistan on issues such as energy infrastructure, including oil and gas, and in encouraging international private investors in both countries to urge the importance of working together opening regional markets that might in due course of time contribute to ease political tensions. It may be worth exploring the possibility of expanding US cooperation in India into a regional plan whereby all South Asian states are able to benefit, thus replacing the specter of Indian hegemony with the prospect of regional cooperation. The implication for such a US policy may be to step forward and to offer some kind of a regional peace guarantee, which would perhaps go a long way in assuring South Asian states particularly Pakistan that their interests would not be compromized by US-India cooperation.

US and Non Military Threats to Security

The end of cold war has led to a renewed focus on non-conventional notions of international and regional security. American engagement in, and assistance to, South Asia to limit environmental degradation, population growth and hydrological problems can fend up potential human calamities. Such an expanded definition of security issues is necessary to cope with the emergent trends of post-cold war South Asia. The US with its substantial experience in dealing with ecological problems could provide technical assistance and collaborate in tackling a range of vexing problems of environmental degradation and resource depletion.

US and Conflict Avoidance Measures

Low-key bilateral, trilateral, and multilateral military-to-military discussions, intelligence exchanges, exchanges of delegations and other transparency mechanisms, all can foster cooperative individuals and institutional ties that may in turn erode the hostile images and suspicious that abound in the relationships, laying the ground work for more substantive cooperation down the road. The US can offer both countries new verification technologies that could help them avoid false alarms and give them the confidence to reduce or redisplay their main forces, simultaneously saving money while enhancing each country's individual security. The US should concentrate on promoting escalation control and conflict avoidance measures. It should consider providing intelligence support to both sides to defuse suspicious and crises, helping to correct exaggerated fears on either side that may help drive unnecessarily destabilising developments.

US and Track II Diplomacy

The US should encourage regular, sustained and multifaceted contact between India and Pakistan in a wide variety of areas including educational, cultural exchanges, travel freedom, telecommunications and sports. It should also promote informal regional interactions, Track II, diplomacy. Since Track I diplomacy has failed to solve the Indo-Pak hostility, track II diplomacy may be used as a conflict resolution model to resolve Indo-Pak differences. In Track II the participants have more freedom to explore the descalation and resolution of conflict. It is designed to assist official leaders by compensating for the constraints imposed upon them by the structural functional compulsions of their domestic politics. Nothing builds more trust and contributes to regional stability than enhanced interaction among scholars, journalists, artists and other human groups belonging to rival group of nations. Unless this interactive process gathers momentum, agreements will remain mere scraps of paper and lurking suspicion persist even after institutionalization of CBMs.

The importance of people-to-people contact hardly needs to be overstressed. In this respect the US can play a major role in bringing about socio-cultural exchanges, people-to-people contacts that would eliminate ignorance and suspicion and sidetrack the conflicting issues that divide these nations. It is the lack of contacts that provide legitimacy to hawkish elements and destabilize the process of normalization. The American Alumni Association like Fulbright, Ford, Salzburg and US universities can play a significant part. This is an important constituency because its members occupy key and influential positions in public life in both the countries. It is rather unfortunate and surprising this has not been properly and effectively utilized so far.

The USIS and think tanks supported by Ford and Rockfeller Foundations have played key roles in encouraging their South Asian counterparts to undertake track II activities and facilitating confidence-building exercises in South Asia. For instance, USIS in Delhi and Islamabad organized a series of 'worldnet' dialogues between India and Pakistani intellectuals. In 1991, a number of South Asia experts invited various research institutions, think tanks and public interest groups involved in conflict resolution in the US under the aegis of USIS. As a result some participants formed the South Network for conflict Resolution[9]. In another USIS sponsored initiative, former diplomat Harold Sandaurs conducted a series of workshops on conflict resolution in South Asia. Under him the USIS launched the 'Nimrara Process" in South Asia which invited an eminent group of Indian and Pakistani citizens including academicians, journalists, ex diplomats and defence personnel for ongoing dialogue at Nimrara, a fort in Rajastan. The groups continues to hold meetings in both the countries. The ground rules of such meetings include no repetition of history, partly because both sides are well aware of each other's public positions and partly for fear of getting bogged down in past differences. The first meeting held in November 1991, stressed that the two countries must change their political language for each other. It was suggested that the two countries should use their present 'modest basket' of CBMs to build a joint fence against any accidental drift towards war, gradually continuing progress of mutual trust and confidence. Without such positive steps, serious cooperation between the two countries is not possible. A concerted effort to mobilize this constituency is the need of hour. An increasing number of informal and unofficial meetings between them could go a long way in bringing about a transformation in the prevailing tense and suffocating environment. The time has come to let the region know that some of its best intentioned people want the countries of South Asia to come closer and work together so that through economic cooperation, greater political stability and human security is ensured. The initiative of course rests with the US. The US through its embassies in New Delhi and Islamabad could sponsor conferences, seminars and workshops at places like Indo-American Centre for International Relations (formerly American Studies Research Centre) at Hyderabad and its counterpart in Pakistan. Needless to say American Alumni associations have great potential to contribute to mutual understanding between India and Pakistan.

US Diplomatic Activism

In the wake of high tensions in the sub-continent in early ninetees as a result of cross border firing, the US took a tough neutral stand. The US Under Secretary of State for Political Affairs R. Kimmet, publicly called upon India and Pakistan to avoid steps which could lead events to spin dangerously out of control[10]. When India-Pakistan tensions over Kashmir rose to the highest level, the then President George Bush Sr. sent his Deputy National Security Advisor, Rober Gates to urge caution on the two countries. Gates warned leaders of both countries that their relations with the United States would suffer badly if they went to war. He declared that the US would remain neutral and 'aid and spare parts would not be forthcoming for the US supplied weapons. He also made it clear that Washington no longer backed a UN plebiscite as the preferred way to solve the Kashmir dispute but instead supported bilateral India-Pakistan talks in accordance with the Shimla Agreement[11]. This was a significant departure from the earlier American stance pursued throughout the cold war period. It is worth pointing out that the US warning had the desired effect and things cooled down a bit.

However, with the taking over of Bill Clinton as President of the US, the American policy towards the region underwent a change. Initially, South Asia impinged on the larger would view of Clinton Administration almost solely in terms of the nuclear issue. The early focus of the Clinton Administration on the promotion of human rights and non-proliferation and its emphasis on 'preventive diplomacy' fused it with American diplomatic activism on Kashmir. Just when the two sides needed to build trust and confidence, US diplomacy on Kashmir stirred up anxieties in India about American intentions and motivations. What appeared to be a small US initiative rattled Indian sensitivities on two scores: the question of territorial integrity, and the nuclear-weapon optino. What For the US regional security in South Asia was largely a case of going through the nations. Significantly towards the end of its first term, there were indications that the Clinton Administration might be pursuing an agenda in South Asia that would see elements of some fresh thinking to sort out some of the crucial problems of the region. For instance, President Clinton made a determined effort to seek a solution to the Kashmir conflict. The Clinton Administration invested quite a bit of political capital in creating the right atmosphere for a peace process to be started. In order to accomplish this objective, the US ambassadors accredited to New Delhi and Islamabad were asked to do the necessary spadework. The reason why the US made such a demonstrative effort concerned the need for creating a far more comprehensive bilateral framework in which not only Kashmir and the Indo-Pak cold war could be tackled, but several other issues including a non-nuclear regime for South Asia to be endorsed by India and Pakistan in association with other states in the region could be handled. The blueprint for a South Asia camp David' type accord between India and Pakistan was drafted by Stephen Cohen, an informal consultant to the State Depart and a respected authority on South Asia in 1995. It was discussed by leading Democratic Senators with President Clinton and other US policy planners. It was almost agreed that the plan would begin to take shape as one of the major foreign policy initiatives of the second Clinton Administration after the November 1996 election as it calls for a bipartis an approach. The plan comprised of a seven point strategy to implement what Cohen calls the Camp David Process for South Asia.

Cohen's Makes the Following Points:

1. It must be bipartisan. He advises Democratic senators to take a "respected Republican senator" along if they go to the President.

"Our engagement in the Middle East has been bipartisan and has survived several changes in administration", he has pointed out.

2. It will take time. He has given example of Cambodia and South Africa. He hopes that a new generation of leaders in the region will speed up the process.
3. The President should not broker the deal though his support, perhaps, through a meeting between the two Prime Ministers at the White House or Camp David, should be evident. Only when the two sides are ready to negotiate - and not hope to manipulate the US through Congress, as they do now-should the President get involved.
4. A special emissary who has the time and enjoys a good reputation in both countries is needed. The state department and the White House are ruled out. Cohen suggest George Shultz, who single-handedly revived the Middle East peace process. Mike Armacost, who was a special emissary once, and Haul Sanders, father of the Middle East Peace process, can also be considered.
5. Only technical aid and economic investment, instead of military assistance, should be promised. That American investors will assure regional progress if there is peace should be the argument.
6. Congress can influence the course of events positively by presenting a united front. Aid may be made conditional on progress towards regional discussions.
7. The Indians know they are in deep trouble in Kashmir and would not want to alienate the US. A "fair, consistent and long-term American effort" will be welcome. "Thoughtful" Indians know it is in their interest to cooperate with Pakistan so that they can get down to the task of economic development and social change[12].

In May 1997, President Clinton ordered a comprehensive policy renew of South Asia because he felt the US had neglected the sub-continent consequently it was decided that a multi-basket approach to India should be taken by the US government. Most importantly, it was decided no issue would be held hostage to another[13]. The President's own sense of his historical legacy had led him to desire to a role in peacemaking in South Asia. He had played an active personal role in defusing other tension spots like West Asia, the Balkans etc. He repeatedly spoken of his willingness to play the role of mediator or facilitator between India and Pakistan. Accordingly a number of elements were initiated into US policy towards the region. In the first place emphasis was laid on the need for sustained engagement of the sub-continent. Secondly the US realized that India had the potential to emerge as a major power in the intendial system. Third, there was some effort in the US to find way round the Pakistan factor, which had always habbled Indo-US relations. The US signalled that it would no longer treat India and Pakistan as confined tensions who must always be paired together in American thinking in the region. Lastly, US emphasis appears to shift from direct and active intervention in Kashmir dispute to promotion of an intensive dialogue between India and Pakistan. This new US line was certainly more sophisticated than the earlier one.

In the wake of nuclear tests by India and Pakistan in 1998, the US delivered demarches to both the countries to undertake wide-ranging military CBMS to reduce the danger of a war. The US strongly encouraged India to resume dialogue with Pakistan after the nuclearization of the sub-continent which finally led to Lahore peace process. There is no denying the fact that Washington exerted pressure on Pakistan right from the start of Kargil crisis, both at the bilateral and multilateral levels. President Clinton's telephone admonitions to Nawaz Sharif, the then Pakistani Prime Minister, the G-8 communique and raising of the issue at the south Asia Task Force meeting in Kiev were illustrative of this effort. It culminiated in the visit of Nawaz Sharif's visit to Washington and his promise to ensure the withdrawal of all Pakistani and Pakistan supported forces from the Indian side of the line of central. However, the US did not act out of love for India or India's Kashmir policy. The US is hardly driven by altrusim in the matters of the international relations. The US had its own reasons to take tough stand against its traditional ally Pakistan. The joint statement issued by the US President and Pakistani Prime Minister on July 5, 1999 was a manifestation of the increasingly significant role the US thought itself destined to play in what it considered to be potential areas of conflict. President Clinton said that he would take a personal interent in encouraging an expectation resumption and intensification of those bilateral efforts, once the sanctity of the line of control was fully restored[14]. The Presidential interest has underscored in a far-reaching policy speech made by Strobe Talbott the Deputy Secretary of State at Brookings. It mentioned 5 crucial areas of interfere. The last one dealt with the underlying causes. The long standing tensions and disputes between these two countries. No amount of diplomatic exertion on our part or anybodyelse's on non-proliferation or any other subject is going to have very much effect unless and until India and Pakistan can literate themselves from their own enmity. And what we and others can help through our good offices with both, that liberation is going to occur only through direct high level, frequent and above all productive, dialogue between the two of them. In that spirit we hope the direct contacts between India and Pakistan will not only complement but will eventually supersede the efforts of the US. A breakthrough between India and Pakistan would allow us, the US to get on with the task the President Clinton set before us before the tests. And this was the task of developing the kind of broad gauged forward looking bilateral relationships with these countries[15]

Two points are worth making. First, an undefined breakthrough between India and Pakistan was clearly to be a precondition to development of a broad ganged, forward looking bilateral relationships. Second, the US role was necessary to ensure the productiveness of Indo-Pak dialogue. Obviously, till General Musharaf, interrupted the momentum, there had been no objection raised with respect to the consultative mechanism which included India conducting several rounds of dialogues with the US. That is very significant at the very least in terms of confidence-building. The Pakistan conducted a similar dialogue with the US. The Indo-Pak dialogue was thus for been the teriary aspect of the trilogue. Setting an ambitious agenda for herself in the new millennium, President Clinton identified general priority areas including easing Indo-Pak ties that would engage his attention[16]. Then in his annual National Security strategy report to the congress, Clinton who kept "easy terms between India and Pakistan on top of his agenda, said: "We seek to persuade India and Pakistan to refrain from weaponization or deployment of nuclear weapons, testing or deploying missiles capable of diverting nuclear weapons and further protection of fissile materials for nuclear weapons as well as to adhere fully to international non-proliferation standards and to sign the CTBT[17]. The US efforts to induce or coerce India and Pakistan to alter their behaviour have not succeeded. The American effort to help resolve the Indo-Pak conflict has met with little success. However, the US has been quietly playing a pivotal backstage role was apparent from the Lahore process and Kargil war. But man it has taken to scripting parallel Indo-Pak moves. Desperate to secure a foreign policy legacy during his final days no office. Clinton continues to meddle in Kashmir, underlined by his special December 20th statement. The incoming Bush team is likely to fully exploit the lee way and leverage. New Delhi conceded to the caretaker Clinton Administration on Kashmir.

Limitations of US Diplomatic Activism

Commenting on the Washington role in the evolving new détente in the region Karl Inderfurth, the outgoing Assistant Secretary of State for South Asia at his farewell meeting with South Asian journalists said, "on the accomplishment side would be that from being the backside" of the American diplomatic globe, the region was finally getting the attention primarily it deserved, that the US apart from successfully reintroducing itself to India had begun to deal with countries in the region on their own merits. As a 'disappointments', the US would have liked more progress on ending conflict in the region; the nuclear tests of 1998 and the Kashmir conflict had caused great concern; and Washington had been trying to use its influence and support to see parties reduce, tensions between India and Pakistan, including over Kashmir[18] . Earlie Robin Raphel, Inderfurth's predecessor, making a sober appraisal of South Asian situation admitted.: "Our efforts to dissuade both parties (India and Pakistan) from pursuing and escalating along this course are unremitting but regrettably not as successful as we would like" she added. While we recognize that the US had limited ability to influence the situation, regional stability must remain high on our agenda. To be effective, any US approach has to take into account the legitimate security needs of regional states[19] . According to the Task Force Report the US interests would be served by helping India and Pakistan to develop a "normal" bilateral relationship with one another. The US needs to realistically determine the limits of its power. Moreover, it is doubtful that Washington passers sufficient resolve or domestic booking to raise its coercive action to the level that might make India and Pakistan alter their policies. More importantly, the US governmental structure is not well suited to pursue the desired policies in the region. The separate South Asia bureau at the State Department created at late as 1992 has been given only a small staff, including for example, only one deputy assistant secretary of State. At the Pentagon the region is divided between two commands, with Pakistan in one and India in the other. At the National Security Council and the Central Intelligence Agency, South Asia is handled as one of four subregions in the Near East and South Asia Directorate. One consequence of the latter structure is that South Asian issues are treated intermittently and secondarily by relevant regional bureaus, while attracting constant and primary attention from functional experts in non-proliferation. This further distorts the lens through which India and Pakistan are perceived. Needless to say maintaining the current approach limits US influence and jeopardizes US interests with two increasingly important countries in an increasingly critical part of the world[20].

Conclusion

A number of factors have made South Asia more important to the US today than it was a decade ago. Given the incipient nuclearization of the region, the prospect of a nuclear war necessitates US involvement in the region. As a global power and the only super power, the US cannot remain oblivious to the security concerns of the one fifth of humanity. Besides, the region has became a major source of narcotics and terrorists. In addition, South Asia migrants to the US form a new and unprecedented budge between the US and the countries of the region. Ensuring stability in the sub-continent is the US overwhelming foreign policy goal. This flows from both regional and global imperatives.

Earlier the region's strategic value was measured solely in terms of the cold war struggle with the former Soviet Union and varied with the mercurial cycles of US-Soviet geo-political competition. With the end of the cold war, the US has a unique opportunity in South Asia of strengthening bilateral relationship with individual countries. Its relationship with the states is no longer confined by the constraints of cold war, for example, of seeing who was toeing whose live in terms of US-Soviet bipolar struggle. Now the US can deal with issues, face to face and judge each issue on its merit.

The efforts to end the South Asian conflicts is an essential element of promoting US interests in the region. For instance, on South Asia, strategic Assessment 1998 notes. "American interests in the region are suggested to include encouraging India and Pakistan to resolve their differences peacefully, containing the proliferation of weapons of mass destruction (WMD), promoting a climate of regional trust and cooperation and encouraging regional states to embrace core values[21]

Though the stand off between New Delhi and Islamabad is strictly bilateral, the process of resolution need not necessarily be bilateral. When India, Pakistan and US periodically assert that Shimla Agreement represents the best and the only way forward, is it is at best a philosophical trvism. The reference really is to the broadest possible guiding principle enshrined in Para 1, 2 of the Shimla Agreement which says: "The two countries have resolved to settle their differences through peaceful means, through bilateral negotiations or by any other peaceful means mutually agreed upon between them." This paradigm shift to the second half of the statement provides the underpinning for the way forward for all the interested parties.

In the absence of adequate political will in India and Pakistan to settle the dispute, the continued expansion of the CBMS regimes is of considerable importance. A robust set of CBMs can help avoid the spirals of misperception and hostility. As rightly suggested by the Task Force Report the US should call upon both the countries to implement fully and unconditionally existing CBMs and also to negotiate and implement additional CBMs. It may prove extremely difficult to persuade India and Pakistan to undertake all these steps. Needless to stress that they would contribute to Indian and Pakistan security and welfare and to an improvement in relations between each of them and the US.

In moving towards closer relations with India, the US should seek to preserve constructive relations with Pakistan by emphasising the economic dimensions of the relationships that had been subordinated during the cold war period. American policies in all spheres should be designed to avoid aggravating tensions between the two countries.

To sum up, being a significant partner in the politics of the Indian sub-continent and being the lone super power, the US is in a position to contribute positively in conflict resolution and confidence -building in the region. The US needs to better understand the complexity of the détente and regional contexts of these two countries, to revise some of its own foreign policy goals, to more judiciously prioritize and choose among conflicting aims and prophels, to scale back move of its expectations, to more effectively gagne the long-term effects of its strategies, to recognize the units of its influence, to use more carrot and less stick ad to state its policies in a more circumspect and precise manner. The US must temper its expectations about what it can do to help to put an end to India-Pak conflict. It should continue to encourage New Delhi and Islamabad to hold regular links about their entire relationships, free from any linkage to progress on Kashmir. It should offer to provide technical means to verify troops movements or withdrawals and to demarcate complete border area. The US could also use its resources to promote non-official track II diplomacy between the rivals. It should support the expansion of non-official transactions such as people to people contact like cultural, educational and professional exchanges. Washington has the economic levers, bilaterally as well as through its clout in multilateral lending agencies to make any impact on an economically vulnerable Indian Sub-continent. Despite limitations, the US role will be crucial is persuading Indian and Pakistan to exercise moderation while talking to each other. Formal mediation, however, is not possible as India will simply not accept it. The US role in engaging India and Pakistan on two separate tracks will have to be discrete and cautious. A little US covert pressure and some lucrative incentives will go a long way in promoting peace in the region.

One finds in full agreement with the Task Force's reports general premises that India and Pakistan deserve upgraded priority in US foreign policy and this policy should be give a more broadly conceived agenda than in the past. The recommendations of the Report are as follows:

(a) Seek to discourage further proliferation and establish a more stable plateau for Indian and Pakistani nuclear weapon and missile competition;

(b) Seek close bilateral political and military cooperation over the long term, especially with India;

(c) Support modest diplomatic efforts in concert with others to help calm the Kashmir situation and steer it in the direction of eventual settlement;

(d) Support the progress of democracy and promote economic liberalization in both countries;

(e) Encourage a normalized and more cooperative working relationship between India and Pakistan;

(f) Revamp relevant existing U.S. legislation;

(g) Restructure bureaucratic organizations within the U.S. government to create separate divisions dealing with South Asia.

The new US policy as suggested by the report has the potential to bring real and important benefits to the US, India and Pakistan, the region and the broader international community. However, the US policy to encourage confidence-building in South Asia involves a neutral position. In brief, South Asia, while posing fresh challenges for the new

US Administration, also presents it with tremendous opportunities. If President George Bush Jr. follows an activist sovereign policy, he may have to follow Clinton's policy towards South Asia. a lost would depend on the choice of his new team of officials primarily responsible for shaping US policy towards the region. It is worth emphasize of that the US remains the only country which is in a position to ensure that democratic problems do not jeopardize the South Asian beseiged elites in the two countries to get out of the ethnic/religious tensions. With the US interaction, an example could be set for a very different South Asia.

References

1. Eric Gonsolves, South Asian Cooperation: An Agenda a vision for the Future, in L. L. Mehrotra, H. S. Chopra and Gert W. Jueck (eds) SAARC-2000 and Beyond, New Delhi, 1995, p. 3.
2. Jasjit Singh, 'Arms Build up in South Asia: Impact on the Process Peace and Development in the Region', in Mehratra and Chopra, SAARC-2000, *op.cit.* p. 19-11.
3. Pervez Iqbal Cheema, Arms, Build up in South Asia; Impact on the Process of Peace and Development in the Region", in Mehratra and Chopra, SAARC - 2000, p. 23.
4. Arun P. Elhance and Moonis Ahmar, "Non-military CBMs" in Michael Kerpen and Amit Sewek (Eds) Crisis Prevention, Confidence Building and Reconciliation in South Asia, New Delhi, 1996, pp. 135-36.
5. A new US Policy Toward India and Pakistan, Report of an Independent Task Force, sponsored by the council on Foreign Relations, New York, 1997, p. 7.
6. Inderfurth, Karl. G. at the confirmation hearing before the Senate Foreign Relations Committee, Times of India, July 12, 1997.
7. American diplomatic activism on Kashmir mid 1990's had raised misplaced hopes in Srinagar and Islamabad and these need to be firmly corrected. Rabri Raphel for instance showed pour judgement and a remarkable facility to make tactless in injudicious remarks throughout her tenure as Asstt. Secretary of State of South Asia. She was perceived in India as being a strongly opinionated pro-Pakistan bias.
8. A New US Policy Toward India and Pakistan, Report of an Independent Task Force, *op.cit.*, p. 40.
9. Novinita Chadha, "Enemy Images: The Media and Indo-Pak Tension", in Michael Kerpen and Amir Sewek, *op.cit.*, p. 184.
10. New York Times, April 20, 1990.
11. *Ibid.*, May 16, 1990.

12. Indian Express, New Delhi, July 3, 1996
13. Bill Clinton, US President, White House Press Report, Washington D.C. 9 February, 1999
14. *The Times of India*, July 6, 1999
15. *The Times of India*, November 19, 1999
16. *The Times of India*, November 9, 1999
17. *The Times of India*, January 8, 2000
18. *The Hindu*, January 12, 2001
19. *The Times of India*, December 7, 1995
20. A New US Policy Toward India and Pakistan, Report of an Independent Task Force, *op.cit.*, p. 46
21. National Defense University, Institute of National Strategic Studies, Strategic Assessment 1998, pp. 53-54.

19

FDR, Nehru and India's Freedom Movement

Few statesmen in the twentieth century have achieved the status of Franklin D. Roosevelt. He belonged to that galaxy of great leaders who wielded gubernatorial power. His vision went far beyond his own nation and embraced the entire human race. His ideas and actions produced a profound effect on the peoples' minds the world over. He made them feel that America's concern for the rights of man was no less than what it was at the time of its own war of independence. He was an ardent champion of freedom from tyranny and oppression, poverty and hunger, want and fear. In his message to the US Congress on 6 January 1941, Roosevelt defined "the four essential freedoms": freedom of speech and expression, freedom of worship, freedom from want and freedom from fear.[1] These were substantially incorporated in the Atlantic Charter. With the signing of the Atlantic Charter and subsequently its publication under the signatures of Churchill and Roosevelt, the latter ensured the commitment of the US to the cause of freedom of the colonies.[2] It kindled a fresh ray of hope among the subject people which was strengthened by the speeches delivered by Roosevelt. In his annual message to the Congress on 6 January 1942, Roosevelt reiterated the lofty ideals of the Charter through the following declaration :

> *Our objectives are clear, the objective of smashing militarism imposed by warlords upon their enslaved people — the objective of liberating the subjugated nation—the objective of establishing and securing the freedom of speech, freedom of religion, freedom from want and freedom from fear*

anywhere in the world. We shall not stop short of these objectives.[3]

The cumulative result of all this was that Roosevelt found himself in a position where hundreds of millions of people all over the globe, especially in Asia, looked to him for deliverance. As Jawaharlal Nehru noted in an article : "President Roosevelt has spoken eloquently about this future and about the four freedoms, and his words have found an echo in millions of hearts".[4] In other words, Roosevelt had become the one hope of mankind during the dark days of the Second World War.

Interest in India's National Movement

In keeping with their liberalism, Americans in general sympathized with India's desire for independence. There was also a strain of anti-colonial sentiment in the US policy. However, before President Roosevelt, American interest and sympathy for India's independence was academic, idealistic and unofficial. It was because of Roosevelt that the American interest in Indian nationalism began manifesting at the official and diplomatic level. With the outbreak of the Second World War, India became vital for the US in her fight against Japan. American strategy and War planning could hardly succeed without the full cooperation of the Indian people. The Indian National Congress was of the firm opinion that only a free and independent India would be in a position to gladly associate herself with other nations which would be to the mutual benefit of all, particularly during times of external aggression. The Roosevelt administration realized this, and rightly so, and the first manifestation of the new attitude of the US was the decision to establish direct ties with India.[5] Simultaneously, with the setting up of the American Mission in India, the Roosevelt administration began to consider the wisdom of approaching the British for the grant of dominion status to India.

With the steady deterioration in the War situation, Roosevelt got convinced by August 1941 that time was ripe for directly approaching the British Government. He authorized Winant, his Ambassador in London, to raise with the British Government two issues: first, the grant of Dominion Status to India and second, the working out of a new relationship among India, China, Australia and New Zealand. However, Summer Welles, the Assistant Secretary of State, was not too sure about the wisdom of Ambassador Winant taking up such a question as of India's political status at the official level. He commented : "Were the President disposed to take the matter up, I would imagine he would wish to discuss it in a very personal and confidential way with Mr. Churchill".[6] Roosevelt was quite willing, according to his son Elliot, to raise the issue of India's independence with the British Prime Minister. During their meeting in the mid-Atlantic Ocean, Roosevelt stressed on the need to develop industry, to improve sanitation and to raise the educational level and standard of living in the colonies. At this Churchill growled, "You mentioned India". "Yes", the President responded, "I cannot believe that we can fight a war against a fascist slavery, and at the same time, not work to free people from all over the world from a backward colonial policy".[7] There is no US record of the discussion, but Churchill is reported to have said: "I reacted so strongly and at such length that he never raised it (India) verbally again".[8]

After the fall of Singapore on 15 February 1942, the need for Indian support to the War effort further increased. On 25 February, Roosevelt took another initiative. He instructed Averell Harriman, his Special Representative in London, to sound Churchill about a "new relationship between Britain and India". After a discussion with Churchill, Harriman informed Roosevelt that the Prime Minister of Britain remained strongly opposed to "stirring the pot".[9] Churchill, at the conclusion of his talks with Harriman, sent a cable to Roosevelt on 4 March stressing that it would not be proper to throw India into chaos on the eve of invasion.[10] Roosevelt was not convinced with Churchill's reasoning and firmly believed that a reasonable gesture had to be made to conciliate the Indian people. He put forth a plan and contended that the American experience with the Articles of Confederation might serve as a helpful precedent for the solution of problems concerning India. He suggested that the British should immediately establish "a temporary dominion government" in India, headed by a small group representing different religions, regions and princes that could be the foundation for a more permanent government.[11] Fully conscious that his suggestions would displease his friend Churchill, Roosevelt concluded his message diplomatically:

> *For the love of Heaven, do not bring me into this, though I want to be of help. It is, strictly speaking, none of my business except in so far as it is a part and parcel of the successful fight that you and I are waging.*[12]

Roosevelt's plan, though not very effective in accelerating India's independence, yet it did emphasize its legitimacy. Looking in retrospect, the remedy suggested by Roosevelt was worth giving a try. The problems faced by both the US and India, though not exactly the same, were quite similar. For example, problems of cultural pluralism and the ones relating to regional and sectional government, representing various castes, religions, etc., did none the less sound sensible.

Cripps and Johnson Missions

Under mounting American pressure, the British War Cabinet approved the idea of issuing an offer of post- War independence and of taking steps to give the Indian leaders a governmental role during the War. It also decided to send a senior figure to discuss the proposal. Sir Stafford Cripps was selected for the onerous task. The Cripps Mission to India was undertaken with the primary purpose of placating America. As Churchill explained to the Viceroy :

> *It would be impossible, owing to the general American outlook, to stand on a purely negative attitude and Cripps Mission is indispensable, to prove our honesty of purpose.*[13]

This fact was duly appreciated by the Indian leaders like Jawaharlal Nehru.[14] Cripps carried with him the Draft Declaration and a confidential copy of the same was sent to Roosevelt to win the confidence of the President. Roosevelt, however, was not satisfied with the proposals made by Cripps. While talking to Bajpai, the Indian Agent General, on 2 April, he criticized the Cripps' proposals as not going far enough, expressing the view that the British should have offered Indians virtually complete independence.[15]

The Cripps' proposals were definitely an advance over all the earlier British offers. The essence of these proposals was the solemn undertaking by the British Government that independence would be granted to India if demanded by a constituent assembly after the War. However this was qualified by a big "if". The provision relating to the defence of India was also Machiavellian. In fact, Cripps Mission was nothing more than a Churchillian device to please Roosevelt.

The Cripps Mission coincided with the appointment of Colonel Louis A. Johnson as President Roosevelt's Personal Representative to India, though originally he was appointed as the head of the War production mission in India. But before his departure a decision was taken to change his role and he was designated as President's Personal Representative. On reaching India Johnson made all possible efforts to resolve the deadlock. Realizing that the Cripps Mission was heading for a failure, Johnson suggested to Roosevelt to intercede with Churchill in order to save the Cripps Mission.[16] Roosevelt, however, did not concur with this suggestion as he feared that this might further complicate the situation.

Roosevelt's refusal notwithstanding, Johnson continued his efforts to save the Cripps Mission. On 9 April he sent another cable stating that Nehru was willing to accept the modified defence proposal and that Wavell and Linlithgow had also agreed. Johnson wrote with a patriotic fervour: "The magic name over here is Roosevelt; the land and people would follow and love America".[17]

Cripps, on the other hand, reported to Churchill that because of the efforts made by Johnson, there was hope of securing India's consent. He urged Churchill to express gratitude to Roosevelt for the efforts made by Johnson.[18] But things took a different turn. The Viceroy complained to Churchill that Johnson gave the impression as if he was acting under the directions of Roosevelt while mediating in the Indian crisis.[19] Churchill told the Presidential aide Hopkins, who happened to be in London during those days, that in case the War cabinet rejected Johnson's proposals, it would cause embarrassment to Roosevelt. Hopkins, thinking it appropriate to downplay Johnson rather than risk a public relations problem for the President, declared that Johnson was not representing Roosevelt while making efforts to resolve the Indian crisis. The President did not wish to be placed in a situation where contending parties would turn down his proposals. Accordingly, Churchill sent a cable to the Viceroy stating that Johnson was not acting on behalf of the President.[20] After the rejection of Cripps' proposals, Johnson, in a cable to Roosevelt, aptly summed up Cripps' failure as: "London wanted a Congress refusal".[21]

Roosevelt's Reaction

Churchill, aware of Roosevelt's interest in the Cripps Mission, sent a copy of the Cripps' message to the Prime Minister conveying the reasons for the Mission's failure. Roosevelt was displeased at the failure of Cripps Mission in the light of Johnson's report. He believed that this could have been avoided. He was not in agreement with Churchill's statement that the British had done everything in their power to reach an understanding. Roosevelt instructed Hopkins, who was still in London, to urge Churchill to make every effort to prevent a breakdown of talks. Refuting Churchill's assertion that "public opinion in the US believes that the negotiations have been broken down on general broad issues",[22] Roosevelt stated :

> *The general impression here is quite the contrary. The feeling is almost universally held that the deadlock has been due to the British Government's unwillingness to concede to the Indians the right of self-government, notwithstanding the willingness of Indians to entrust technical, military and naval defense control to the competent British authorities.*[23]

In his last minute bid to save the Cripps Mission, Roosevelt asked Churchill to postpone the departure of Cripps Mission from India until another attempt was made to prevent a breakdown. Roosevelt reiterated that his earlier proposal of solving the Indian problem on the basis of American colonies on the pattern of American confederation with suitable modifications could be considered for implementation on an experimental basis.[24] Churchill responded to this by stating, though incorrectly, that he could not do anything further since Cripps had already left India.[25] Thus Roosevelt's last minute bid to save Cripps Mission did not yield any results.

British Propaganda and Roosevelt

Graham Spry, a member of the Cripps Mission, toured the US to put across the British viewpoint. He asserted that Cripps' proposals were to the liking of the Americans and that Congress should have accepted them.[26] Roosevelt, however, did not share this view. When Spry met him on 1 May 1942, Roosevelt pointedly asked if the British cabinet switched instructions during the later stages of Cripps negotiations.[27] Roosevelt also criticized Cripps' proposals during his meeting with the British diplomat Sir Ronald Chambell and told him that the idea of offering parts of India the right to secede "sounded terrible to Americans after the civil war".[28]

Johnson's Plea

When Washington turned down his proposal of issuing a statement on the Pacific War Aims that would appeal to the Indian nationalists, Johnson urged Roosevelt to take up the matter with Churchill. He sent a cable to Roosevelt on 4 May stating that "America alone can save India for the UN cause".[29] Presumably influenced by his earlier inability to move Churchill, Roosevelt accepted the State Department's appraisal that Johnson's proposal was unlikely to succeed and would only make matters worse in India. He cabled back a polite but firm rejection.[30] This signalled the end of Johnson's mission. He left India on 16 May, never to return again.

Quit India Movement

Roosevelt and his administration were not happy with the launching of the Quit India Movement as they thought that it was bound to adversely affect the War effort. As the US looked upon the British War effort as essential for the success of the Allies, American attitude towards India's independence underwent a change. This stiffening of the American attitude was in line with their thinking that defence was to be given priority over independence. Thus, the earlier policy of extending diplomatic support to India gave way to the policy of neutrality and non-intervention. In response to Chiang Kai Shek's plea that Roosevelt, by virtue of his being the brain behind the publication of the Atlantic Charter, should take steps in favour of India's independence, the latter retorted :

> *... irrespective of the merits of the case, any action which slows the War effort in India results not in theoretical assistance, but in actual assistance to the armed forces of Japan.... I wish Mr. Gandhi could understand that the very worst thing that could happen to the people of India would be victory by Axis powers ...and we have not the moral right to force ourselves upon the British or the Congress Party.*[31]

Gandhi's Correspondence with Roosevelt

Conscious of America's misgivings and the implications of the Quit India Movement, Mahatma Gandhi wrote a personal letter to Roosevelt, explaining India's stand. The letter was drafted by Nehru.[32] Gandhi reiterated that India would be willing to cooperate with the Allies provided it was given freedom. In his reply, Roosevelt skirted round Gandhi's call for help. Instead, he expressed the hope that "our common interest in democracy and righteousness will enable your countrymen and mine to make a common cause against a common enemy".[33] Even this somewhat disappointing reply could not be delivered to Gandhi as by the time it reached Delhi, he had been imprisoned.

US Mission Plea for Roosevelt's Intervention

Meanwhile, the American Mission at New Delhi earnestly tried to find out what transpired in the minds of Indian leaders with regard to their negotiations with the British. In the wake of the comments made by Nehru[34] and Maulana Azad,[35] the Mission made a last ditch effort to avert the Civil Disobedience campaign. The Mission, on the basis of its assessment of the situation, requested the President to intervene. A tentative draft of the proposed declaration to be made by the President was also sent. It was suggested that the US should stand guarantor to the British pledge of independence immediately after the War and help the Indian leaders in setting up a provisional Wartime government.[36] Since the Indians held Roosevelt in high esteem and trusted him greatly, a declaration by him was quite in order. The Congress party was willing, as indicated by Nehru, to resume negotiations provided a guarantee from a third party was forthcoming. However, these comprehensive and well-researched suggestions of the Mission met the same fate as those of Johnson's primarily because of Roosevelt's disinclination to challenge Churchill further on India.

The early collapse of the Quit India Movement, its failure to have any significant impact on the War effort and the success of British repression swung the American public opinion once again on the side of India's independence. Letters, interviews, reports, editorials and articles supporting the cause of India's independence flooded the American press.[37] Public enthusiasm in favour of India rose to such heights that it became impossible for the US Government to remain indifferent. In view of the strong public opinion, it decided to explore yet again the possibility of effecting some understanding between the British and the Indian leaders. Since Johnson's departure, the post of President's Personal Representative was lying vacant. Philips was chosen for this crucial post and entrusted with the responsibility of studying the situation and suggesting suitable ways for resolving the deadlock. Thus, by the end of 1942, the US had reverted to its earlier policy of diplomatic intervention in the Indian tangle. Philips was sent to India to keep the British 'reminded of Roosevelt's interest in India's freedom.[38] The sending of such an experienced and outstanding diplomat as Philips to India amply testified to America's renewed interest in India.

Gandhi's Fast and Roosevelt

Soon after Philips' arrival in India, Gandhi went on a fast with effect from 9 February 1943 as he was greatly distressed by the violence which ensued in the wake of the Quit India Movement. The fast brought America prominently into the picture. The Indian press criticized Roosevelt and his Personal Representative for their failure to condemn the indifferent attitude of the British towards Gandhi. Philips was flooded with letters and telegrams enquiring if something could be done from Washington to end the crisis. The fact that the Indians were looking to the US and her President for the resolution of the crisis resulted in British resentment, so much so that even Philips' request to see Gandhi in prison was turned down by the Viceroy. The news of the efforts made by Philips to meet Gandhi received a favourable press coverage in India, thus improving the US image. When doubts were raised about Gandhi's survival, Hull, the Secretary of State of the US, apprised the British Ambassador Halifax of the strong feelings of the President that Gandhi should not be allowed to die in prison. Roosevelt telephoned Hull during the course of his meeting with Halifax to emphasize his "extreme embarrassment about sitting with hands folded doing nothing on an issue that was likely to have grave international reaction".[39] Although Halifax urged Hull not to publicize the issue, the State Department let the press know about the US concern for Gandhi's health.[40] Churchill, on the other hand, felt that any American intervention would cause great embarrassment to the British Government.[41] Roosevelt assured that no further statements would be issued by the US Government on this matter, but in case Gandhi died, he would be constrained to issue a statement to the effect that his Government had all along been expressing apprehensions about the possibility of Gandhi's death.[42] The mounting tension, however, subsided with the decision of Gandhi to end his fast.

Philips' Plan

After the conclusion of Gandhi's fast, Philips suggested a plan to Roosevelt for putting an end to the deadlock. The plan envisaged a meeting of all political groups in India under the chairmanship of an American. This was considered necessary as a token of America's interest as well as a guarantee of British offer of independence to India.[43] Roosevelt characterized Philips' plan as "amazingly radical"[44] and asked Hopkins to refer Philips' plan to Eden who in turn recommended that it be filed.[45]

In his last report, Philips reported to the President : "I see only one remedy to this disturbing situation, and that is, to try with every means in our power tc make Indians feel that America is with them and in a position to go beyond mere public assurances of friendship".[46] At the instance of Roosevelt Philips returned to Washington at the end of 1943. On his return to Washington, Philips met Roosevelt who seemed pleased with the former's performance in India. Roosevelt appeared to have concurred with Philips' appraisal of the Indian situation and asked him to see Churchill, who happened to be in Washington at that time, and convey to him his impressions without any inhibitions. Philips sensed Roosevelt's reluctance to talk to Churchill on the Indian issue, for Churchill had earlier rebuffed him.[47]

As directed by Roosevelt, Philips met Churchill on 23 March 1943 and apprised him of India's lack of faith in the assurances given by the British that independence would be granted after the War. He also pleaded the case for the formation of a provisional coalition at the centre with limited powers at the domestic level. As expected Churchill reacted sharply and said : "Take India if that is what you want. Take it by all means! But I warn you that if I open the door a crack there will be the greatest bloodbath in all history".[48] The outcome of the meeting was duly reported to Roosevelt who seemed rather amused but glad that Philips had spoken so frankly.[49] Without the President having to risk a direct clash with Churchill over India, the message had been put across. Philips told Roosevelt that India was looking to him for help, and the continued presence of President's Personal Representative in India could put the President in a false position unless the British attitude changed. Roosevelt agreed with Philips and said he would consider sending Eden to India to assess the situation and to have a discussion with all the parties and groups concerned, including Gandhi. And subsequently during Eden's stay in India, Philips too would be sent to India in his capacity as the President's Personal Representative so as to convince India of the President's deep concern for the Indian cause.[50] What happened to Roosevelt's suggestion in this regard is not clear. But Philips never returned to India and his mission thus came to an end.

Roosevelt's failure to act on Philips' recommendation was disquieting and raised Indian doubts whether the US was genuinely concerned about the Indian cause vis-a-vis the British. Gandhi's reasoning was that since America had become the predominant partner in the Allied cause, she was a partner also in British guilt.[51] He observed: "President Roosevelt talks about Four Freedoms. Does that include freedom to be free"?[52] Such sentiments were widely echoed in India. Roosevelt got alarmed, and in his bid to erase such anti-American sentiments, he issued the following statement on 1 February 1943:

> *The American objectives in India as elsewhere in continental Asia are to expel and defeat the Japanese in closest collaboration with our British, Chinese and other allies in that theater. . . . Nobody in India or elsewhere in Asia will believe, as we do at home, that their job is to ensure the defeat of Japan without which there can be no opportunity for any of us to enjoy and expand the freedom for which we fight.*[53]

Roosevelt's statement helped to some extent in allaying Indian disappointment concerning US policy. A few months later, when Philips' final report to the President was published, the US standing with India got a further boost. When the British pressed for an official disavowal by the US Government, Hull successfully argued with Roosevelt against this on the ground that the State Department was in agreement with Philips' views.[54] The US refusal to repudiate Philips angered the British, thus further strengthening the bonds between the US and India.

After the failure of the bilateral dialogue, Roosevelt tried to make India an international issue. At the Teheran Conference at the end of 1943, Roosevelt referred to the problem relating to India while talking to Stalin.[55] Aware of the fact that India was a contentious issue, Stalin diplomatically evaded discussion on this saying that the Indian question was rather a complicated one. Thus Roosevelt's effort to internationalise the issue proved to be of no avail.

Barely a month before his death, Roosevelt again expressed his concern, about colonialism in Asia. Talking to State Department Adviser Charles Taussig, Roosevelt commented that much of the Orient was ruled by a handful of Whites much to the former's resentment. He declared : "... our goal must be to help them achieve independence — 1,100,000,000 potential enemies are dangerous. *Churchill does not understand this*".[56] The emphasized words aptly reflect Roosevelt's dilemma throughout the War in dealing with India. There was an inherent contradiction between the US support to the British as an ally and, at the same time, espousal of the Indian cause. It was extremely difficult to reconcile the two contradictory positions.

Roosevelt and Nehru

While analysing the role of Roosevelt during India's struggle for freedom, it seems pertinent to discuss at length the kind of relationship established between Roosevelt and Jawaharlal Nehru who had become the foreign policy spokesman of the Indian National Congress. After the Democrats came to power in 1933, Indian nationalists, notably Nehru, began to look to the US as a potentially powerful supporter of their struggle for freedom. Roosevelt gained immense popularity in India by virtue of his New Deal domestic reforms and his anti-colonial attitude. Roosevelt's support to the Indian cause was widely appreciated in India and was often referred to by Nehru who seems to have developed an instinctive admiration for Roosevelt. He had hailed Roosevelt's attitude towards the Czech Crisis. In an article, Nehru spoke admiringly of Roosevelt's efforts to discourage Hitler from following policies that might lead to war:

> *President Roosevelt has sent another message to Hitler, a dignified, moving appeal in which the real point at issue is stressed. What a vast difference between what he says and how he says it and Mr. Chamberlain's pronouncement! Even the printed word shows that there is a man behind it.*[57]

Nehru was convinced that once the War was over, Roosevelt would play a leading role in persuading Great Britain, France, the Netherlands and other imperialist powers to abandon their outmoded views on colonialism. He observed:

> *For my part I admire President Roosevelt and consider that he has been shouldering a very great burden worthily. I think he will inevitably play a great part in the future.*[58]

Nehru, who had succeeded in gaining favourable attention in America as an articulate and sensitive Asian leader through his famous *Autobiography*, presented India's case for independence for the informed US audience through articles in *Foreign Affairs*[59] and *Atlantic Monthly.*[60]

Nehru's firm faith in Roosevelt and his belief that the burden of the future would ultimately fall on the US inspired confidence in him.[61] In February 1942, when American Ambassador Winant urged Roosevelt to use his personal influence with Churchill on behalf of India, Nehru reacted : "The next hundred years, it has been said, are going to be the century of America. America is undoubtedly going to play a very important role in the years and generations to come".[62]

Nehru had come to establish a personal rapport with Roosevelt. In February 1942, Roosevelt sent a friendly message to Nehru through Edgar Snow and insisted that Nehru write to him. "When you get there and see Nehru, say hello for me. I wish you would ask Nehru to write me a letter and tell exactly what he wants me to do for India. You can send it through our diplomatic pouch".[63]

After the breakdown of Cripps negotiations, Nehru addressed directly to Roosevelt in the hope of securing his active involvement in the Indian problem :

> *I am venturing to write to you as I know you are deeply interested in the Indian situation today and its reaction on the War. The failure of Sir Stafford Cripps Mission to bring about a settlement between the British Government and the Indian people must have distressed you, as it has distressed us.*[64]

He concluded by saying :

> *To your great country, of which you are the honoured head, we send greetings and good wishes for success. And to you, Mr. President, on whom so many all over the world look for leadership in the cause of freedom, we would add our assurances of our high regards and esteem.*[65]

The sentiments expressed by Nehru in his letter were not much different from those of Roosevelt's who responded by sending a friendly and prompt reply. Expressing his deep gratification at the message, Roosevelt assured Nehru that the US would "to the utmost extent of its ability"[66] help India against Japanese aggression. Roosevelt's reply, however, was disappointing as no mention of Indian independence was made in it.

Colonel Johnson, Roosevelt's Personal Representative, praised Nehru as "magnificent in his cooperation with me. The President would like him and on most things they agree .... He is our hope here".[67] Johnson sent a cable to Roosevelt on the eve of the Congress Working Committee meeting emphasizing that Nehru's hands would be immensely strengthened if a statement on Pacific War Aims was jointly issued by the British, China and the US, assuring freedom and self-determination to India.

Nehru told the US Mission Political Officer, L. Berry, that the Congress would be willing to extend its cooperation to the War effort if Britain declared India independent and established a provisional government.[68] Nehru's ideas were very much similar to Roosevelt's own pet solution for India — form a provisional government and work out the details later.

Equally remarkable is the revelation by Congress leader Acharya Narendra Deva that Nehru was opposed to the launching of the Quit India Movement because of his belief that once India joined the War, Roosevelt would somehow manage to persuade the British to resolve their differences with the Congress party. According to Acharya :

> *Jawaharlal's intellect never really approved of the decision (to undertake the Quit India Movement). During our imprisonment in Ahmadnagar Fort, he conferred more than once that in his view the step had been hurriedly taken, and that it might have been possible to bring Great Britain to terms with the help of American pressure.*[69]

On hearing the news of Roosevelt's death, Nehru recorded the following observations in his prison diary :

> *This news came to us as a great shock .... I was really upset and at night I was restless and dreamed of him. I had long wanted to meet him. My mind was full of the far reaching consequences of his death—in the US as well as in the world.*[70]

In fact Colonel Johnson had earlier suggested to Nehru to visit Washington and see President Roosevelt. Nehru seemed agreeable to the suggestion but because of Johnson's rather sudden departure after his meeting with Nehru, the programme could not materialize.[71]

Conclusion

From the above, it becomes evident that Roosevelt evinced keen interest in India's struggle for freedom and that his sympathies were with India. He was a supporter of greater concessions to India, leading ultimately to independence. Roosevelt left no stone unturned in his persuasions with the British Prime Minister on this subject. It was mainly because of this constant pressure that the Cripps Mission was sent to India. First, Roosevelt sent Colonel Johnson to India in keeping with the situation prevalent in the subcontinent. Subsequently, he sent Philips with the same mission. These missions, though unorthodox in terms of conventional diplomacy, attracted a great deal of attention in India. At the diplomatic level, too, Roosevelt wasted no opportunity in impressing upon the British that India must be granted independence. Last, but not the least, from a purely pragmatic point of view, Roosevelt realized the significance of India's support to the War effort and was convinced that only independence could ensure the wholehearted involvement of the Indian people in the fight against Nazism and Fascism.

Roosevelt had definite reasons to push India's case with the British. In the first place, as mentioned at the outset, he had a love for liberty of all people of the world. Secondly, when Roosevelt entered the White House, the New Deal liberals, influenced by the anti-imperialist traditions of the Democratic Party, sympathized with India's desire for independence. Thirdly, pressure was building up in the US to extend the provisions of the Atlantic Charter to India as well.

While Roosevelt was openly sympathetic towards the Indian aspirations for independence, he did not prove very effective in pressing India's case with the British. At times, he appeared to be inhibited in expressing his unequivocal support to the Indian cause. As the head of the single most powerful nation on the globe, Roosevelt certainly could have asserted more. He seems to have abdicated his responsibility as the co-author of the Atlantic Charter.

While analysing the factors responsible for a country's response to a foreign issue involving two external parties, it is important to consider that a country's response in this respect is determined more by promotion of national interest than abstract moral and ethical considerations. At a time of crisis, particularly when War is in full swing, military considerations assume the most crucial importance in the calculations of the policy-makers.[72] An evaluation of Roosevelt's attitude towards the Indian national movement can best be made in the light of these factors. The US support to the British as an ally and, at the same time, espousal of the Indian cause were apparently contradictory. During the War times, Allied unity had to be given top priority, and giving concessions to India at a time when it was heading towards a crisis situation, would have irked Churchill no end. America's role during the War years was in the final analysis not determined by the lofty ideals pronounced by the founding fathers and echoed on the international scene by Woodrow Wilson and Roosevelt, which often had to take a back seat. In deference to the larger goal of Allied unity, Roosevelt was not prepared to raise the issue of India's freedom publicly and put America's prestige at stake. Cordhell Hull in his *Memoirs* recorded that it was because of the fear of offending the British sensibilities that the US had to take a rather unhelpful attitude.[73] Roosevelt could hardly fathom Gandhi's tactic of launching the Quit India Movement which he thought was certain to disrupt the War effort. In the American eyes, it was one thing to launch a Civil Disobedience movement in peacetime, and quite another in the midst of a War against fascism. Hopkins told the British diplomat Chambell that Roosevelt remained anxious about India, although he was not sure what could be done. Even if Nehru might say all the right things Roosevelt's Adviser commented : "It would be Gandhi who would decide and we all knew what Gandhi was".[74]

To sum up, a study of Roosevelt's role during the Second World War years remains a tragedy of good intentions self defeated. Despite being sympathetic to India's cause, Roosevelt could not do much. However, it would not be correct to say that Roosevelt was content to remain, in effect, a mute onlooker and to follow a policy of "silence" and "inaction". Overall, Roosevelt's policy and the stand taken vis-a-vis India's struggle for freedom undoubtedly gave a substantial impetus to the nationalist movement. As an Indian scholar put it:

> *In the long run, Roosevelt's concern with the Indian question was bound to accelerate the march towards independence, especially since the concern was shared by non-official opinion.*[75]

India remembers with gratitude Roosevelt's support which sustained her leaders during the national movement.

References

1. *The Public Papers and Addresses of Franklin D. Roosevelt, 1940 Volume, War and Aid to Democracies* (New York, 1941), p. 672.
2. Article 3 of the Charter laid down : "They respect the right of all people to choose the form of government under which they live, and they wish to see sovercign rights and self-government restored to those who had been forcibly deprived of them".

3. *The Public Papers and Addresses of Franklin D Roosevelt, Humanity on the Defensive* (New York, 1942), p. 35.
4. S. Gopal, ed. *Selected Works of Jawaharlal Nehru*, Vol. 12 (New Delhi, 1979), p. 171.
5. Thomas Wilson was appointed the first American Commissioner to India. Sir G.S. Bajpai became the Agent General for India in the United States.
6. *Foreign Relations of the United States* (hereinafter *FRUS*) (1941), Vol. III, pp. 178-81.
7. Roosevelt, *Elliot, As He Saw It* (New York, 1946), pp. 35-37.
8. Winston S. Churchill, *The Hinge of Fate* (Boston, 1950), pp. 208-09.
9. *FRUS*. Vol. I, p. 608.
10. Churchill, op.cit., p. 209.
11. *FRUS*, Vol. I, op.cit., pp. 615-16.
12 Ibid.
13. Nicholas Mansergh, ed. *The Transfer of Power*, Vol. I (London, 1970-1983), pp. 394-95.
14. See Jawaharlal Nehru, An Autobiography, With Musings on Recent Events in India (London, 1942).
15. Mansergh, Vol. 1, op.cit., p. 609.
16. FRUS, Vol. I, op.cit, pp. 626-27, 28.
17. Ibid., pp. 697-98.
18. Mansergh, Vol. I, op.cit., p. 697.
19. Robert S. Sherwood, *Roosevelt and Hopkins* (New York, 1950), p. 524.
20. Ibid.
21. *FRUS*, Vol. I, op.cit., pp. 631-32.
22. Ibid., pp. 633-34.
23. Ibid.
24. Ibid., p. 632.
25. Ibid., pp. 634-35.
26. Mansergh, Vol. II, op. cit, pp. 89-92.
27. Ibid.
28. Ibid., pp. 576-77.
29. *FRUS*, Vol. I, op.cit., pp. 648-49.
30. Ibid., p. 650.
31. Ibid, p. 716.
32. Ibid.
33. S. Gopal, ed. *Selected Works of Jawaharlal Nehru*, Vol. 12, op.cit., p. 378.

34. *FRUS*, Vol. 1, pp. 702-03.
35. Nehru told Lampton Berry of the American Mission in New Delhi : "Let the British Government make a declaration acknowledging the independence of India here and now, and requesting all the various parties in India to get together and form a provisional government. This provisional government, after its formation, would then negotiate with the British Government in the best of goodwill as to how together they could best organise and promote the War effort to the greatest possible extent". It was a clear proof of Nehru's anxiety to avoid a conflict.
36. Maulana Azad, the Congress President, was of a similar view and proposed the following : (1) Let the British make an absolute promise of independence after the War and let the UN or President Roosevelt alone guarantee fulfilment of the promise; and (2) Let the UN or President Roosevelt alone offer to arbitrate the question of an interim settlement and he (Azad) would guarantee that he would get Congress to accept the offer.
37. *FRUS*, Vol. I, op.cit., pp. 690-94.
38. *Congressional Record* (Washington, 1942), Second Session of 77th Congress, Vol. 88, Part 10, pp. A3463-64, A 3841, A3952.
39. Dennis Kux, *Estranged Democracies, India and the United States 1941-1991* (New Delhi/Thousand Oaks/London, 1992), p. 30.
40. *FRUS*, 1943, Vol. IV, pp. 196-97.
41. Ibid., p. 196.
42. Ibid.
43. Ibid., pp. 196-97.
44. William Philips, *Ventures in Diplomacy* (Boston, 1952), pp. 379-80
45. Hess Gary, *America Encounters India, 1941-1947* (Baltimore, 1971), p. 106.
46. *FRUS*. 1943, Vol. IV, pp. 217-20.
47. Ibid., pp. 220-22.
48. Philips, op.cit., pp. 389-90.
49. Ibid.
50. Ibid.
51. M.K.. Gandhi. *My Appeal to the British* (New York, 1942), p. 40.
52. Louis Fischer, *Empire* (New York, 1943), p. 15.
53. Department of State Bulletin. Vol. X, 241, 5 February 1944. p. 145.
54. *FRUS*, 1944, Vol. V, pp. 241-42.
55. *FRUS*. 1943, Vol. IV, p. 486.
56. *FRUS*. 1945, Vol. I, pp. 121-24.
57. *National Herald (Lucknow)*, 28 September 1938.

58. S. Gopal, ed, *Selected Works of Jawaharlal Nehru*, op.cit., p. 200.
59. 1938.
60. April 1940.
61. S. Gopal, *Jawaharlal Nehru* : A Biography, Vol. I (Oxford, 1975), p. 260.
62. M.V. Kamath, *The United States And India 1776-1976* (Embassy of India, Washington, 1976), p. 128.
63. S. Gopal, op.cit., p. 290.
64. Idem, ed, *Selected Works of Jawaharlal Nehru*, Vol. 12, op.cit., pp. 212-13.
65. Ibid.
66. *FRUS*, Vol. I, pp. 636-37.
67. Ibid., pp. 704-07.
68. Ibid., pp. 685-89.
69. Cited in H.S. Gould and Sumit Ganguly, ed, *The Myth and the Reality — US-Indian Relations From Roosevelt to Reagan* (Oxford, 1993), p. 27.
70. Prison Diary, 14 April 1945: S. Gopal, ed. *Selected Works of Jawaharlal Nehru*, Vol. 13, p. 608.
71. S. Gopal, ed, *Selected Works of Jawaharlal Nehru*. Vol. 12.
72. M.S. Venkatramni and B.K. Shrivastava, *Roosevelt, Gandhi and Churchill: America and the Last Phase of India's Freedom* (New Delhi, 1983), pp. 348-49.
73. Cordell Hull, *The Memoirs of Cordell Hull* (New York, 1942), Vol. II, p. 1494.
74. Mansergh, Vol. 11, op. cit., pp. 674-75.
75. Bimal Prasad, *The Origins of India's Foreign Policy : The Indian National Congress and World Affairs, 1885-1947* (Calcutta, 1962).

20
US-Russian Relations

The cold war has ended, but international politics continues. The great threat we faced for 40 years is gone, but the system of relations among sovereign states that makes war possible has not come to an end. The world is still a dangerous place, or it is at least potentially dangerous in a way that has been true for 2,500 years.

Introduction

The danger now, is not the Soviet Union but uncertainty[1]. The unprecedented changes in the international political scene in recent years have led to consequences in the relations among all nation-states and between each nation state and the global system. The earlier assumptions and presumptions, and interpretations of each other's behavior in any particular situation have undergone radical transformation. This necessitates study and analysis of any bilateral relationship with a fresh perspective. The cold war involved a confrontation between the two global super powers that often brought the world to the brink of nuclear disaster. After the end of the cold war, there was a great deal of optimism in the west that Moscow would cease to be a threatening force and would instead become a cooperative member of the international community. Russia's embrace of democratic principles, its cooperative engagement in arms central and its participation in threat reduction efforts fostered the hope that the world would indeed be a much safer place. In an equally important measure from the perspective of the West-Russia embarked upon a policy which stressed good relations with its neighbours. Significantly, Russian troops were withdrawn from Germany, eastern Europe and a number of former Soviet republics. After the emergence of a new Russians state, initially the foreign policy of the new state had a strong pro-western orientation. The then Russian Foreign Minister Anderi Kozyrev, who was a key proponent of this policy, far owned closer relations with the west on both pragmatic and philosophical grounds[2]. Echoing the views of many western experts on international politics, he argued:

The main thing is western countries are pluralistic democracies. Their governments are under the control of loyal public institutions, and these public institutions practically rule out the pursuance of an aggressive foreign policy. In the system of western states the problem of war has essentially been removed[3].

Guides by this perspective, Kozyrev with the strong backing of President Boris Yeltsin, initiated a course whose object was to bury all traces of cold war rivalry and to wing the full support of the west by demonstrating that the new Russian state was fundamentally different from its Soviet predecessor. To this end, Moscow supported sharp cuts in nuclear arms and signed the strategic Arms. Reduction Treaty (START II) which was designed to bring this about. Russia was cooperative at the United Nations, refrained from using its security council veto in May 1992 in favour of western proposals for aiding Serbian expansion in Bosnia. Significantly, Moscow voted for these sanctions despite Russia's traditional ties with Serbia and widespread sympathy in the Russian parliament for Serbia. All these measures were clearly arrived at to indicate that Russia had decisively rejected the anti-western character of Soviet foreign policy and could now be counted as a constructive partner in building of a new post-cold war international order. On the other hand, the window of opportunity for the US to influence reform in Russia opened most widely in the fall of 1991. Both Bush and Clinton Administrations opted to assist rather than contain Russia. Both President Bush and then presidential candidate Bill Clinton pledged to deliver billion of dollars to Russia during the 1992 presidential campaign. Given the 40-year legacy of cold war distrust, rivalry and confrontation, this policy shift was a real achievement. In other words the US-Russian relationship experiences a brief honeymoon.

Cold Peace

However, the honeymoon in East-West relations did not last long. By early 1994, influential figures in Russia and the West were warning of deteriorating relations. For instance, William Parry, the US Secretary of Defense cautioned that even a revival of some new version of the cold war was possible[4]. The question arises what went wrong? What are the prospects for constructive US-Soviet relations? In the first place, by 1993, it became evident that the Russian policy of friendship towards the west was not meeting expectations. The transition - a market economy was proving to be much more difficult than originally envisioned. Despite extravagant grant promises little western aid was actually reaching Russia. Foreign investment in Russia was equally modest. Consequently, Russia's policy was sharply criticized by members of parliament and by various foreign policy experts. It was argued that the Russian government, in its quest for the west's friendship, supported western and especially American policies even when they were not in the Russian national interests. In doing so Russia was no longer behaving as a proud and independent power[5]. Moreover, the critics alleged that the government, in its excessive concern for western goodwill, was neglecting other states that were especially important to Russia, such as China, India, Korea and Saudi Arabia[6]. They argued that more attention should be devoted towards building good relations with these countries and less towards developing links with the west. According to the critics of the pro-western policy of Yeltsin government it had extracted a great price in terms of Russia's international prestige, autonomy and national interest. This storm of protest provoked by Russia's pro-western policy is one reason why this policy began to change by the end of 1992. Besides, a sharp increase in crime and rampant corruption undermined peoples' confidence in the government and weakened its ability to adhere to its original foreign policy agenda. The deterioration of the economy and decline in the standard of living also affected Russian foreign policy. The Yeltsin government was also vulnerable to this criticism because of the deterioration of conditions in the near abroad. Instability and conflict on its borders are of great concern to Russian government. All this provided a strong base for a more assertive Russian foreign policy. The vacillation in Russian policy toward the west was attributed by most American commentators to Russia's Soviet or indeed pre-Soviet imperial legacy. As one commentator put it: Russia can pose a major regional threat if it moves toward reimperialization. This scenario has been dubbed ...Russia, denoting the possibility that, embittered by its economic and political troubles and humiliations, Russia may attempt to recover its past glory by turning to ultranationalist policies, particularly the reincorporation of - or hegemony over- part or all of the odd internal empire the so called Near Abroad[7].

Another important factor which contributed significantly to the cooling of relations between the two countries is the element of deep-rooted instructive hostility. The role of hatred of Russia among the American policy makers and media hardly needs to be overstressed. For them, whenever Russian and American interests clash, Russia is automatically to blame. An interesting example of the Russo phabe school among the US policymaking elite is General William Odom. He summarizes the whole of Russian history as follows: The lesson is clear; liberalism in Russia prospers only after major defeats, and once the regime has regained its self confidence and achieved détente with the west, Russia returns to domestic repression and imperialism[8].

This historicism of summing up hundreds of years of immensely varied national history in this way should be apparent. On the other hand the element of deep-rooted instructive hostility is equally strong the Russian side.

In an age when American foreign policy is increasingly a reflection of domestic politics and electol expenditure, Russia's lack of a consistent lobby in Washington is a serious handicap. On the other hand, a strong domestic constituency in favour of western assistance has failed to emerge in Russia because most people could see little tangible benefit from it in their daily lives. Last but not the least, deep contradictions between Russia and the US in geopolitics and global strategy have always existed. These contradictions have increasingly manifested themselves in serious disputes over major international issues, resulting in US-Russian relations entering a period of so-called "cold peace".

Points of Frictions

The US-Russian relations began to deteriorate due to NATO's eastward expansion, American ambitions in caucasus and Central Asia and airbombing of Yugoslavia, became more tense, due to Russia's sending troops to Chechnya and the US attempt to establish the National Missile Defence System (NMD). It appears pertinent to analyze the impact of all these factors on the US-Russian relationship.

NATO Expansion

Among the areas in which US policies toward Russia constitute a danger to Russia's security and give Russia a genuine cause for concern - is the expansion of NATO. Russian opposition to NATO's expansion into eastern Europe - its old sphere of influence -reflects the complex nature of Russia's current relations with the west. Russia has its own distinctive interests and perspectives which set it apart from the west and prevent it from fully sharing the wests sense of common identity and purpose. The west widely supports the post-cold war continuance of NATO as an instrument of trans-Atlantic cooperation, as a means of keeping the US from disengaging from Europe, as a mechanism for anchoring Germany to the alliance and reassuring its nervous neighbours, as a low-east insurance policy offering protection in a turbulant world. But the Russian perceptions are very different. NATO is viewed with great suspicion as a legacy of the cold war and as an organization which was directed against the erstwhile Soviet Union in the past and might be aimed at Russia in future. From the Russian perspective, the buffer zone between their country and the west narrowed and the NATO alliance is seeking to further strengthen against them. The Russians also perceive that the US is helping France and Germany accomplish that which neither Napoleon nor Hitler could to themselves-extend the borders of Western Europe in the direction of Moscow. From the Russian viewpoint, the US is acting as a defacto European power. By later 1993, Russian opposition to the expansion of NATO was loud and clear. The bitter Russian reaction to NATO expansion stems partly from a belief that the alliance has betrayed promises made when the Soviet government allowed the revolutions in Eastern Europe, and even more importantly, agreed to the reunification of Germany. These included a clear and implicit promise not to expand NATO to include the former Soviet bloc in eastern Europe. The real danger from Russia's point of view is that NATO's east ward expansion would lead it to become embroiled in post-Soviet disputes, and on the side opposite to Russia. NATO had shown its willingness to intervene in other countries conflicts. Significantly, Azerbijan, Georgie and Maldova have suggested NATO's role in Kasov as a model for NATO intervention in their own disputes with separatist regions. Russians have reasons to fear that they or the side they back in a dispute would not get a fair hearing in Washington and that they would be automatically treated as the enemy. Thus, the Russian government firmly opposed the extension of NATO membership to the states of eastern Europe[9]. This strong negative reaction in Russia is indicative of the fact that as much as Russia wants to heal the scars of cold war, to integrate into the international community and to utilize western economic aid and technical know-how, it is still far from being an integral part of the Atlantic community. Russia stand apart from the West because of its historical experiences, its geographical location, its aspirations for the great power status, and the outlook of its influential elites[10]. In response to Russia's strong opposition and because the US and other key NATO members were themselves uncertain as to whether they really wanted to be committed to the defence of new members in the East NATO announced a compromise plan in January 1994 named the Partnership for Peace. The PFP is open to all of the former Soviet Union. However, participation in the PFP offers a junior status well below full NATO membership. There are no firm security commitments and there is no timetable guaranteeing the eventual admission to NATO as a regular member. Russia felt concerned that PFP would serve as a counterweight to Mascow's power in both Central Europe and the Commonwealth of Independent states because its existence would encourage the post-comment States on Russia's border to look westward rather than eastward for security. Finally the PFP was seen as likely to have undesirable consequences for the Russian economy because participation will be encouraged to adopt NATO specifications for their military equipment. This would further reduce the interest of east European countries in Russian arms and thus weaken the already ailing Russian military industry. However, despite these objections to the PFP, the Russian government gradually moved toward joining it. The Russian government evidently decided that the costs of not participating in the PFP outweighed the disadvantages of membership. Attempting to make the best use of a delicate situation, the Russian government eventually announced its unwillingness to join the PFP, provided that NATO agreed to sign a declaration acknowledging Russia's special status as a great power. However, the countries of Eastern Europe strongly objected to anything that would relegate them to second class status and could be taken as a recognition of Russian dominance in the region. Consequently, Russia failed to get the recognition it sought. Eventually on 22 June 1994 an agreement was signed making Russia the 21st member to join the PFP. A watered down statement was also signed which vaguely acknowledged Russia's important role in world affairs but did not confer any special privilege on Moscow[11]. The inordinate delay and the accompanying acrimony and diplomatic wrangling is a vivid reminder of the distance that remains between Russia and the West. Further evidence of this gap is to be found in the voting of 22 June 1994 in the state Duma on a resolution aimed at blocking Russia's membership in the PFP. It failed by only 9 votes[12]. In short, the expansion of NATO has only served to widen the distrust Russia has for the US and to heighten Russia's dependence on nuclear weapons. By expanding NATO the West appears to be treating Russia harshly. This harshness has the potential to harden Russia's resolve to regain its former military stature, especially if future Russian governments were to embrace communism. As Galen Carpenter states in his book, NATO Expansion: Staying out of Europe's Wars": The allies myopic policy of alternately treating democratic Weiner Germany as an international non-entity and as a probable future aggressor led to tragedy. Those who are tempted to take advantage of Russia's weakened position risk causing a similar tragedy[13].

The action to expand NATO only further threatens Russia and cannot be interpreted as encouraging the full participation of Russia in the peace of Europe. In fact, the new NATO does less to ensure peace than the former structure. Russians interpret expansion as an aggressive act and many in the US seem agree with them. For instance, according to Lewis Greddis, Professor of History at Yale University.

Peace settlements work best when they include, rather than exclude former adversaries[14].

By expanding NATO, the US has helped design a world of the past. The current area of NATO expansion - Central Europe is already of no vital interest to the US. This new burden would divert US resources and energies from focussing on security efforts to support engaging markets in Asia. The US is now needlessly obligated to protect more European countries than before and it is not clear what has been gained from this action while a secure Europe is vital to US security and economic well-being, the NATO expansion was not necessary to assure that security.

Chechen Issue

The issue of Chechnya has also become an important factor leading to tension between the US and Russia. Russia regards the issue of Chechnya as between a pretext of American intervention into its internal affairs. It is afraid that this issue will arouse a series of ethnical religious, territorial and resource issues, thus providing more pretexts for the US to interfere in its domestic affairs. After the acceptance of Poland, Hungary and Czech as its members, the NATO has already expanded towards the borders of Russia. At present, the US is engaged in encouraging the Baltic countries to join NATO to enlarge its military presence there in an attempt to narrow down Russian space in its turbulent sphere of influence. Russia is also worried about US intensified penetration into the Caspian and Caucasus regions, rich no oil and gas resources. Undoubtedly, this has piled difficulties for Russia. In the beginning, when Russia launched an attack against the terrorists in Chechnaya, the US immediately expressed concern about it. With the gradual escalation of war, the US media has given enormous publicity to the peoples casualties and the 'humanitarian disaster in Chechnya, Russia and the US sharply disagreed on the issue of Chechnya at the summit meeting of the Organization for Security and Cooperation in Europe held in November 1999. President Clinton openly exerted pressure on Russia and President Yeltsin reacted sternly to it. Russia clearly understand that the US interference in Kasov has constituted a serious threat to Russian interests and intensified instability of Russia and its neighbouring states. Russia believes that the US support of Albanian splittists of Kasov will probably encourage splittists in Russia and other countries of CIS. Furthermore, it is feared that the war in Kasov might become a pattern of US intervention into the conflicts within former Soviet Union and Russian territory. These events would inevitably lead to the tide of a large scale split. Therefore, Russia must suppress the armed splittists in Chechnya. Despite protests and opposition from the West, the new Russian President Putin has repeatedly stressed that the Chechen issue is an internal affair of Russia and engaging in the war in Chechnya is necessary to save the state honour of Russia. This issue and a series of issues arising from it pose a new challenge to the US-Russian relations.

Yugoslavia

Yugoslavia is the hot bed that ignited the first world war. Failure to resolves the Yugoslavian question now will allow it to fester as a potential flashpoint for future armed conflict between Russia and the West. Russia has long viewed the Balkans with avarice for its potential to provide access to the Mediteranian. Russia also has a cultural affinity for the Serbs. Significant differences remain between Russia and NATO in their approaches to the resolution of conflict in the former Yugoslavia. Western policymakers were angry when Moscow suddenly announced in February 1994 that it had reached an agreement with the Serbian forces to send peacekeepers to the hills around Sarajevo, thereby complicating potential air strikes against Serbia artillery by NATO. Fears were expressed that Moscow was once again positioning itself as the supporter of forces opposed to the west. The Russian government does not appear to be motivated by a desire to challenge the West in the former Yugoslavia. As a matter of fact the Russian government was under tremendous pressure to do something to support the Serbs. The NATO operation caused genuine anger in Russia which was reflected in often hysterical rhetoric about NATO genocide". But Russian policy over all was helpful to NATO. Significantly Russia did not supply Yugoslavia with new weaponry by sea. It only moved a symbolic force to Kasov, not its entire Bosnia contingent, and in the end agreed to NATO's terms for its deployment. The Russian position is striking because Kasov provided Moscow the opportunity to try to inflict some damage on NATO. A Russian government as nationalist or anti-western as many American commentrators allege would have encouraged Misoevic to fight on India while it could have compelled NATO to accept a compromise or launch a ground offensive that would have widened existing splits in the alliance. In the end, Russia's behaviour was more that of a discontented US client-state than that of an enemy. The differences between the US and Russia on this issue should be viewed as natural. Even the closest allies have divergent interests and perspectives. Constructive diplomacy can minimize and contain the resulting friction.

Russian Sphere of Influence

One of Russia's key national defence interests is preventing foreign power influence in the security issue of the Commonwealth of Independent States[15]. However, the US opposes the concept of a Russian sphere of influence. For instance Ambassador-at-large and special Advisor to the Secretary of State for the NIS, Stephen Sestanovich testified to the Congress on May 20, 1998: We absolutely reject the idea of a Russian sphere of influence, the reality is that the region will benefit from a cooperative, constructive Russia that trades with its neighbours and that helps to resolve differences with and among countries[16].

By mid 1993, a broad consensus had emerged among Russian policymakers in favour of a kind of Russian Manroe Doctrine. Prodded by influential foreign policy critics, President Yeltsin embraced the view that the entire territory of the former Soviet Union constituted a sphere of vital Russian interest where Russia had a special responsibility for maintaining peace and order. The Russian government went so far as to urge the international community to endorse Russia's role as regional policeman. In a speech on 28 February 1993, President Yelstin declared: Russia continues to have a vital interest in the cessation of all armed conflicts on the territory of the former USSR. Moreover the international community is increasingly coming to realize our country's special responsibility in this difficult matter. I believe the time has come for authoritative international organizations, including the United Nations to grant Russia special powers as guarantor of peace and stability in the region[17].

Specific proposals along these lines were presented by the Russian government to the UN[18]. Needless to say this has been cited by many western commentators as the evidence of continued existence of an imperial mentality in Russia. Significantly, in all regions of the former Soviet Union, the US policy is now devoted to rolling back Russian influence. This trend is acknowledged by American diplomats and has been made explicit by US sponsorship of the GUAM consultative groups of Georgea, Ukarine, Azerbijan and Maldova, which informally links the members of CIS whose interests are opposed to those of Russia. GUAM is intended to function as a kind of counter CIS and has contributed to hardening the desire of that already maribund institution. American backing for GUAM became evident when the agreement by which Uzbekistan joined the group was signed in Washington in April 1999, a date deliberately chosen to coincide with NATO's 50th anniversary summit in the same city. Most worrying for Russia is American support for increased Turkish influence in the region, demonstrated by Washington's advocacy of an oil pipeline from Azerbijan to the Turkish Medeterian part of Ceyhan long after most western oil companies had decided that this route was economically unviable. US policy was originally motivated by a desire to keep a new main route for Azerbijan oil exports out of Russia's hands. Russian fears of Turkey have their roots in the long history of conflict between the two countries. These concerns greatly increased with the realization that Russian conventional forces in the caucasian and Black sea regions were now inferior to those of Turkey. US policy in Causes and Central Asia suggests that the Clinton administration adopted a modified version of the programme advocated by Kussinger Brzezenski of containing and isolating Russia by creating a ring buffer states around its neigbours. The policy of rolling back Russian influence and replacing it with that of US risks drawing America into a local conflict in the former Soviet Union on touching off a war between Turkey and Russia.

Russia's New Military Theory

After the war of Kasov broke out, the Russian Defence Minister repeatedly announced that it would reuse its military theory. Since Putin became Prime Minister, the work to revise this military theory has been expedited. On October 9, 1999, Russia come out with a draft of the new military theory, stressing that the threat of direct aggression against Russia and its allies exists, and that such a threat can be prevented only though active diplomacy and keeping conventional and modern troops on high alert. The threat listed include intervention in Russian internal affairs, disregarding and encroaching on Russian interest while resolving international security issues, preventing Russia from being an influential power in the multipolar world, intentionally weakening the UN and OSCE, taking military actions without the authorization of the UN and in violation of international arms control and supporting extreme national and religious splitting activities within Russia. In early January 2000, Putin approved the concept of Russian state security adopted by the Federal Security Conference. The concept expressed clear opposition to a single power world, and reaffirmed the desire to establish a mutipolar world. The concept also stressed the desire that Russia will play an active role during the process. These announcements clearly illustrate that Russia's main external threat comes from the west.

National Missile Defence System

The US has been pressing Russia to approve amendments to the 1972 Anti Ballistic Minite Treaty (ABM) which out laws any kind of National Missile Defence system (NMD). Washington says it kind of a needs to protect the country from what it calls rogue states. On the other hand, Mascow regards the ABM treaty, which guarantees a balance between Russia and the West, a corneostone of global strategic stability. It has sof far threatened to tear up all arms accords with the US, if Washington went ahead with holding a NMD systems. Moscow has refused to modify the ABM treaty suspecting the Washington, real purpose is to lay the ground work for a later rapid expansion of the defences, which would nullify the deterrent value of Russia's strategic forces.

Of late, the US has clearly expedited the implementation of the National Missile Defence System. The biggest hurdle is the ABM signed by the US and the former Soviet Union in 1972. Therefore, Russia to give up this treaty. Starting in 1999 the US attitude towards abrogating the treaty has undergone great transformation since the end of the cold war. It is argued that the ABM can no longer meet the needs of the former Soviet Union, a signatory party had disappeared. The US has attempted to do away with this treaty by linking its disintegration with economic aid to Russia. The Russian government has always held a disapproving attitude toward various attempts of US intimidation. In November 1999, Moscow announced the successful launching of a short-range intercept missile. This was a warning. On December 1, 1999, Russia together with China and Belarus issued a draft resolution to safeguard and honour the ABM at the UN General Assembly and this draft resolution was passed. With Russia's strength weakening in recent years, the importance of nuclear weapons as a trump eard to safeguard state security and propagate the image of a big power has become an outstanding function. Actually, whether the ABM can be effectively safeguarded or not does not only concern Russian interests but also has a bearing on Russia's international image and stability of political power. On this critical issue, no elected Russian President can easily compromise with the US. Therefore, the sharp conflict between the US and Russia will also become a major factor preventing the development of these bilateral religions in the near future. Significantly, during his visit to Moscow, President Clinton had brought an ultimatum to Moscow. US domestic political pressure in favour of NMD made its deployment inevitable, so either Moscow agreed to his proposal to amend the ABM treaty to allow a limited American NMD directed against 'rogue states', as Washington calls North Korea and Iraq, or it faced the risk of seeing the next US President go for a full-scale missile shield against Russia and China. Moscow's consent to his plan, Clinton argued would boost the prospects of the Democratic Party candidate while its rejection would play into the hands of his Republican party rival George Bush Junior who has been calling far just scrapping the ABM treaty. Russian President Putin's immediate goal at the summit was to persuade President Clinton to defer a final decision to deploy NMD system. And this goal appears to have been accomplished. In their joint statement the two presidents vowed "to continue consultations on ABM Treaty'. Simultaneously Moscow launched a diplomatic offensive to expose Washington's hidden motives in pushing for a missile defense and to rally international opposition to the plan. Putin's startling offer to join hands with the US in holding a common defence against terrorist missiles attacks exposed Clinton's bluff. By predictably turning dawn the Russian proposal the US President unwillingly admitted that an American NMD was designed to shield the US not against 'rogue states' but against Russian and Chinese missiles. Interestingly, soon after Clinton's departure, Putin extended his proposal for a joint nuclear defense to Western Europe. He pointedly did it on a visit to Italy which is a vocal critic of an American NMD. Putin's initiative has no more chance of being accepted in the West than his earlier proposal that Russia join NATO, but its purpose is to stir Europe's concerns that a US missile defense would tigger off an arms race that would leave. Europe defenceless. After all the first thing Russia would do if nuclear arms control collapse would be to redeploy its medium-range missiles targeted at NATO states in Europe. The US pursuit of NMD system could push Russia and China into a closer alliance significantly the joint statement issued after the recent summit between Russian President Putin and Chinese President Jiang Zemrin called on the international community to heed continuously the activities of a certain country (implying the US) to develop a missile defense system which is detrimental to the global strategic balance. In addition to registering their pique at US plans for an anti-missile system for North American and Asia, Russia and China stressed their opposition to international intervention in domestic conflicts on humanitarian grounds. However, like any partnership based more on a common adversary then on shared values, this new type of cooperative relationship between Russia and China is vulnerable to their diverging interests.

Areas of Cooperation

The Kremlin's recent threat to bomb Taliban bases in Afghanistan was at least partly meant to demonstrate Russia's willingness to forge a common front with the west against Islamic extremism. The armed conflict of Afghanistan and Taliban sponsored terrorism was central to the joint discussion between the deputy foreign minister of Russia A.P. Lasynkor and the US Deputy Secretary of State Karl Inderfurth on May

25-26, 2000. The necessarily of strict fulfilment of the resolution and declaration of the UN on the political regularization of the Afghan crisis was stressed by both sides. Interestingly, it was agreed that: "If Kandhar were to ignore the opinion of world community, this would necessitate review of further measures by the Security council of the UN.

The joint declaration expressed "concern over the growing influence of extremist groups in Pakistan threatening the internal stability of the country". Both urged the Taliban to transfer Osama Bin Laden "into the hands of justice" and to take accelerated steps to dismantle the terrorist infrastructure functioning in the territory under its control. Russia joined the US in emphasising the need for both India and Pakistan to demonstrate restraint, reject violence and respect the line of control in Kashmir as "inalienable elements" to stabilize the situation in the region. The moratorium on conducting nuclear Tests in South Asia was taken note during the discussion with both Russia and the US agreeing that New Delhi and Islamabad should continue their efforts toward signing the CTBT as an important step related to the non-permissibility of nuclear and missile arms race in the region. In an attempt to win the Wests trust, President Putin pushed through the Russian parliament ratification of START II nuclear arms treaty with the US and CTBT. Overruling objections from the Russian military, Putin renewed Russia's contracts with NATO freezed after the Alliance's attack on Yugoslavia. On the other hand, faced with the prospect of prolonged instability, ethnic conflict, and a power vaccum that might allow inroads by outside countries on the forces of radical Islam, many in the west do not appear averse to Russia taking on the role of regional policeman. So long as Russia acts with circumspection, securing the consent of relevant governments wherever possible and using a minimum of force the US and other western countries are prepared to accept Russian predominance in the region. In effect, a tacit understanding appears to be emerging between Russia and the West. A measure of Russia's cooperation with the west is not only dictated by a sober and patriotic assessment of Russian interests and Russian weaknesses. It is also implicit in the nature of the contemporary Russian state, economy and society and above all in the interests of Russia's ruling elites. Russia's elites are loath to endanger their interests by allowing Russia to engage in a major clash with the west. Significantly, the main threat to the continuation of a constructive relationship between Russia and the west does not arise in the realm of foreign policy but from the explosive situation within Russia. The economic crisis there continues to deepen, law and order are breaking down and there is real danger that the continued deterioration in the population's standard of living may lead to an upsurge of anger against the west for supposedly foisting and alien unworkable economic programme on Russia. The US and other leading western states need to do what they to avoid fuelling an anti-western backlash. Foreign assistance is vital but it is also essential to avoid giving offence to Russian self-respect and appearing to dictate painful measures.

New Russian Leadership

During his visit to Russia President Clinton discovered a major change of mood in Mascan. Gone were the days when a personal relationship between "friend Bill" and "friend Baris" was sometimes a decisive factor at US-Russian summits. President Clinton met an assertive and pragmatic President Putin, a tough negotiator determined to ensure that Russia is treated as an equal partner. Putin demonstrated Moscow's new negotiating style and a new foreign policy agenda that calls for building constructive relations with the west without sacrificing the country's national interests. Putin had publicly stated that Russia will greatly develop its defense industry in order to improve its own economic situation. He also pledged to further increase defense expenditures in order to deal with threats from home and abroad. In another statement Putin said that Western democracy is not suitable for Russia and he would lead Russia dawn the third road of not blindly believing western liberation and pursuing communism anew. Last but not the least in a speech delivered after his assuming the post of acting President, Putin hinted that Russia is deeply worried about the US being a huge power in the world. He said that Moscow will strive to establish a multipolar world. All this is indicative of the fact that Russia under the leadership of Putin would take a tougher stand against the west.

US Policy - An Overview

From the above, it becomes evident that the US is offering Russia a relationship in which Moscow is eventually bound by many of the constraints on its international behaviour expected by members of NATO without receiving NATO style security guarantees in return. This implies acceptance of NATO expansion to include those members west decides shall become makers; acquiescence to US policy in Kosov and Bosnia; acceptance of US abrogation of the 1972 ABM Treaty, thereby greatly diminishing the effectiveness of Russia's nuclear deterrent, acceptance of US term governing relations with Iran, Iraq, North Korea and other US-declared rogue states even when this means considerable trade losses for Russia; severe limits on Russia's arms trade; acceptance of the US as sole mediator in the West Asian peace process; acceptance of US decisions concerning various aspects of trade with other sates, and acquiescence to a growing role for the US and American strategies in other states of the former Soviet Union in terms set by the US. Finally, of course, it implies a complete abandon of the former Soviet role in Central America. In other words, it means a subordinate role for Russia in an American dominated European security system. From Russian perspective, the US had defined Russia as the enemy. All other efforts well disguised, to convince Russia to the contrary failed to change this basic fact. Russia has learned to distrust the US. Under the circumstances, it would be illogical for Russia to accept partnership with the US - a euphemism for full acceptance of US domination of Russia's foreign policy. Russia cannot simply accept American terms for relations between the two countries. This refusal is partly because of national sentiments but more importantly because the US eventually demands from Russia subjection and obedience without providing added defense and security. Any stable hegemonic system protection and advancement in return for service. Russia receives no direct security in return for the retreats and concessions it has made. No nation would willingly agree to sacrifice its interests even if it is for the sake of humanity on terms dictated by another power in its own interests.

A country that simply seeks to gain acceptance of all its interests is not engaged in diplomacy but bullying and the response will be not a desire for compromise but anger and resistance. To understand the depth of Russians anger at recent American policies, it is worth remembering that Russian believe they have already made an immense sacrifice and humane international order, and a 'common European home'. This sacrifice was called the abandonment of the Soviet bloc and the Soviet Union itself.

American Apprehension

Many in America fear that the new Russian government would retreat from democracy and return to embrace communism. It is also feared that Russia would retreat from its cooperative policies on nuclear arms control and non-proliferation. The US is also concerned that Russia would attempt to reestablish its control over its former empire. It is argued that Russia is still capable of conducting an all-out nuclear attack on the homeland of the US. However, the facts are otherwise. Since its defeat in Chechnya, Russia has been revealed to be militarily too weak even to intimidate most of its smaller neigbours, let alone the mighty US. As Kasou amply demonstrated, Soviet-era military technology is no match for US technological superiority. Russia appears incapable of seriously harming American interests. The only alliance that could cause serious harm to the US would be between Russia and China. However, a full anti-American, Sino-Russian alliance is unlikely to materialize. China's prospects for economic growth and prosperity are crtiically dependent on access to the American market, which vastly outweighs any possible economic advantages of links with Rusia. And for Moscow, the west, not China, is both the crucial market for Russia;s exports of raw materials and the source of outside investment. Secondly, while the US does not have any potential claim on Russian territory, Russia and China have serious territorial disputes. The treaties of Argun and Peking by which Russia acquired hundreds of thousands of square miles of Chinese territory north of the Amur River and east of the Ussuri river, are the last of the nineteenth century "unequal treaties" to remain in force. Thus, if Russia were to become a junior partner in a Chinese-led anti-American alliance, it would be humilating and dangerous.

Need for a New American Strategy

Russia in 2005 is not the same as Russia in 1992. It is high time for the US to recast its policy toward Russia in a manner that avaids the mistakes of the past and capitalizes on the opportunities of future. As the conditions within Russia and the challenges facing it change, US policy-makers must rethink some basic assumptions and redesign their policies accordingly. Disagreements over Iraq, Iran or Serbia; past failures regarding aid programmes, and tensions between Russia and America are arguments not for abandoning engagement but for rethinking and reinvigorating it. The bases of the US strategy of engagement with Russia were sound. The challenge before the US it to work to regain Russia's trust, not exacerbate its mistrust. It is in the US national interest that Russia have a strong economy, enter into the community of nations, as a nation with political, economic and military standing, and be a force for stability in the region, rather than anarchy and destabilization. America should bear in mind that the first government to emerge following the Russian revolution was a democratic one. had that government survived, the US might have been able to avoid the 15 tri billion cost of the nuclear arms race. The plight of Russian economy is miserable. Russia desperately needs to make radical reforms in its economy US aid to Russia should be sustained at higher levels and private investments should increase. Sustained funding for economic support to Russia could be obtained from the savings that would accure from not expanding NATO further. A healthy economy is critical to Russia's transition to reliance on conventional military force, rather than nuclear and also to balance China's growing military and economic strength in the region and the world. A new American regional strategy toward Russia is the need of hour. Since stability in Eurasia and Central Asia is vital to US national interests of defending the homeland, enhancing its economic well-being, maintaining a stable world order, and promoting democratic values. Given the more intense and better understood threats, a review of existing US policy towards Russia is warranted.

Conclusion

The euphoria that accompanied the end of cold war and the birth of new Russia has long since dissipated. The end of the cold war was supposed to lead to the integration. Instead it has led to further division. There is no denying the fragility of current East-West relations. The honeymoon did that last long. It has been replaced by a mature recognition of the importance of sustaining the relationship through improved communication understanding of each others viewpoint and hard work. In June 1992, President George Bush and Boris Yeltsin solemnly affixed their signatures to a document on mutual relations entitled the "Charter for American Russian Partnership and Friendship" and the term partnership has been widely used ever since. However, continued disagreements between Russia and the west make it clear that such talk is, at least, premature. Yet, if the term partnership is misleading because it suggests a much more harmonious relationship than in fact exits on the ground. It would be equally mistaken to view Russia as an adversary or enemy in the way that the Soviet Union was during the cold war days Today, Russia is less than a partner but much more than an adversary. President Clinton rightly summed up US-Russian relations at the end of his visit to Moscow in these words. We are not destined to be adversaries but it is not guaranteed that one will be allies.

References

1. Jeff Chackel, "Russian Foreign Policy: Back to the Future?", RFE/RL, *Research Report,* 16 December 1992, pp. 20-26.
2. *Izvestia, 2* January 1992, as translated in *Current Digest of Post-Soviet Press 44,* February 1992, p. 22.
3. *New York Times,* 15 March 1994.
4. Vera Talz, *Russia,* "Westernization continues to challenge National Patriots", RFE/RL, *Research Report,* 11 December 1992, pp. 1-9.
5. Sergei Stankevich, "Russia in search of itself", *National Interest,* No. 28 (Summer 1992), p.p. 47-51; Valadimir P. Lukin, "Our Security Predicament", *Foreign Policy,* No. 88 (Fall 1992), p.p. 57-75.
6. The Near Abroad includes Estonia, Latvia and Lithuania, Belarus, the Ukarine, the Caucasus, and the Central Asian States of Kazakhstan, Tajikistan, Kyrgyzstan, Uzbekistan and Turkmenistan.
7. Zalmay Khalilzad, "Losing the Moment? The United States and the World order After the Cold War", *Strategy and Force Planning,* Naval War College Press.
8. Dimitri K Simes, "Russia's Crisis, America's Complicity", *National Interest,* Winter 1998-1999.
9. Suzanne Crow, "Russia asserts its Strategic Agenda", RFE/RI, Research Report, December 1993, p.2.
10. *New York Times,* 23 June 1994.
11. RFE/RL, *Daily Report,* No. 118, 23 June 1994.
12. Cited in Kathleen T.O'Halloham, "A New US Regional Strategy Toward Russia", *Strategic Review,* Summer 1999, p. 60.
13. Lewis Gaddis, "The Senate should Halt NATO Expansion", *New York Times,* 27 April 1998.
14. Cited in Kathleen T.O'Halloharn, *Strategic Review,* p. 58.
15. Cited in Suzanne Crow, RFE/RL, *Research Report,* December 1993.
16. Ibid.
17. See Zbignew Brzezenski, *The Grand Chessboard; American Primacy and Its Geostrategic Imperatives,* New York, 1997.
18. *Asian Age,* May 27, 2000.

an adversary. President Clinton rightly summed up US-Russian relations at the end of his visit to Moscow in these words: "We are not destined to be adversaries, but, it is not guaranteed that (we) will be allies."

References

1. Jeff Checkel, "Russian Foreign Policy: Back to the Future?", RFE/RL Research Report, 16 December 1992, pp. 21-22.
2. *Izvestiya*, 3 January 1992, as translated in *Current Digest of Post-Soviet Press*, 12 February 1992, p. 22.
3. *New York Times*, 13 March 1993.
4. Vera Tolz, Russia: Westernization continues to challenge National Identity, RFE/RL *Research Report*, 11 December 1992, pp. 1-9.
5. Sergei Stankevich, "Russia in search of itself", *National Interest*, No. 28 (Summer 1992), pp. 47-51; Vladimir P. Lukin, "Our Security Predicament", *Foreign Policy*, No. 88 (Fall 1992), pp. 57-75.
6. The Near Abroad includes Estonia, Latvia and Lithuania, Belarus, the Ukraine, the Caucasus, and the Central Asian States of Kazakhstan, Tajikistan, Kyrgyzstan, Uzbekistan and Turkmenistan.
7. Zalmay Khalilzad, "Losing the Moment? The United States and the World order After the Cold War", *Strategy and Force Planning*, Naval War College Press.
8. Dimitri K. Simes, "Russia's Crisis, America's Complicity", *National Interest*, Winter 1998-1999.
9. Suzanne Crow, "Russia asserts its Strategic Agenda", RFE/RL Research Report, December 1993, p.2.
10. *New York Times*, 12 June 1994.
11. RFE/RL, *Daily Report*, No. 118, 23 June 1994.
12. Cited in Kathleen T.O. Halloran, "A New US Regional Strategy Toward Russia", *Strategic Review*, Summer 1994, p. 40.
13. Lewis Dudde, "The Senate should Halt NATO Expansion", *New York Times*, 27 April 1998.
14. Cited in Kathleen T.O. Halloran, *Strategic Review*, p. 38.
15. Cited in Suzanne Crow, RFE/RL, *Research Report*, December 1994.
16. Ibid.
17. See Zbigniew Brzezinski, *The Grand Chessboard, American Primacy and its Geostrategic Imperatives*, New York, 1997.
18. *Asian Age*, May 27, 2000.

21

US Strategy in Central Asia

Inaugurating the Central Asian Institute at the John Hopkins School of Advanced Studies, Washington in October 1996, James F. Collins, Special Advisor to the Secretary for the New Independent States defined the US objectives in the Central Asian region as follows:

1. Support for the independence, sovereignty and security of each of the Central Asian states.
2. Assistance in the establishment of free market economies and democratic governments committed to equal opportunity and human rights for their citizens.
3. Integration of these states into the world community of political and financial institutions as well as their participation in the Euro-Atlantic security dialogues and co-operation programmes.
4. Encouragement of these states to pursue peaceful relations among themselves and with their neighbours for regional cooperation and to resolve local conflicts with international mediation.
5. Prevention of any trafficking in weapons of mass destruction or their elements across the region or the borders.
6. Enhancement of US commercial interest and the expansion and diversification of global energy supplies.

The highest American priority, however, was to denuclearize these Central Asian states in exchange for political, diplomatic and economic support. In this respect Washington cooperated with these states to dismantle and transport fissile material to the US. The departure of the last nuclear warhead from Kazakastan in 1995 was a significant achievement in support of non-proliferation.

The US appears to be taking keen interest in defining the interests, goals and strategies of Central Asian states. It roped in all the five republics into partnership for peace and organization for security and cooperation in Europe. By admitting the Central Asian states into the NATO membership and the Conference on Security and Cooperation in Europe (CSCE) process, Washington is not only seeking to enlarge the European Security complex but also intends to provide fresh mechanisms to address Central Asian security concerns. Turkey has been pushed in this regard by Washington as an anchor to encourage the programme of cooperation and engagement with these states.

The promotion of democracy and free market are among the principal objectives of the US Administration. According to Strobe Talbott, the former Deputy Secretary of State, political and economic reforms in Central Asia would contribute to stability in a strategically vital region that borders China, Turkey, Iran and Afghanistan and that has growing economic and social ties with Pakistan and India. It is increasingly in the US interest to encourage that development of stable, democratic systems and market economies in these news states and to minimize the social, ethnic, religious and other sources of conflict that could destabilize the region.

While numerous US programmes have had a beneficial impact, other initiatives have been criticised by locals as patronizing the very governmental structure, which are in need of reform. The US efforts have been subjected to criticism for viewing democratic and market reform as something to be imposed from the top. Despite the stated commitment of the US to expand the role of grass-root efforts, US-Central Asian partnerships in small non-governmental organization (NGOs) have played a relatively minor role in overall assistance programmes.

As US assistance networks are expanded there, they must be restructured to take account of population whose support for reform may be more complex and ambivalent than observers may have thought previously. The US efforts must be sensitive not only to the social safety nets, cultural values and traditions of Central Asia but also to the uniquely evolved mixture of Soviet and Middle Eastern political and economic systems in these new countries, which may be quite different from other parts of the world. Americans must understand that it is possible to encourage democracy in the Muslim world without establishing themselves as enemies of Islam. The fear of Islamic fundamentalism that seemed to drive so many of the US initial efforts in Central Asia has also been viewed as leaving a destructive legacy that may have only encouraged the growth of this fundamentalism.

Central Asia's enormous resources made the region increasingly attractive to the US business community. The region has been identified as one of the most promising unexplored oil-rich regions in the world. The $20 billion Chevron oil venture with Kazakastan and the western consortium to exploit the oil fields in the Caspian sea are among the world's largest and particularly most lucrative oil and gas ventures, and the number of other US companies seeking opportunity for entry into this field has grown exponentially in the past few years. Besides exploiting oil and gas deposits, the US companies are seeking influence in Uzbekistan, Kyrghgyzstan and Tajikistan, whose vast deposits of gold appear to be more lucrative than oil.

With these parameters, American's interests in Central Asia's stable development are vital. Domestic stability of all five states is a policy goal of the US. Conflict resolution is a prerequisite for any successful energy development plans to be executed there in the region. Any conflict there would have profound repercussion on the US commercial interests. However, with slashes in foreign aid, the scope for direct US governmental programmes aimed at supporting Central Asian states economically and politically is limited. Given the limits on its foreign aid, Washington will have to encourage its European and Asian partners to take leading roles.

The primary focus of the US should be on legal and technical assistance in tackling issues such as environmental protection, drug-control and weapons proliferation. The US can also channel its efforts through international organizations that provide social progress such as refugee relief, health-care and family planning. Particularly useful US roles might include providing technology and skills especially in dry land agricultural technologies such as drip-irrigation that could reduce water use and help farmers shift from cotton production to a more balanced agriculture. One of Central Asia's most crucial needs is to train experts who can play neutral roles in the transition to market economies and democratic political systems. Unmatched US capacities in higher education could be especially useful.

To sum up, the US as the sole remaining super power has great stakes in Central Asia. The first challenge for a constructive US role in Central Asia is to bring American attention to the region. The responsibility and care that the US attention to Central Asia demands at the moment can only come from foreign policy experts and not form public forces driven by market mechanisms. It is absolutely necessary for the US policy makers to respond to the basic aspirations of all the Central Asians. An effective US policy must seek to address their aspirations as central goals, rather than suggesting that the Central Asia's main concern is to check the Iranian influence.

Last but not the least, the prevailing tendency to lump all the Central Asian states together as one entity should be discarded. All these states are anything but homogeneous. The fact that all of them once belonged to the same now-defunct-communist superpower is surely not reason enough to pretend that they are of equal importance to the US. Differentiation among them is a necessity. The US policy should be oriented towards each of the individual states and not to all of them as a whole. The real challenge to the US is to correctly assess the American interests in the region. The US has to formulate a policy towards the region, which should be based on quest for real solution.

22
Changing U.S. Priorities in Central Asia

A mix of oil, ethnic conflict, Islamic resurgence and strategic location between Russia, China, South Asia and West Asia makes Central Asia extremely pivotal as a geo-strategic region. The US as the sole super power wants to control this region because of its rich resources and strategic location.

U.S. Interests

After the Soviet retreat from Central Asia, the region is in a great strategic and ideological vacuum. The US now feels that it would lose strategically to Iran in the region, should the latter succeed in establishing its foothold there. The prime US Security concern about Central Asia was the existence of enormous stockpiles of nuclear weapons and enriched uranium. The immediate concern of US centered around the possible leakage of nuclear weapons and fuel from these republics to potential recipients like Iran. The first US priority was to denuclearize this region in exchange of US political, economic and diplomatic support. Last but not the least, the enormous economic potential of Central Asia made the region quite important for the US too. The region has been identified as one of most promising unexplored oil regions in the world. It has become even more important for the US policy markers in view of the growing US dependence on oil imports from this region.

Thus the initial move of the US in Central Asia, after the break up of Soviet Union, was a modest and cautious one. Significantly, independence came to Central Asia at a time when the US researchers and analysts were warning about a fundamental confrontation between the Islamic world and the western world. The debate in the US even suggested that a conflict between the western and Islamic world might replace the cold war and that the two might compete to determine Central Asia's future. And quite in line with such hypotheses, gradually, the US developed an interest in the region, following the apprehensions of possible Islamisation of the new states.

Keeping all these factors in view, by mid-1994, the US has formulated its specific policy for this region. It now regards Central Asia as a region of vital strategic significance for the US. Apart from the geo-strategic dimension of the region as the gateway to West Asia, East Asia, South Asia, and Russia, the vast natural resources are seen to be of utmost strategic importance for the US. The twin goals of the US policy in Central Asia have been spelt out as: to encourage democratic values, and to introduce market economy. To maintain a policy of enlargement and engagement, the US has established political stability, regional peace and the maturation of market economies as policy goals for the Central Asian states.

Turkey and Pakistan as Strategic Levers

The US has sought to involve Turkey's cultural, linguistic and ethnic influence alongwith its Islamic heritage, for leverage in Central Asia. The factors that place Turkey in an advantageous position, amongst other regional powers are the close historic, linguistic, cultural and ethnic ties it shares with several of the Central Asian republics. It is thus easier for Turkey to present itself as a more authentic actor in the region than any other state. Besides Turkey, Pakistan is also acting as a tool of the US machinations in Central Asia. Pakistan's close proximity to Central Asian states makes it imperative for the US to boost Pakistan militarily in order to make it a spring-board for its plans in the region. The US regards Pakistan as potentially a major stabilising factor in Central Asia. Significantly, Pakistan is carefully pursuing the possibility of piping natural gas supply from Turkmenistan through Afghanistan. Consequently, piping oil along the same route could also supply oil to the US, reducing its reliance on the Gulf oil. If the US wants to have economic access to Central Asia, there could be an effective land route through Jammu and Kashmir as well. In the context of the US policy in Central Asia, as stated by experts like Dr. Kissinger, the inescapable conclusion is that the US would like to take advantage of the centrifugal political trends in Jammu and Kashmir to further its own interests in the Central Asian region.

The US as the only remaining super power has great stakes in Central Asia. The heightened US interest in the region is chiefly due to the growing competition for influence in this part of the world by other interested powers. Resolution of the conflicts in the region and the promotion of democracy and free market are the principal objectives of the Clinton Administration and the US policy makers seem to be trying their best to define the interest, goals and strategies of Central Asian states.

The Nuclear Non-Proliferation Issue

A careful analysis of the US policy towards Central Asia reveals that in order to denuclearize the region, the US played its cards adroitly. On 23 May 1992, the US signed the Lisbon Protocol which dealt with the Strategic Arms Reduction Treaty (START) with Kazakhstan, Russia, Belarus and Ukraine (those states on whose territory strategic nuclear weapons of the former Soviet Union are located). In December 1993, Kazakhstan ratified the Nuclear Non-Proliferation Treaty (NPT). On 13 December 1993, the US and Kazakhstan signed an umbrella agreement that provided the legal framework for the provision of funds for the Safe and Secure Dismantling (SSD) of nuclear weapons. In March 1994, an additional agreement was signed to assist in the process of converting defence industries to industries for civilian purposes. The departure of the last nuclear head in 1995 from Kazakhstan was a significant achievement in support of non- Proliferation

The Lure of Oil and Gold

So far as exploitation of the economic potential of Central Asia is concerned, US companies like *Chevron* have already moved into Kazakhstan to exploit its oil resources. Besides exploiting oil and gas deposits, the US companies are seeking influence in Uzbekistan, Kyrghizstan and Tajikistan, whose vast deposits of gold appear to be more lucrative than oil. In February 1997, the *USOPIC* investment corporation announced its decision to insure the US *Newmont Gold Company* operating in Uzbekistan against political risks. The *Intertech* which happens to be the largest gold producing company of the US has established itself in the Kyrgiz gold business. An effort is being made to export a market oriented economy and culture. As a part of this, new projects are being floated with American technology and financial assistance.

23

US-China Axis : Implications for India

The significance of Sino-US relations has been emphasised several times by President Clinton terming it the most important relationship that the US maintains with any country on the face of the earth. Beijing is Washingtons newest strategic partner and the new flavour is broad-based engagement in political/economic/military spheres and vigorous endorsement of Beijing as the second pillar of stability in the post-cold war period. The US policy towards China can be summed up as deep engagement and active endorsement.

Reasons for Proximity

Interestingly, it is the same China that Clinton denounced during 1992 election campaign and accused George Bush of pursuing a policy that continues to coddle aging rulers with undignified contempt for democracy, for human rights and the need to control the spread of dangerous weapon ideologues". However, after entering the White House he felt convinced that the two countries would be better off working together than apart. What could be the reasons for President Clinton's so insistently vociferously pro-China tilt? One reason may be that Clinton is in some way beholden to China, and is under the threat of exposure by those who support China. According to the US media reports Clinton Administration's China policy is motivated by contracts or even illegal campaign donations. The alleged campaign donations from Beijing as well as by American aerospace company Loral space and communications had forced it to ignore illegal Chinese transfers of sensitive nuclear and missile technology to countries like Pakistan and Iran. Secondly, commercial interests seem to be Washington's overriding consideration. China's clout in international affairs comes from its economic strength. US is dependent on China in a variety of ways. Apart from a massive trade imbalance which American companies are anxious to remedy by cornering the huge Chinese market for themselves, US firms would also like to exploit China's potential as a destination for investment. Moreover, China has enormous financial clout and cannot be dictated in the way other Asian countries have been. As a result of its economic strength, China has the political ability to sustain an autonomous security policy in defiance of non-proliferation concerns of the US. Last but not the least, president Clinton who is halfway through his second and last presidential term, appears to be increasingly obsessed with his imprint on presidency and on American history. He feels, therefore, that he has to do something dramatic. China is big enough and potentially great enough to enable Clinton to have his place in history, if he could turn Beijing around to be a partner and honest friend. Clinton believes that gradual democratization of China and its trade links with Washington may convert the yellow peril into a golden friendship.

US is dependent on China in a variety of ways. Apart from a massive trade imbalance which American companies are anxious to remedy by cornering the huge Chinese market for themselves, US firms would also like to exploit China's potential as a destination for investment. Moreover, China has enormous financial clout and cannot be dictated in the way other Asian countries have been. As a result of its economic strength, China has the political ability to sustain an autonomous security policy in defiance of non-proliferation concerns of the US.

Domestic political compulsion for the ruling elite as recommended by special customers and domestic interests groups are increasingly shaping foreign policy options thereby eroding the inviolability of the once sacred long term interest which is now subservient to primacy of market forces. Thus, President Clinton who lambasted George Bush's China policy as "mollycoddling dictators" now feels that sanctioning China might backfire if Beijing retaliated. Thousands of American export jobs could be lost would have tarnished his presidency Clinton argues that despite differences the US cannot turn its back on China, the world's most populous nation, a growing military power with an economy expected to be the largest in the world within the next half century. US relations with China, according to Clinton, will in large measure help to determine whether the new century is one of security, peace.

Implications for India

The strategic partnership between Washington and Beijing has stirred up anxieties in other Asian countries including India. Its impact is being felt throughout the region and beyond. India bristles at the hegemonistic mentality behind the US-China axis. It has a significant impact for India by way of redefining its geo-political space and deeper strategic interests.

There seems to be a deliberate attempt on the part of the US to let China become a decisive say in matters relating to South Asia as was obvious form P-5 meeting at Geneva. President Clinton remarked on the eve of P-5 meeting. "Let me now express my appreciation to China for chairing the P-5 meeting. This is further evidence of the important role China can play in meeting the challenges of the 21st century, and the constructive Chinese leadership that will be essential to the long term resolution of issues involving South Asia". In his speech of the National Geographic society President Clinton said that China had a key role to play in the resolution of problems between India and Pakistan. Close on the heels of Clinton's remarks came the G-8 meeting on nuclear tests at London for which is a calculated insult to India, China was also invited to contribute her views mainly at the instance of the US. After the G-8 had in effect punished India and intervened in favour of Pakistan by proposing to constitute task force on Kashmir Clinton decreed that China will have a policing role in South Asia. Much to the dismay of India, Clinton during his China visit went on to display a strange addiction to engaging with China, despite ground realities in that country that went beyond all cherished principles of America. Clinton's suggestion that China should intervene in diplomatic parleys to resolve the Kashmir dispute has further complicated already tense Sino-Indian relations. It is well known on whose side Beijing has been so far in the pre and post nuclear scenario. Significantly Chinese spokesman joined hands with the White House spokesman Mike Mccurry saying that China was concerned that a pro-active policy against Pakistan, if it continued to train and arm Kashmiri militants. Clinton's suggestion reveals a hidden agenda. Taken together, it is clear that the US is trying its best to whitewash China's role in proliferation of missiles and nuclear weapon components to Pakistan. Clinton is equating Chinese along with Pakistani security interests vis-a-vis American one.

The shifting pattern of accommodation and contention between the US, the principal global hegemon and China, its most important challenger will help determine the contours of the Asian and world order well into next century. The crucial issue of the US-China relationships is whether it will contribute to peace and stability in Asia and enable accommodation of China in a democratic global order. The US preference for dealing with China in a bipolar framework overlooking the need to embed China in a balance of power in Asia in the primary concern of Asian nations.

The emerging US-China axis in Asia has became the main foreign policy task for India. Containing India is a key part of strategy aimed at ensuring Chinese hegemony over Asia. US and China share a give and take relationship. America recognizes Beijing's influence in Asia in return for not challenging America's global role. For India which regards China's rise to be the principal challenge, the US strategy is dangerous because it is built around the same objective of dominating Asia. US is unwilling to focus on China's proliferation aid to Pakistan which hurts Indian security interests. As in 1971, India has to deal with an US-China-Pakistan axis with possible Chinese hegemonism tacitly backed by the US.

The shifting pattern of accommodation and contention between the US, the principal global hegemon and China, its most important challenger will help determine the contours of the Asian and world order well into next century. The crucial issue of the US-China relationships is whether it will contribute to peace and stability in Asia and enable accommodation of China in a democratic global order. The US preference for dealing with China in a bipolar framework overlooking the need to embed China in a balance of power in Asia in the primary concern of Asian nations. While US engagement with China is the right policy in a poly-centric Asia, exclusive bipolar engagement to the neglect of a stable balance of power among US, Japan, Russia, China and India will not serve long term US interests.

24
Indo-Canadian Relations into the 21st Century

India and Canada share a lot of things in common. Both the countries arc multicultural and multiethnic societies their roots in the constitutional law and political structure are very much the same, both are federal states and are governed by a parliamentary system of governance: both of them have been classified as middle powers both of them have general traditions of liberalism and both as key centres of their regions have special responsibility[1] towards their respective regions.

Historic Backup

In the early years, there was a fundamental convergence in the approach to international affairs between New Delhi and Ottawa, on such issues as the Commonwealth, the United Nations and the situation in Asia. Leaders of both countries saw themselves as representatives of middle powers who were interested in influencing international affairs in a constructive manner. They shared an identity of perceptions on the need to enhance relations between Asia and the West, to promote multilateral organisations and to foster Third World development. Canada became 'involved in the Indian subcontinent because of the Kashmir dispute. Canada's relationship with India intensified because of a common middle power perspective which led the two nations to cooperate in the Commonwealth of Nations. The 1950s and 1960s was the period of intense Canadian involvement in South Asia, as security concerns like containment of China coincided with humanitarian assistance considerations. The lack of congruency which surfaced over issues like Korea. Indo-China and Hungry transformed a once special relationship between India and Canada into one characterized by ambivalence.[2] The 1970s saw retrenchment in Asia by Canada. During P. Trudeau Administration Africa rather than Asia became focus of Canadian aid effort which adversely affected Indo-Canadian. ties further. The indignation felt by Canada, at the Indian detonation of an atomic device produced with Canadian nuclear materials marked an obvious low points in bilateral relations. Canada's interest in South Asia rekindled in 1980s because of the Soviet intervention, in Afghanistan confict in the Persian Gulf, concern about nuclear proliferation and issues related to immigration and 'terrorism' originated from the subcontinent. It took the bombing of an Air India plane with considerable loss of Canadian life to once more focus Ottawa's attention on South Asia.

Post-Cold War Scenario

Fundamental changes in the international system have made it obligatory for every nation to review its foreign policy postures. Each country, super power or regional power has to adopt its policy to the new agenda of the impending era with its special economic, social and environmental challenges. Any bilateral relationship is bound to be affected and influenced by the changing global scenario. Indo-Canadian ties cannot be an exception. This relationship has to be adjusted in the light of spectacular transformation of international relations. As grand realities that determined the Indo-Canadian relations have changed, bilateral relations between the two countries have to be restructured. With the end of the cold war, the Canadian and Indian policy-makers are called upon to re-evaluate their bilateral relations in view of the rapidly, changing international situation. In the 'Cold War' period American factor dominated the India-Canada relations. Both had to contend with their differing views of the American role in global politics. In .the post-cold war period however that problem has been dissolved. In an increasingly integrated globe India and Canada have a new relationship to determine. In the rapidly evolving post-cold war world, there has been a broadening of the security agenda to encompass non-traditional threats to. security issues such, as poverty, crime, pollution, terrorism, narcotics trafficking, diffusion of weapons in society and other non-military threats. For both states, this in turn raises the problem as to how such international threats can be accommodated within the current global and regional multilateral frameworks and what types of reforms might be necessary to address these challenges.

People to People Contact

People to people relation is conditioned by the fact that there are four hundred thousand people in Canada who originally came from the Indian subcontient.[3] This social connection is now becoming more politicized. Ottawa's interest in South Asia stems from the fact that the Indian subcontinent is Canada's leading source of immigrants. The Indo-Canadian population offers a basis for contacts between the two countries and if Canada maintains a reasonable open immigration policy, the exchange increase further. In the 21st Century, South Asian people with their large number will, have greater impact on the country with the smaller population. That the Canadian government once again took notice of the subcontinent is reflective of the fact that relations with India, because of the high value of immigration from the country, have become an important domestic issue. The flow of people from India clearly provides corrosive as well bonding dimensions to bilateral relations.

Economic Cooperation

As the world moved into the 21st Century, international relations are most likely to be determined by economic factors. Economic considerations assume an expanding role in international affairs in the context of the post-cold war developments. Canada's position as a donor of aid to India was significant in the. past. Canadian assistance is viewed as desirable by India since unlike assistance from the United States, it is regarded unconnected with geopolitical and strategic considerations and more genuinely geared to development requirements. It was in the Commonwealth that very first Canadian development programme was established. Over the past four decades India has received over two billion dollar in direct and making it the largest recipient of Canadian external assistance. The focus of bilateral ties is shifting from aid to partnership as several Canadian non-governmental organisations have relationships with their Indian counterparts.

Indian economic liberalisation has created opportunities for Canada to invest and to expand trade in India. Within South Asia, India is Canada's leading trading partner. There is substantial room for expanding Canada's trade with India. Both India and Canada have succeeded over the last two decades in incrementally changing the composition of their exports to each other from primary commodities to higher value added manufactured products. Canada has been particularly successful in diversifying its exports with its factor endowments and global competitiveness. India's growing middle class population provides a stable foundation on which to build a larger market for Canadian products and services in the 21st Century. The following observation by R. Terrence Sellen a member of the Trade delegation sponsored by the Western Economic Diversification (a Federal Government Agency) to the 9th Engineering Trade Fair held in New Delhi in February 1991 is worth citing:

"India is an interesting market because of the size of the population their continues to be more than five million new buyers in the market place every year."[4]

The long-term case for commercial cooperation is based. upon existence of support complementarities in the economics of the two countries to make them mutually gaining partners in trade and trade-related activities. Canadian industry is very much interested in infrastructures like telecommunications, power, roads and all those spheres that India needs to modernize in order to attract foreign investment, to develop industries so that they could be cooperative in the world market economy. Canada can use India as a production procurement and trading base for capturing the growing markets of the SAARC (South- Asian Association for Regional Cooperation). Canada is now looking to diversifying its international business beyond the United States. This is where India fits in appropriately. India is a safe country with a clean record of honouring her international commitments.

The advantages offered by the Indian market include a stable democracy with an independent judiciary, a large pool of enterpreneurial, management, engineering and scientific expertise and a huge and developing market. The advantages offered by the Indian market appear to outweigh the disadvantages. The potential for Canadian involvement in India is enormous. While increase opportunities for investment will receive Canada's interest in India, a more stable political environment will be required, if improved ties are to be sustained.

Thrust Areas of Cooperation

The thrust of Canada's exports of India include technology related engineering products, transport equipment, telecommunications equipments, food processing equipment, grain rolling equipment and technology, raw materials, drugs and special vaccines. On the other hand, the thrust of Indian exports to Canada include readymade garments. leather products, gem and jewellery products, marine products and sports goods.[5]

Environment

Another significant issue that both countries are cooperating is environment. Environment is a vital dement in Canada's development cooperation programme. It is a sixty million dollar programme aimed at developing environmental projects in India to help the environment all over. On environmental question, both Canada and India are exposed to external pressures. No jurisdiction in either country can act with complete disregard of international repurcussions. Both countries are open to the influences of a developing national and international community of opinion. Mega projects now come under for more domestic scrutiny than in the past. In abstract terms, one can see the play of forces at work in each country. It is not by coincidence that Canada first established a Department of Environment in 1971 and India only nine years later.

Academic Exchange

Academic exchanges between the two countries are organised for a long time. There are exchanges between Canadian universities and Indian universities and there are visits by scholars and scientists between the two countries. The popularity of Canadian studies in India is increasing. The current academic exchange between India and Canada shows no interest in defining the mainstream culture, but great interest in alternatives, in the voices of the neglected, ignored and disenfranchised. In this shared concern, the boundaries between Indian and Canadian breaks down.[6]

Non-Military Threats to Security

In recent years, the two countries have been brought together on the issues of international terrorism and narcotics. On these two international issues of non-military threats to security there is significant scope for interaction between India and Canada. Though in India the concept of non-military threat to security has received recognition, there has not been much effort to form a coalition of interests with developed countries like Canada. This could be a very fertile area for interaction between the two countries.

Mutual Advantage

India and Canada are not required by their national interests to work together but the possibilities for mutual advantage are many. As international relationships change, and as India renegotiates its links with what was the USSR. Canada, as a member of the Summit Seven Group and also as a voice at the major international meetings at which economic problems are discussed, is of vital importance to India. On the other hand, India has emerged more often as a decisive voice in many international debates because of its size and economic and strategic strengths and its influence is frequently sought by Canada.

Canada and South Asia

India's relations with other South Asian countries have a major influence on its relations with Canada. Canada has always supported whatever openings there were to encourage good relations between the countries of South Asia. Any regional organisation in South Asia can count on Canadian contribution for programmes beneficial to the region as a whole. If on the other hand, there is a war in any of the South Asian countries, the result is adverse for Canada's relations with the region. For Canada, South Asia is essentially the relationship between India and Pakistan. Canada was concerned by the partition of the sub-continent. Accordingly, it got involved in mediating the Indo-Pak conflict and in particular, in finding a mechanism for the amicable settlement of the Kashmir dispute. It also became, a participant in the UN-peacekeeping contingent, a step that has kept it 'involved' in the affairs of the sub-continent for over four decades. Canada is acceptable to India in that role as a preferred alternative to the United States. When the relationship between India and Pakistan is good. Canadian involvement in the sub-continent is at its height. When there is discard between India and Pakistan, there are immediate consequences for Canadian involvement in the region. Canada has of course, direct bilateral relationships with both countries which are to some extent seperate. But these relationships became almost irrelevant in time of Indo-Pak conflict. There is broad political 'support within Canada for the thesis that, other than in a humanitarian, context, and by supporting UN peacekeeping. Canada should not be involved directly in situations of conflict.

To sum up, India and Canada have a number of common characteristics. They are parliamentary democracies: ethnocultural, racial, religious and linguistic diversity, independent judiciary and membership in Commonwealth. Besides, people of India who have migrated to Canada provide strong ties between India and Canada, the growing middle class population in India provides a stable foundation on which to build a large market for Canadian products and services in the 21st Century Canada is now looking to diversifying its international business beyond the US. This is where India fits appropriately. There is enormous potential for direct Canadian investment in India. Canada could be a worthy partner for India in confronting the new world disorder. Conscious efforts to build linkages between India and Canada must be made if the two societies are to be more closely related. It is not enough to strengthen official channels between the two countries but outmoded myths have to be discarded, obvious impediments have to be reduced, changed international realities have to be taken into account. Only then the people of two countries would be benefitted and contribute to the .improvement of the international situation. It is high time that perceptions affecting smooth relationship are changed, so that both countries could develop stronger ties. Even though India has a tremendous potential to attract Canadian investment, converting it into reality is a challenging process. What is required is a firm determination and will on both sides. The need of the hour is to restructure policy in vital .areas of cooperation which are bound to increase, in the coming century.

References

1. See Reid. Escart. Envoy to Nehru. Oxford. New Delhi. 1981.
2. Kapur, Ashok, Canada and India *in Ruberioff. ed.* Canada' and South Asia: Political and Strategic Relations.
3 Longmuir. Gardon, Indo-Canadian Relations. Journal of Peace, Studies. Vol. 1(3-4), March-June. 1994.
4. The Indian Express. New Delhi. 16 April 1991.
5. Oarday, H. Gar. The, Current State of Canada's Relations with South. Asia *in Ruberioff. op. cit.*
6. Branden, Michael, India and Canada: Origins and Assessment of the Shastri Institute.

25

Pressure Groups in Canada

Pressure or interest groups constitute a significant element in the political life of all modern societies. The development of pressure groups represent a response to increasing functional differentiation and the break down of traditional type of authority. A pressure group may be defined as "an organised association which engages in activity relative to governmental decisions"[1]. The chief characteristic of the pressure group is the fact that it strives to persuade governments to pursue the policies it advocates. In doing so it deploys various techniques of persuasion. They differ from political parties. While political parties are large agencies, the pressure groups are small. The main objective of political parties is to control government but pressure groups want to influence government decisions in their favour. Political parties contest elections but pressure groups influence by other methods such as lobbying, propaganda work, etc. In countries like the US and Canada, where there are two dominant political parties, the distinction between parties and pressure groups is evident. But in countries like India where many small parties compete, minority parties often represent very narrow interest of one group and the distinction thus becomes less clear.

Political scientists have identified the following as the contributions of pressure groups to liberal democratic politics. In the first place, pressure groups are a major source of mediation between the government and the individual, articulating aggregate opinions and protecting the individual from undue control by state. Second, they provide a mechanism for political representation which supplements the electoral process, assisting the political, system by marshalling support for issues and providing ideas for public policy. Next contribution of pressure groups is that they allow the political processes to be more responsive, than the electoral process to social and economic differences in society. Last but not the least, such groups feed the government valuable information, both facts and opinion, which can be used to formulate policies and test policy proposals.[2]

Pressure groups have always been an integral part of the Canadian political system. The everwidening activities of government have stimulated the creation and consolidation of these groups in Canada. They operate in and help to mould the federal political system. Paul Pross identifies four prime characteristics of pressure groups in Canada. First, they have a formal structure of organisation which gives them continuity. Second, interest groups are able to articulate an aggregate interests. Third, they attempt to act within the political system to influence policy outputs. Fourth, they try to influence power rather than exercise the responsibility of government themselves.[3]

Pressure groups in Canada reflect a wide range of issues and concerns. The number of these groups is extraordinarily large. However, only two typologies of pressure groups have had lasting acceptance in Canadian Political Science. Engleman and Schwartz divide them into economic and non-economic categories, then subdivide the first into agriculture, labour and business groups. The non-economic category is further divided into nine subtypes.[4] The multiplicity of pressure groups in Canada becomes evident when one takes into account the activities of some of the largest and most active groups.

Business groups are especially active in political persuasion, since the economic viability of the business they represent is quite often directly dependent on government policies. The largest business association in Canada is the Canadian Chamber of Commerce, with 650 local charters and board of trade, 125,000 affiliated members and 5,000 corporations. Another organisation which aims at influencing government policy in such fields as corporate regulation and taxation is the Canadian Manufacturers Association. Representing 80 per cent of Canadian manufacturing its membership is between 8,000 and 9,000 companies. It is funded by this corporate membership. The various financial interests are also well-organised. The Canadian Life and Health Insurance Association represents all companies of insurance business. The Canadian Bankers Association represents all 58 banks. Small business is centralized as an interest group by the Canadian Federation of

Independent Business. Business groups also try to influence government foreign policies. The most significant of these. groups is the Canadian Business and Industry International Advisory Committee.

Agriculture has two major organisations. The largest is the Canadian Federation of Agriculture. It is composed of provincial federations of agriculture and many commodity organisations such as the Canadian Park Council. The Fisheries Council of Canada is the largest organisation representing fishing interests. Labour happens to be a powerful force in Canadian politics. The major umbrella organisation is the Canadian Labour Congress. Unlike most interest groups, Labour Congress supports one political party the NDP. Another major workers association, the Canadian Federation of Labour is emprised often building trade unions. It differs from the CLC in emphasising cooperation with the government and in being non-partisan. Another prominent category of economic interest groups comprises those represent of consumers. The consumers Association of Canada represents the interests of Consumers to government. This function often brings it in conflict with both business and labour. In a separate category are professional workers. The Canadian Bar Association, the Canadian Association of Broadcasters and the Canadian Council of Professional Engineers, among others attempt to secure government policies conducive to their professional interests; perhaps, the best-known group in this category is the powerful Canadian Medical Association.

The category of non-economic, groups is possibly the largest. Religious interests are fostered by the Canadian Council of Churches, the Canadian Conference of Catholic Bishops and Christian Movement for Peace. Ethnic representation is made by groups such as the Canadian Jewish Congress, the Arab Palestine Association, the Ukrainian National Association, and the Canadian Palish Congress. Women are represented by the National Council of Women, the Voice of Women and the YWCA.

A permanent organisational structure is very important because it helps the group act cohesively. Organisations that represent business interests are among the best developed or most institutionalised, as the Canadian Bankers Association illustrates. The result is that the CBA has been drawn into the sub-government that devices and administers many policies of significance to the financial community. A sharp contrast can be drawn between the organisational, development of the CBA and that of most non-business groups. Take for instance, the groups that seek to represent the interest of social welfare recipients. There is not one association that represents social welfare recipients, but several, including the National Anti-poverty Organisation, the National Council of Welfare, the Canadian Council on Social Development and a host of other consumer groups that are concerned with additional issues. In contrast to the financial security and autonomy which the CBA enjoys, these organisations are all dependent on Canadian government for their funding. None of them have sufficient staff resources to generate expert information necessary for appreciable input into government policy. Their differences hamper any efforts to mount a united front before government.

In Canada professional lobbyists are based in Ottawa and the provincial capitals to represent interest groups and bring their concerns before politicians and public servants. Given the complexity of government, lobbying is essential. Lobbyists provide valuable assistance to government and parliament is that they assemble facts which are necessary for informed decisions. Lobbyists are particularly useful to governments because they furnish information which enables politicians to develop policies that will gain votes. The lobbying strategy chosen by an interest group depends largely on the type of group it is, its resources and the type of issues involved. Some groups concentrate on the pre-parliamentary stages of government, while others prefer buttonholing MPs. However, no amount of persuation will be effective unless public opinion is in agreement with a lobby or at least not hostile to its demands. Within the policy process, access is available through individual MPs via the committee system or caucus and, of course, the cabinet. But interest groups operate outside the narrow confines of Parliament. The bureaucracy is concerned with policy in earliest formation and is often the most important focus of lobbying. Such activity has led to complaints that interest groups bypass Parliament and the elected representatives. The close relationship between civil servants and pressure groups is due to several reasons. Civil servants are often required by their ministers to initiate and draft or to research and evaluate policy proposals for cabinet, to give advice on the public acceptability of these policies and even to help educate and inform public about them. Interest groups which do much information collection in their respective spheres are often approached by bureaucrats for their expertise. Their specialized knowledge provides pressure groups with the opportunity to affect policy formulation. The intervention between pressure group leaders and politicians or bureaucrats is characterized by a spirit of cooperation that has been termed as "an ethos of mutual accommodation.[5] Since responsibility for initiation and control of legislation is in the hands of government, the cabinet is the real target for pressure groups activity. Some interest groups relations with cabinet are more formalized. Every year certain large national groups are invited to present an annual brief to the whole cabinet. This recognition, which has been achieved by only a few organisations, such as the CLC, is greatly valued. The committee system is yet another attractive access point for interest groups because the very purpose of committees is to gather information. Although pressure groups normally prefer to transmit their demands directly through bureaucracy or legislative system, political parties form a further possibility for access to decision making. Interest groups try to influence party policy resolutions because it is political parties who supply the government leaders; party decisions therefore may become government policy decisions. However, being identified with one political party is a two-edged sword that many groups prefer to avoid.

No one policy process is necessarily like another. Although public servants, the cabinet, MP other interest groups, the media and the public opinion are generally members of most policy committees, how and when they affect policy proposed differ from issue to issue. Thus policy process knowledge will need to be rather sophisticated. Alarmed in the mid-70s with their ignorance of governments agenda, business and professional groups in Canada have since taken a number of measures to enhance the sophistication of their process knowledge. One root has been to hire a professional lobbyist. A more frequent root taken by group organisations has been to restructure their organisation to create government affairs divisions staffed by individuals whose sole responsibility is to monitor government and media sources. The influence of pressure groups is significantly affected not only by characteristics of groups themselves but equally, by characteristics of the governments with which they interact. How authority is organised within the political system affects the ability of groups to realize their goals.

The concerns about the role of pressure groups in Canada are three fold: First, the substitution of the groups for the elected representative diminishes the influence of individual Canadian. Second, interest groups by definition promote specialist interests likely at the expense of the public interests or good. Third, source of uneasiness with their legitimacy rests on the claim that the process which form interest group are not characterized by the same openness as in legislative or electoral process. The biggest controversy concerning pressure groups centres on the question of providing equal access to all interests. Diametrically opposite views prevail in Canada. On the one hand a President of the Retail Council of Canada has argued that "Almost every special interest group, be they disabled, the poor, the native people, have formed their own interest groups and legislators and civil servants pay at least as much attention to these groups as to the older established lobbies of business and labour."[6] On the other hand, an activist associated with the status of women has argued that although groups representing women, labour, minorities and the unemployed exist, they are virtually ignored.[7] Some skeptics complain that pressure groups are associated with unethical means such as bribery or blackmail in influencing government decisions in their favour. There are people who even harbour the suspicion that they are evil because they conflict with the fundamental attributes of democracy.

Conclusion

In today's big, complex modern society, it is necessary for persons with similar interests to come together to form organisations with greater power and voice than a number of isolated individuals would have. Moreover, they are useful to government for purposes of consultation. If a government plans legislation affecting farmers, it is valuable for all concerned to have consultation between interested parties before the bill is made law. The legitimacy of organised interests can be defended on following grounds. First, interest group activity can be seen to be rooted in the basic democratic rights of freedom of association and freedom of expressions.[8] Second, the right of groups to advocate or petition is deeply rooted in our traditions.[9] Together these two themes are encapsulated in the US Madisonion doctrine that the autonomous expression of interests (through freely organised groups) is a hallmark of liberal democracy.[10] Organised interest groups can also be defended as necessary to meet the requirements of the modern interventionist governments. The creation of the welfare state and the institution of the government in the market place created a need for expertise. To sum up, the legitimizing interest group activity in Canada has been an incremental process. Earlier they were regarded as a 'hidden', if not evil empire. Now their legitimacy or even desirability has been accepted. Pressure groups are now a widely accepted part of the Canadian political culture. The interaction between these groups and the political system is characterized by an ethos of mutual accommodation or cooperation in which the interaction is deemed mutually worthwhile. The fact that interest groups are accepted within the political culture implies that there is a legitimate channel for complaints and frustrations; and opportunity for citizens to articulate viewpoints and defend them, so that citizens do not have to resort to extra-legal behaviour to be heard. Thus, pressure, groups provide a crucial and culturally acceptable link between citizen and public policy. However, issue oriented groups, though they have a well-defined role to play in the system, tend to be considerably less favoured by the relatively closed nature of the Canadian policy structures than are the more fully institutionalized groups. Although Canadian policy process is more structured and heiracrchial than that in the US, it too places considerable strains or group resources as time and energy must be spent monitoring the progress of issues through the system. The Canadian political system is based on representative and responsible government and both these aspects need to be considered in the case of interest group activity. The issue of pressure groups in politics did not end when their existence was publicly recognized. The question of the most appropriate structure for interest groups input is yet to be resolved.

References

1. Salisbury, Robert H. Interest groups, *in Fred* I. Greenstein and Nelson W. Poslby, *ed.* Handbook of Political Science, Vol. 4, Addison-Wesley, Mass, 1975, p. 175.
2. Etzioni, Anitai. Making interest groups work for the public. Public opinion, Vol. 5 (4), Aug-Sept. 1982, pp. 53-55.
3. Pross, Paul. Pressure groups : Adaptive instruments of political communications, *in* A. Paul Pross *ed.* Group behaviour in Canadian politics. McGraw Hill Regerson, Toronto, 1975.
4. Engleman F. C. & M. A. Schwartz. Political parties and the Canadian social structure. Prentice Hall, Canada, 1975.
5. Jackson Robert J. & Michael M. Atkinson. Canadian legilature system. Cage, Toronto, 1980, p. 36.
6. Kernaghan Kenneth and David Diegel. Public administration in Canada. Methuen, Toronto, 1987, pp. 410-11.
7. Hertog, Jahanna den. Lobbying and interest group representation : A comment, *in* William Neilson & James Mac Pherson *eds*. Legislative

process in Canada. Monteral Institute for Research on Public Policy, 1978, p. 221.

8. Scott, Roget. ed. Interest groups and public policy. MacMillan, Melbourne, 1980, p. 240.
9. *See* Submission on Bill C-82, The Lobbyist, Registration Act, Canadian Bar Association, April 9, 1988, pp. 1-2.
10. Hague, Rod and Martin Sarrop. Comparative government .An introduction. Macmillan, London, 1982, p. 79.

26

India's Case for Permanent Membership of the UN Security Council: Reactions of the Major EU Member States

In the post—Cold War era, there is a general consensus that the UN Security Council needs to be reformed to make it an effective institution of international peace and security. The modalities of the reform are, however, being vigorously debated. There is also a widespread view that conscious efforts need to be made to strengthen the UN through democratisation of its structure and procedures.

The Security Council, which met for the first time at the summit level in January 1992, acknowledged the need to strengthen the UN in the following words: "All member-states expect the UN to play a central role at this crucial stage. The members of the Council stress the importance of strengthening and improving the UN to increase its effectiveness."[1]

The focus of the current debate is on the subject of the composition and functioning of the Security Council, which has extraordinary powers flowing from its representative character. Article 24 of the UN Charter underlines that when the Council discharges its primary responsibility in peace and security matters, it does so on behalf of the entire membership of the organisation.

The composition of the Security Council has for long been criticized as highly non-representative of the current global realities. At the time of its creation in 1945, there were five permanent and six non-permanent members from fifty-two nations represented in the General Assembly. Now, the General Assembly having reached a membership of 185, there is a strong case to increase the membership of the Security Council. The report of the UN Secretary-General notes that the enlargement of the Security Council has evoked broad agreement.[2] It is argued that two unrepresented geographical regions, namely, Africa and Latin America alongwith the under-represented Asian region, must get their due share.

The question of making the Security Council more representative both qualitatively and quantitatively has received the priority attention of member-states for the last couple of years. The General Assembly has been seized of the matter since December 1992, when the views of the member-states were solicited with regard to the equitable representation and increase in the membership of the Security Council.[3] In 1993, the General Assembly established an open-ended Working Group to facilitate a full and frank exchange of views. The question is no longer whether to enlarge the Council membership, but how soon and in what form.

India's Case

India formally staked its claim to a permanent seat on the Security Council in September 1992 when its Minister of State for External Affairs, Eduardo Faleiro, while addressing the General Assembly, marshalled a wide range of arguments to espouse India's case for permanent membership. He observed how, together with economic criteria, it was necessary to give weight age to certain other relevant issues at the time of expanding the Security Council. The population and size of a country as well as standing in the region needed to be given due weight age in the matter, he said.[4]

India, the largest democracy in the world, is a major regional power in Asia and accounts for 73.4 per cent of the South Asian landmass and 76.5 per cent of its population. It has one-sixth of the world's population and has a huge market with free enterprise. It is the eighth largest industrialised country in the world. It has been one of the founding members of the Non-Aligned Movement and played a leading role in the foundation of the South Asian Association for Regional Cooperation (SAARC) and ratification of the South Asian Preferential Trading Arrangement (SAPTA).

India's consistent role in promoting the purposes and principles of the UN Charter may also be noted. As a founding member of the UN,

India has been steadfast in its support to the world body. Its contributions to the maintenance of international peace and security, its unique record of supporting UN activities and measures against colonialism and racism, its unwavering commitment to the cause of disarmament and development stand out as an outstanding success of India's foreign policy since independence. India is amongst the handful of member-states whose record, particularly since the early 1950s on all key issues having a bearing on strengthening or weakening the UN system, have invariably been in support of maintaining the UN on an even keel.[5] Historians of India's role in the UN have observed: But after independence, the Charter became Nehru's most consistent criterion for judging international conduct and a compendium of ideals to which his government could subscribe. He felt that if there was hope in the world for a new dispensation that might lessen conflict and promote international justice it might lie in the reconstructive effort that the UN could undertake; if a new age was indeed at hand, of greater human welfare and equality, and of peace and cultural developments, then the foundation and first evidence of that epoch would most readily be apparent within the framework of the new organisation.[6]

During the half century of the United Nations' existence, India has contributed significantly to UN peacekeeping operations. It has participated in over twenty-five peacekeeping operations in four continents, including some of the most sensitive and protracted. Starting with Korea in 1953-54 and including the operation in Vietnam, Congo, Middle East, Cambodia, Haiti, Somalia, El Salvador, Mozambique and Rwanda, Indian peacekeepers are currently in Angola, Bosnia, Herzegovina, Liberia and Kuwait. India has tried to set up a role-model through its activities associated with these operations and has been one of the few countries which sustained large-scale troops commitment over prolonged periods. The dedicated commitment of its personnel in these operations to the objectives of the UN Charter has been duly acknowledged by members of the international community and UN officials.

India has also served six terms in the Security Council as a non-permanent member. It may also be noted that India has never been a defaulter in its contribution to the UN. The US, Russia and France, which besides South Africa are the major defaulters in this respect, are permanent members of the Security Council.

India fulfils both the conditions required for the membership of the Security Council as envisaged in the UN Charter, namely, with regard to its contribution to peace and security, and in terms of its geographic position. By any reckoning, India's contribution to the promotion of the objectives of the UN cannot be regarded as inferior to or less valuable than that of any other member of the UN, including any permanent member of the Security Council.

Kofi Annan, the UN Secretary-General, during his visit to India on the eve of the twelfth NAM Ministerial Conference, unequivocally supported India's claim for a permanent seat in the Security Council. In his view, New Delhi could serve well as the voice of the developing countries in the decision-making forum of the UN.[7] The former Secretary-General, Boutros Ghali was also in favour of including India alongwith Brazil and Nigeria, Germany and Japan as permanent members of the Security Council.[8]

However, the political and economic realities of the world do not always endorse the justness of a cause. No major power or regional group has come forward to support India's case, explicitly or impli-citly. Even the non-aligned group failed to take an agreed, clear stand endorsing the claims of any aspirant. In today's world, a booming economy is more appealing to nations than commitment to international principles and one's track record in the maintenance of world peace and other such qualifications.

The US attitude has been particularly unhelpful for India's entry into the Security Council. While openly campaigning for Germany and Japan, Washington is cold towards the idea of India becoming a permanent member. Pakistan also is competing for the seat. In the US view, the Asian countries should debate and decide whether any single country will be nominated as the permanent member or the permanent membership should be rotated.

Reaction of EU Countries

Although there is increasing recognition of the need to review the composition of the Security Council, there are wide differences of opinion. At the India-EU Troika meeting at Luxembourg in September 1997, while discussing the reform of the UN, India tried unsuccessfully to seek EU support for its cause for a permanent seat in the Security Council. In the absence of any EU declaration on the subject, it may be pertinent to analyse major EU members' reactions to India's candidature.

Great Britain

As a permanent member of the Security Council, Great Britain regards the expansion of the Security Council as relative loss of its position and would prefer it if there is no addition to Security Council membership. It is apprehensive that the inclusion of Germany would enable it to exert more influence in Europe, and especially the EU. In response to the UN Secretary-General's request to submit written comments on a possible review of the membership of the Security Council, the British government expressed satisfaction over the performance of the Security Council in the post-Cold War period.[9] It maintained that the changes which have taken place in the international situation in the past few years have for the first time enabled the Security Council to operate effectively as a collegiate body; that as a result the Security Council has begun to play the role envisaged for it at its establishment as the primary means of resolving regional and other conflicts; that it has assumed the position the founding fathers intended for it at the centre of world affairs. Britain further pointed out that in the past few years the Security Council, in exercise of its primary responsibility for the maintenance of international peace and security and working with an unprecedented degree of consensus, has responded to challenges in various parts of the world states; this is borne out from the fact that the members are increasingly turning to the Security Council for assistance; that they need a Council which remains able to respond rapidly and effectively. The British comment concluded by arguing that the present arrangements allow for the equitable representation of states from all regions working with permanent members able to assume global responsibilities; that neither a protracted debate on enlargement nor precipitate action should be allowed to diminish the Security Council's effectiveness.

The British attitude is obviously unhelpful for India's entry into the Security Council. Keener British awareness of India's sensibilities on this issue would have been welcome. It is worth pointing out that the current Labour Party leadership is wedded to the policies first spelt out by the late John Smith, Tony Blair's predecessor. John Smith was a friend of India and in a speech at Oxford went to the extent of supporting India's membership of the UN Security Council.

France

France also is bothered about the possible change in power balance in the Security Council and has not shown enthusiasm for expanding the Security Council. Its reply to the Secretary-General's request for comment on the matter noted that the Security Council had, in effect been able to resolve or to arrive at a common position on a variety of conflicts affecting international peace and security for several years now;[10] that the Council's effectiveness is in part because it has a limited number of members, which permits the achieving of compromise and reaching decisions which generally reflect a consensus agreement within the United Nations as a whole; that the ten non-permanent members of the Council ensure an equitable geographical representation of member-states.

France conceded that the increase in the number of member-states of the General Assembly and the political and economic changes over the past decade do indeed prompt consideration of an enlargement of the Security Council. Any contemplation of an increase in the number of permanent members, it stated, must take account not only of the relative weight acquired by certain states by virtue of their level of economic development but also of their participation or willingness to participate in peacekeeping operations and the interest evinced by them in discharging global responsibilities in the field of international peace and security.

France thus favours expansion of the Security Council. It supports the candidature of Japan and Germany. But beyond saying that the present power structure at the Security Council needs a change as it reflects the international position after World War II, the French are unwilling to commit themselves. France is perhaps the only permanent member of the Security Council which is not too averse to the idea of inclusion of any country from the developing world.

During his visit to India President Jacques Chirac of France, while heaping praise on India for its brave reforms and economic growth, refrained from committing his country to support for India's candidature in the UN Security Council. Referring to France's position as a member of the Security Council, he limited himself to saluting India's considerable contribution to the UN peacekeeping force.[11] France is of the view that it would be quite India's vocation to be a member of the Security Council. Vocation in French would mean that India can consider itself for membership of the Security Council. It looks like a futuristic French proposition.

If, however, France could be persuaded through diplomatic channels to show greater understanding of India's sensitivities and concern on issues such as membership of the Security Council, India could expect a fair deal. But the key question is whether France could assert its independence of the US, as has usually been its vein in the past, and concede India's case on its merit. In the post-Cold War period, on other critical issues, such as the NPT and CTBT, France has departed from the traditional track and shown solidarity with the other Western powers. Perhaps, it believes that its own larger global interest demands it to move in unison with the big powers of the Atlantic community. On the recent Iraqi crisis, France moved out of the US trappings and got alongwith Russia and China to oppose any military adventurism against Iraq. There is thus not all hope lost about France treating India's case on its merit, and lending support to it as and when its vocation requires. Much, of course, would depend on how India plays its cards on the diplomatic chessboard.

Germany

Germany seems quite enthusiastic about expansion of the Security Council, being itself a hot favourite for inclusion in the select club. Its response to the Secretary-General's query on the matter shared the view expressed in the General Assembly resolution that the changed international situation and the steadily increasing membership of the UN necessitates reconsideration of the present composition of the Security Council.[12] It expressed its willingness to assume the responsibilities which permanent membership of the Security Council entails.

While supporting India's candidature—because India has all the preconditions to be a permanent member of the Security Council.[13] Germany ambivalently says that the question which country should represent Asia should be decided by the region. India has also to contend with Pakistan's diplomatic campaign to thwart its ambitions at the UN.

Conclusion

The present membership of the UN Security Council is in need of expansion if only to reflect the steady rise in UN membership. Any expansion of the Security Council has to take into consideration the membership of the developing countries from Asia, Africa and Latin America, for these regions are not adequately represented.

India's claim for a permanent seat in the Security Council is related to the rectification of the distortions of the UN as currently structured. Denying such membership to the largest democracy is inequitous. Issues wholly irrelevant to India's entitlement to a permanent seat should not any more stall a decision in its favour. India has a strong case for joining the Security Council both in terms of nurturing its own core interests and values and in shaping the global agenda.

The major EU powers are not readily forthcoming on the matter. The UK and France view the expansion as relative loss of their powers. Going by the round of negotiations, it seems that the existing veto-wielding powers are going to stick to their privileged positions rather than share it with other member-states. They fear that the induction of countries from the developing world could have an adverse impact on their preponderance as big powers in the Security Council.

India's case may not be easy to push through and permanent status will not be offered on a silver platter. India needs to pursue its claim through a well-thought out diplomatic strategy. It has to negotiate a complicated concessions package with the Asian group of countries, in particular with its South Asian neighbours and the permanent members of the Security Council. India has to convince the world powers that it is not anti-West, but its stance on peace and genuine disarmament should be interpreted in right earnest. A change in India's self-image is necessary before it succeeds in its endeavour. For this, India will need to give up its preoccupation with subregional disputes and look to the larger interests of the world.

To be admitted as a permanent member, India needs the support of both the General Assembly and the Security Council, including the existing five permanent veto-wielding powers. Indian diplomacy has to pay closer attention to the European Union because it has two permanent members, cultivating not only the key EU members individually, but the EU collectively. The EU now wields considerable supranational authority over its members who have ceded to it. Its control over their policies is increasing day by day.

References

1. See text of the statement read out by John Major, Prime Minister of the United Kingdom at the end of the Security Council meeting, 31 January 1992. *Link* (New Delhi), 1 March 1992, pp. 29-30.

2. Boutros B. Ghali, *The 50th Anniversary Annual Report on the work of the Organisation, 1996*. UN, New York, p. 9.
3. UN *Newsletter* (New Delhi), 44/51 (19 December 1992), p. 2.
4. *Hindustan Times* (New Delhi), 27 September 1992.
5. For details, see, K.P. Saksena, "The UN in India's Foreign Policy Strategy" in: M.S. Rajan et al. (eds), *The Non-Aligned and the UN* (New Delhi, South Asian Publishers, 1987), pp. 188-90.
6. Charles H. Heimsath and Surjit Mansingh, *A Diplomatic History of Modern India* (Bombay, 1971), p. 84.
7. *The Pioneer* (New Delhi), 7 April 1997.
8. *International Herald Tribune*, 14 August 1992.
9. Report of the Secretary-General, on the Question of Equitable Representation and increase in the membership of the Security Council, Official Records of the United Nations General Assembly (GAOR), Forty-eighth session, (A/48/264), pp. 90-1.
10. Ibid., p. 41.
11. *The Statesman* (New Delhi), 26 January 1998.
12. GAOR, Forty-eighth Session (A/48/264), pp. 43-4.
13. Federal Minister Kinkel's Visit to India, *German News* (New Delhi), Vol. XXVIII, March 1997, p. 50.

27
Relevance of Non-Alignment

A heated public debate is on about the validity and contemporary relevance of NAM and Non-alignment (as a foreign policy option for individual country) in this unipolar world. According to the critics, non-alignment is no longer relevant because of the changed international conditions. It is argued that the policy of non-alignment had some utility in the cold war days. It was evolved to meet a particular type of situation. It had its origin in the reaction of certain countries to the cold war. The word was bipolar and there was considerable tension between the two superpowers. The two main contenders for political ascendancy had almost reached the point of extermination. It was the desire to preserve independence as district form merely formal sovereingnty which led some nations to resist absorption into one or the other of the power blocs. It is argued that the international system is no longer bipolar and the Cold War is over.

That the post-war international political scene has undergone a sea change is a fact which cannot be questioned. Revolutionary changes have taken place in the world. However, these changes have only confirmed the continuing validity and relevance of non-alignment. Non-aligbment derives its origin from certain perennial Yearing of nation states for a safe, fuller and better life. It would, therefore, remain of abiding significance. It was not dependent upon international political circumstances which are subject to change. It is worth pointing out that the relevance of non-alignment was heightened by the Cold War, not limited by it.

Similarly, the abatement of tension between the superpowers, the emergence of new detente, does not end the tasks of non-alignment.

Only in a very narrow and short-sighted view is the relevance of non-alignment measured entirely in terms of fluctuations of the politics of Cold War. It is true that non-alignment was a child of the Cold War but during the decades of its existence it has acquired an importance of its own. Only the negative connotation of non-alignment has been partly eroded by the collapse of bipolar rigidities.

From the outset, there has been no lack of inquisitors, who looked upon non-alignment as heresy and distorted its meaning. The critics of non-alignment both well-intentioned and tendentious, have become prisoners of etymological narrowness conveyed by the literal interpretation of the term. The principal objective of non-alignment has been and remains to exercise independence of judgement and action in foreign affairs. Non-alignment is permanent significance because it springs from the determination of countries to safeguard their independence; to contribute effectively to the betterment of international relations; and creating international atmosphere more conducive to social and economic development. These principles are as valid today as they were in the fifties. In fact, the world has no other alternative.

Non-alignment is a political concept that strives for the remodelling of international society, as a whole, and not merely any single aspect of it, though inevitably the nonaligned nations had stressed particular aspects at a particular period of time. Political independence is incomplete without economic emancipation. While power blocs and military pacts have not lost their lusture, there are militant alliances which continue to dominate global trade. From political freedom, the NAM is progressing towards economic independence. The nonaligned nations have been working for a legitimate share in world exports. The determination of the quality and quantity of foreign aid from developed to developing countries is also a task for the nonaligned nations. Economic cooperation between the developed and developing states forms part of the three-fold strategy advocated by the NAM. The three stands are: (a) reliance on their own resources, (b) promotion of cooperation among the non-aligned states themselves, and (c) fostering cooperation with the advanced states, with the object of promoting self relations as would restrict exploitation and contribute towards resolution of the problems of world economy as a whole. In this respect, the nonaligned countries have revised their earlier approaches which were largely vindictive character and insisted on a transfer of part of the advanced countries to the developing ones.

The non-aligned economic paradigm is not substantially different from the general paradigm which developing countries approached the economic issues of the Third World within the group of 77. This paradigm revolves round the notion of changing international economic relations through the liberalisation of foreign trade and the increase of economic aid.

While the challenge of international peace continues to be the predominant concern, the immediate task facing the NAM is the creation of a new, Just and equitable international economic and social order. The struggle of NAM is now entering a new phase when most developed nations of the world appear to be accepting in principle the need for a new international order. The fundamental concern of NAM has always been with global questions of decolanosation and consolidation of freedom, disarmament and development of economies through mutual cooperation among members as well as through a more equitable and Just new international economic order,. All these are interrelated and go to make the package of peace and prosperity for humanity. The package can endure only in its entirety; it is indivisible.

Over the years, the contours of non-alignment have undergone change. Earlier non-alignment was interpreted chiefly in politico- military terms. The economic considerations were occasionally interected in to its interpretation. Non-alignment was seen merely as a strategy for maximising the flow of foreign capital, while minimising the strings attached to it. The idea was that by refraining from alliance with both power blocs, aid would flow to the nonaligned states from both power blocs. In contrast, now nonalignment has come to be seen mainly in economic terms. It is seen today essentially, as a doctrine of economic liberation and a strategy that would enable the underdeveloped states to loosen the ties which bind them to the exploitative world economic order. From a primarily political strategy individually and collectively followed by the new states, NAM has transformed itself fundamentally into a collective economic movement of the Third World countries. It has entered forcefully into the North-South economic order based on equality and justice. The changing stress does not necessarily imply that the NAM has lost its political mooring, or by implication accepting the view that the political aspect of international politics is the domain of haves while have nots concern themselves primarily with the economic issues. In order to influence the international economic system politics has to be commanded. There is an integral connection between politics and economics.

In brief, non-alignment has not lost any of its relevance even though the rigid attitudes of the Colds War have softened. It has stood the test of time. It has served the useful purpose of protecting and preserving the interests of the Third World countries. It has been the vanguard of the confining struggle against the inperialism, colonialism and racialism. It has focused attention on the major economic issues facing the world and has made a constructive contribution in building up a consensus for the evolution of a new economic order based on the principles of justice and equality. In fact in no other sphere, the exertions of the non-aligned been more fruitful as in pressing the Third World's case for a just international economic order.

To sum up, in contemporary international relations, non - alignment is one of the most powerful trends. Since, its inception, non-alignment has an anti-status quo bias. The NAM could be described as both a movement for moderation in East-West relations, and a commitment to global reform in North-South relations. Over the years, there has been a change of focus from a preoccupation with reducing the level of conflict in East-West relations to a more pronounced stress on changing the basis of North-South relations. The emphasis has shifted from anti-alignment is neither exclusively a result of the bloc confrontation, nor is exclusively linked with economic underdevelopment. It incorporates other motivations and objectives, namely, working for a situation in international relations in which power politics will be eliminated and sovereignty and freedom of choice will be respected. Non-alignment represents the wave of the future.

28
Indian Muslims

> *"Indian Muslim is both Indian and Muslim. The existence of this duality, and the endeavour to stress either one or the other fact rather both, have proven, shall we say, explosive. There has been a failure to intellectualise the duality to hold the two poles synthetically in creative tension. In this duality of the Indian Muslims, both the components, i.e., Indianness and Muslimness are equally valid and interdependent. No one component surpasses or nullifies the other. The undue stress on Indianness assumes the totalitarian form of the principle of Indianisation."*
>
> —*W.C. Smith*

The Indian Muslims constitute the second largest segment of the total population of India. The Muslim situation cannot be understood unless one takes into account the nature of Indian democracy. After independence India has adopted parliamentary democracy as a way of life. It requires involvement and participation of all sections of Indian society. Mere participation, however, is not enough. It should not be confined to the election processes. It must be effective which requires economic prosperity, political consciousness and social and educational advancement.

Keeping these factors in view, do the Indian Muslims have any real say in the governance of the country? Are they equal partners in free and democratic India? Has fairness and justice been shown to them? How much have they benefited in independent India?

The answers are not easy to find notwithstanding constitutional guarantees. The Constitution of India is very clear on this point. It ensures equality of opportunity to all citizens. The founding fathers of the Indian Constitution, having regard to the past history of India and the peculiar circumstances of India wisely decided to adopt a separate group of articles dealing with the rights of .minorities. While the impact of other rights contained in Part III is on the people of India as a whole, that of these rights is only on minorities. The rights of minorities guaranteed in the Constitution may be classified under three separate heads—religious, cultural and educational.

The Constitution guarantees freedom of religion, prohibits religious discrimination on the part of the State and prohibits taxation for the support of religious institutions. The freedoms provided in articles 25, 26, 27 and 28 have been conceived in most generous terms to the complete satisfaction of religious minorities. These provisions embodied in detail one of the objectives of the Constitution declared in the Preamble: "to secure to all its citizens...Liberty of faith, belief and worship."

The Constitution also provides that the script, language and culture shall be preserved, even of a minority group. No other group, even if it be the majority in the country shall impose its own language, script or culture on the minorities (Article 29). Clause (2) of the same article guarantees equal treatment to all citizens in the matter of admission of educational institutions maintained by State or receiving State aid. Clause (1) of article 30 guarantees that "All minorities based on religion or language shall have the right to establish and administer educational institutions of their choice." Clause (2) of the same Article provides that "State shall not, in granting aid to educational institutions, discriminate against any educational institution on the ground that it is under the management of minority whether based on religion or language."

The rights guaranteed under these heads are unique in their thoroughness. An analysis of these provisions makes it clear that the maximum possible freedom has been guaranteed to the minorities. The sole purpose of these rights is to infuse complete confidence in the minorities and to ensure their safety and equal participation in the nation-building.

But in spite of all the constitutional safeguards, any dispassionate observer will find that the largest religious minority, namely, Indian Muslims is not getting a fair deal in free India. Their plight has been miserable. According to a study made by Gopal Krishna it was found that the Muslims as a group were poorer than the national average, their educational levels were lower, their drop-out rates were higher and moreover this was true of Muslims in every part of the country. Despite constitutional guarantees, the Muslims have been discriminated against in almost every sphere of national life. Their percentage in public services has been constantly dwindling. The doors of industry and enterprise in private hands have been kept shut for them. There is highly organised vested interests who exercise powerful influence on the administration and succeed in pushing through the minority interests to a subsidiary position. Consequently, a great injustice is being done to the members of the Muslim community in matters of employment, in grants of licences, permits, contracts and admission to various institutions. Here, it may be argued that there are other groups which are also ill-treated and discriminated against like Harijans. But anti-Muslim feeling is much more in evidence in the country than the anti-dalit feelings.

The text books which are being used in different classes appear to be an attempt to de-Muslimise the Muslim children. The text books militate against Islam and Islamic teachings. Urdu language is facing virtual genocide at the hands of administration. It has become an alien language in the land of its birth. History is being falsified and distorted to provide a justification for Hindu communalism. The facts are, however, otherwise. It was the Britishers who distorted Indian history and gave it a communal twist. After independence, a fresh wave of communalism has swept Indian history writing. Consequently, the Indian history today is full of half-truths, fanciful assumptions, fantastic propositions and wishful thinking. There can be no two opinions that the communal interpretation of history is mainly and basically responsible for the present extremely explosive communal situation in the country. There is no denying the fact that the distorted history creates a very bad impression on children's minds and sows seeds of hatred and enmity.

Above all, frequent communal riots which are actually preplanned and organised attacks on Muslims create an agonising sense of insecurity and alienation among them. More often than not, the rioters are encouraged and are actively helped in looting the property of Muslims. In fact the rioters become more active and aggressive during curfew hours. In every riot, it is Muslims who are greater sufferers and loosers in terms of life and property. The openly partisan and collusive attitude of the civil and police administration in the event of communal flare up has created a feeling among Muslims that they are aliens, second class citizens or totally isolated in their motherland. The sharp increase in riots has led the Muslims to adopt a defensive and static attitude. The modernised Muslim in this situation either withdraws into his shell or in his private postures feels shy of being identified with anything explicitly Muslim. There begins to operate some sort of defence mechanism which may result either in desperation, frustration or militancy. Such a situation does produce an identity consciousness among Muslims which is sustained by a sense of insecurity and non-redressal of their grievances. The allegations of separatism and anti-nationalism levelled against Muslims by Hindu communal groups make the sense of grievance all the more acute.

This is in short the social, economic and psychological state of affairs in which Indian Muslims find themselves today. Under these conditions when Muslims feel insecure in respect of their lives, property and honour, when they find that Urdu is being driven out of its cradle and when they see to their dismay that their share in economic sphere or in public and private sector has dropped to a level much less than their proportion in population they get angry. Consequently, the Indian Muslims as a whole are today frustrated, demoralised, disillusioned and pessimistic.

The situation is very dismal. The state of affairs is really astonishing and merit urgent attention of every thinking Indian. Because the development, progress and welfare of Muslims cannot be isolated from that of entire community. If Muslims are not allowed full participation in nation-building, it will not only be to the peril of Muslims alone but the entire country stands to suffer. The words of Sir Syed Ahmad Khan are worth recalling who had rightly said that Hindus and Muslims are like the eyes of a bride, that is India, if one of them suffers an injury, the beauty of India would be destroyed.

Who is responsible for this sorry state of affairs? How long this situation will continue? How can it be remedied? Such questions agitate the mind of every thinking Indian. An attempt is being made here to find answers to these questions.

It has become fashionable these days on the part of social scientists and political analysts to hold Islam as the ultimate control system of the Muslim politics. According to them the connection between Islam and Muslim politics runs very deep. It is argued that

Islam is responsible for the backwardness of the Muslim community. It is nothing but imagination running wild. The crisis created by the technological leadership of the West produced a resurgence of Islam as well as Hinduism. The centrifugal tendencies now apparent in India are the product of the circumstances which have nothing to do with Islam or presence of Islam in the sub-continent.

It will not be incongruous here to mention the effects of partition on the Muslim community. Before independence most of the Muslims, by and large, enjoyed the same social and economic status as other communities. The aftermath of partition brought misery and sufferings for Muslims. The two-nation theory had taken its toll. The division of the country was the tragic culmination of the communal politics of pre-independent days. The partition created an unprecedented situation which Nehru rightly characterised as "cutting up of a living structure". What the Muslim community got out of partition and independence was a sense of insecurity, frustration and uncertainty. As compared to Hindus, they suffered a greater loss as a result of partition. They paid the heaviest price in terms of culture and political status of the community.

Even after 1947, the introduction of democratic institutions and procedures did not materially change the situation for the Muslim masses. In fact the Muslims find themselves in a dilemma after 1947 as they had never encountered such a situation in the past. The response of the community to the changed realities of the situation has not been satisfactory. The suddenness of the change has rendered them psychologically unprepared to confront it. Splintered and divided, the Muslims have been faced with a crisis failing to discover the true self and the validity of existence as a community. The crisis of the community emanates from partition. After partition todate there has been a slow, sure and continuous process of degeneration of Muslim community.

As a Muslim myself, I venture to assert that the present attitude and outlook of Indian Muslims is largely, if not entirely, responsible for their miserable plight. Their condition can never change to better unless they do not change their present attitude and thinking. According to the Holy Qur'an "Verily God does not change the condition of a community unless and until it changes its own condition." The question arises what is the present attitude of the Indian Muslims? To be precise: negative. The vast majority of Indian Muslims is living in a world of their own. They are not prepared to accept certain hard realities of the present day life. They are an emotional community. They are excitable and they are gullible. They lack a rational approach. They are wasting their time and energy in passing resolutions and submitting memoranda. They are begging for their legitimate rights. They are demanding reservation of seats. As a matter of fact they expect the government to do everything for them.

If the Indian Muslims really wish to get their due and rightful place in Indian polity, the first thing which they should do is to shed the habit of self-pitying. They should at once stop begging for their rights. Rights are not begged, they are taken. They should realise that reservation is no solution to the problem of under representation. Reservation ensures immediate representation but spells isolation in the long run and is therefore suicidal. They should remember that no minority can seek the solution of its problems by expecting the government to do everything for them.

The Muslims should bear in mind that ours is a competitive world. We stand and fall on the basis of our own merit and on the self-confidence with which we face the world. In this age of specialisation, the best is always recognised everywhere. The survival of the community depends upon specialisation, in different fields. Take the example of Jews. They suffered the worst type of persecution in human history yet, because of their unfailing courage, faith and hard work, they are marching ahead on the road of progress and prosperity. They were able to do so because they distinguished themselves in various spheres of life. Consequently, despite being in minority they are dominating a number of countries including the United States of America. There is no reason why the Indian Muslims cannot do the same in India. The only thing required is that they should ruthlessly devote themselves to first class efficiency in every sphere of national life.

The Muslims should remember that communalism cannot be cured through communalism. Two wrongs never make a right. The only effective answer to communalism is secularism. Fortunately, the present leadership of India is committed to a secular set up which is the only satisfactory solution to a multi religious society. Due respect for all religions is not anything un-Islamic. The Muslims should strengthen secular forces so that the overwhelming population does not remain a mere spectator when orgy of violence takes place, but fights actively and politically to ensure peace. Once there is peace and security, the best would come out of the communities including the minority community.

The backwardness of Muslims needs to be tackled with a sense of dedication and purpose. Muslims ought to be persuaded to educate themselves, and those already undergoing education should strive to improve upon their present standards. Education would go a long way in removing ignorance, prejudices, biases and would unfold to them the vast world of economic opportunities. Fortified with academic qualifications or vocational or technical training and know-how, the Muslims would be able to get their rightful share, both in the government as well as in private sector. Thus, instead of concentrating on politics, they should devote their energy and strength to the educational, economic and social spheres. It is worth pointing out that uplift of people in these spheres demands hard and dedicated work and great sacrifice.

The Muslims are fortunate indeed to have the opportunities which democracy alone provides for the expression of their grievances. If they have hitherto failed to use them, it is simply because of want of a leadership at once courageous and enlightened. Courageous enough to realise that this is a national problem. Courage is the need of the hour. The Muslims should prepare themselves to grasp the great opportunity.

The one sure antidote to the Muslim dilemma is a full and wholehearted participation in the national life and a total identification with the national ideal of a democratic, and secular India. It is now the responsibility of the new generation of Muslim intellectuals to come forward and take the initiative. A concerted effort should be made to educate the Muslim masses along correct lines. The task is urgent. The sooner it is realised the better for the Muslims and the country. What is needed is to change the mental outlook of the people and create a new and healthy atmosphere.

29

Muslims and Reservation

The Indian Muslims constitute the second largest segment of the total population of India. Inspite of their regional diffusion, cultural and linguistic segmentation and social class stratification, Indian Muslims have the characteristics of a religious minority group. Before independence, Muslims in India, by and large, enjoyed the same social and economic status as other communities. However, the aftermath of partition brought misery and sufferings for the Muslims. They paid the heaviest price in terms of cultural and political status of the community. Despite constitutional guarantees and safeguards, any dispassionate observer will notice that the largest minority is not getting a fair deal in free India. Their percentage in public services has been constantly dwindling. The Muslim share in government jobs is about four per cent and in civil services less than two per cent - down from twenty four per cent in 1947. There seems to exist a highly organised vested interest who exercise powerful influence on the administration and succeed in pushing through the minority interests to a subsidiary position. Under these conditions when Muslims see to their dismay that their share in public and private sectors has dropped to a level much less than their proportion in population, they get angry. Consequently, demand like reservation in jobs is not surprising but inevitable.

No Solution

According to champions of reservations, the solution to the problem of underrepresentation lies in reservation. But reservation is no solution to the problem of underrepresentation. Reservation ensures immediate representation but spells isolation in the long run and is therefore suicidal. It will not be incongruous here to recall Jawaharlal Nehru's reaction to the decision to do away with communal reservation which he described as a "historic turn in our society". On 26 May 1949. he told the Constituent Assembly, "If you seek to give safeguards to a minority, and a relatively small minority, you isolate it. May be you protect it to a slight extent, but at what cost? At the cost of isolating it and keeping it away from the main current in which the majority is going, at the cost of forfeiting that inner sympathy and fellow feeling with the majority."

Un-Islamic

The argument that since other background classes have been given reservations, why Muslims among the backward classes should be kept out does not hold water as Islam does not recognise social backwardness.

Wrong Comparison

There is a basic flow in the argument that if the policy of reservations for the Scheduled Castes and Tribes is legitimate, so are reservations for the Muslims. However, the social status of the Scheduled Castes and Tribes cannot be compared with any other group in India. The Scheduled Caste are the victims of centuries of social, religious and cultural prejudices against them. In fact, they represent the Indian variant of slavery. They are the real victims of Indian history and the redressal of their historical grievances through reservations is legitimate. The Muslim community cannot claim the same rights as it has never been exploited as a religious community. They cannot advance the argument of injustices of history to claim reservations. Moreover, it is worth noting that in spite of reservations, the status of Scheduled Castes is no better than what is was half a century ago.

Myth and Reality

According to those who accept slogans as substitutes for arguments and facts the need of hour is job reservations for Muslims in government services. It is conviniently forgotten that government jobs do not constitute more than one or two per cent of the total employment. With the privatisation and liberalisation, government jobs will further decrease.

No Difference

Even, if the demand for reservations is accepted for implementation, it is not going to make any difference to the twenty crore strong Muslim community. This is due to the fact that among the backward sections of Muslims, there is a dearth of qualified people to take up responsible positions in government. In any case, the benefits of reservation scheme would be confined to the creamy layer and the purpose behind the reservation exercise would be defeated.

Majority Backlash

The evil effects of communal reservation are too obvious. It might lead to a backlash in the majority community. Communal forces are bound to be strengthened. The real beneficiary would be Sangh Parivar.

From the above it becomes evident that the entire thinking behind reservations on the basis of religion is pernivious. It is fraught with disastrous consequences. In fact, the remedy is worse than the disease. After reservation, the next logical demand would be separate electorate and ultimately would lead to separate homeland. Reservation should follow the principle of social justice. The criterion should be economic backwardness. Certain sections from among the Muslims be identified as backwards enabling them to avail of reservations.

The backwardness of Muslims is an undisputed fact. It needs to be tackled with a sense of dedication and purpose. Muslims ought to be persuaded to educate themselves, and those already undergoing education should strive to improve upon their present standards. Education would go a long way in removing ignorance, prejudices, biases and would unfold to them the vast world of economic opportunities. Employment in government services is not the only means to uplifting a community. Fortified with academic qualifications or vocational or technical training and know-how, the Muslims would be able to get their rightful share, both in the government as well as in private sector. The Muslims should bear in mind this today's world is a competitive world. One stands and falls on the basis of one's own merit and on the self-confidence with which one faces the world. In this age of specialisation, the best is always recognised everywhere. The survival of the community depends upon specialisation, in different spheres. It would not be out of place to give the example of Jews. They suffered the worst type of persecution in human history. Yet, because of their unfailing courage, faith and hard work, they are matching ahead on the road of progress and prosperity. They were able to do so because they distinguished themselves in various spheres of life. Consequently, despite being in a minority they are dominating a number of countries, including the United States of America. There is no reason why the Indian Muslims cannot do the same in India. The only thing required is that they should ruthlessly devote themselves to first class efficiency in every sphere of national life.

30
Jawaharlal Nehru and the Arab World

There is hardly any country in the world with which India has better, warmer and more cordial relations than the Arab world. Undoubtedly, Jawaharlal Nehru was the main architect of Indo-Arab understanding which has been built up into a solid edifice. It was Nehru who laid the conceptual framework of India's Arab policy long before India became independent. By virtue of being the acknowledged and undisputed authority of foreign affairs in Indian National Congress, the main vehicle of national movement he was able to prepare the base for Indo-Arab friendship

Nehru was basically a historian. His study of world history turned him into an admirer of the creative contributions of the Arab to the world civilisation. Besides, he was greatly fascinated by the ceaseless intellectual and cultural contacts between India and the Arab world since time immemorial. While addressing a seminar on indo-Arab relations in 1964, Nehru rightly observed: "Throughout the course of history both the regions, representing two great civilisations have equally benefitted from each other".

Nehru was an Indian to the core but at the same time he was an internationalist in the true sense of the term. The internationalist in him always linked India's struggle for independence with the world-wide movements against imperialism. To him, the Indian and Arab national movements were both integral parts of the tide in history against world imperialism. He was fully conscious of the imperialist designs of Britain not only in India but in countries like Palestine. As a freedom fighter he cherished an emotional affinity with the nationalist stirring in all parts of the Arab world. Nehru shared with many of his eminent Arab contemporaries the belief that the struggle against imperialism was one and indivisible.

While in prison, Nehru spent a good deal of time in pondering over the events in other countries and seriously analysing the world situation. He had keenly followed the events in Palestine and acquired a complete grasp of the issue at stake in that conflict-ridden country. Nehru was fully aware of the fact that the British imperialism followed the same policy of divide and rule in Palestine as it did in India. As he pointed out in his famous work *Glimpses of World History*:

"So England puts Jewish religious nationalism against Arab nationalism, and makes it appear that her presence is necessary to act as an arbitrator and to keep the peace between the two. It is the same old game which we have seen in other countries under imperialist domination; it is curious how often it is repeated."

Stressing the need to sympathize with the Arabs, Nehru argued: "India and Palestine have both their national problems, and both struggle for independence. They have something in common in the struggle, and the opponent is the same... We must, therefore, understand each other and sympathize with each other".

He thus found something common to the Arabs and the Indian people viz. their fight against the British imperialism. His meetings with the representatives of the Palestine Nationalist Movement at Brussels in 1927 gave him greater insight into Palestinian affairs. He was very much influenced by the struggle of Palestinians against the British imperialism. Nehru viewed the Palestine problem in connection with his own country's struggle against the British imperialism. His support for the Palestinian Arabs was derived not only from moral considerations but also from his anti-British and anti-colonial sentiments. To Nehru the Palestine problem was basically one of nationalist struggle against colonial domination.

Nehru viewed the Bafour Declaration of 1917 which favoured the establishment of a Jewish national home in Palestine as "a gross betrayal of Arabs by British imperialism." At the instance of Nehru, the Indian National Congress, the main vehicle of national movement had expressed a complete sense of identification and solidarity with the Palestinian people and passed several resolutions (drafted by Jawaharlal Nehru himself) supporting the Arabs in their struggle against the British and the Zionists. For instance, the All India Congress Committee adopted a resolution at its Calcutta Session as far as back as 1937. The Congress party at its Haripur session in 1938 in a strongly worded resolution denounced the British imperialist designs aimed at depriving the Palestinian people of their homeland and creating the so called National Homeland for the Jews. It further resolved that the method of solving the Palestine problems was by an amicable settlement between the Arabs and the Jews.

It appealed to the Jews not to seek shelter under the British Mandatory Authority and not to allow themselves to be exploited by British imperialism. Again, the All India Congress Committee at its Wardha session in December 1938 passed a resolution deploring that the Jews in Palestine had aligned themselves with British imperialism. All these resolutions obviously reflected Nehru's sentiments. Besides passing the resolutions in order to mobilise mass support, against the anti-Palestinian British policy, the Indian National Congress had several times sponsored the observance of a Palestine Day.

In a speech delivered in London in July 1938, Nehru started :

"This (the problem of Palestine) is a peculiar problem and we are apt to think of it too much in terms of conflict between the Arabs and the Jews. May I remind you to begin with that right through two thousand years, there has never been any real conflict between the Arabs and the Jews in Palestine? It is a problem which has recently arisen, since the War. It is fundamentally a problem created by British imperialism in Palestine, and unless you keep that in mind, you will not solve it".

In an article published in *The Hindu* on 17 December 1938 Nehru categorically asserted that "Palestine is an Arab country and Arab interests must prevail there."

Shortly before the outbreak of Second World War, Nehru observed that the British Empire had "added to its sins by the butchery of democracy and freedom in Central Europe, in Spain, in Palestine."

While the national movement in India under the leadership of Nehru sympathised with the national aspirations of the Arabs, the latter realised that their own emancipation was tied up with the outcome of the Indian struggle. This brought India and the Arab world nearer to each other and close contacts were established between the Indian National Congress and the Arab national parties like the Wafd Party of Egypt.

It is therefore not surprising that the independent India under the stewardship of Nehru felt emotionally and morally committed to the national aspirations of the Arabs to gain rightful place in the comity of nations. As the architect of free India's foreign policy Nehru evinced an abiding concern for Palestine which forms the crux of West Asian problem. One of India's first voles in the United Nations was against the Partition Plan that created Israel. India tried her utmost to avert partition. She alongwith Yugoslavia submitted the plan for a federal state of Palestine. But unfortunately the plan did not find favour with other countries. As a result, Palestine was partitioned and Israel emerged as an expansionist state grabbing a lot more territory than was assigned to it by the United Nations resolution. Nehru was fully conscious of the complications, the creation of the state of Israel had brought into the region. In a speech in August 1958 he pointed out:

"Ever since Israel came into existence, it has been a source of constant irritation to the Arab countries. This was because the Arab countries have looked upon Israel as an outpost from which their freedom might at any time be threatened."

Nehru fully agreed with the fears of the Arab countries. Consequently, in the United Nations and its various forums as well as in various Afro-Asian and Nonaligned Conferences, Nehru's India supported the Arab stand on Palestine. The Indian position on Arab-Israel dispute had always been of the warmest sympathy for the Arab cause. Nehru's opposition to the creation of Israel was based upon ideological as well as emotional factors. Ideologically, India knew from its own experience that partition did not solve basic problems; rather it accentuated them. Emotionally, the long standing friendly ties with the Arabs moulded Nehru's attitude. Apart from the force of history, ideology, tradition and culture which forced Nehru's India taking an almost emotionally pro-Arab stance, there were questions of India's political and economic needs and interests. Undoubtedly the Arab States are the best markets for Indian goods. The Arabs provide a substantial capital for Indian industries. The Arab markets are a source of much needed foreign exchange. Particularly important is the fact that India's growing need for petroleum crude supply is being largely met by the Arab world.

Elsewhere in the Aràb world, India under the leadership of Nehru whole heartedly supported the freedom movements in Algeria, Morocco, Thunisia and South Arabia. This support of India to the Arab cause was totally in line with her declared policy of supporting freedom movements of Asia and Africa and her adherence to the principles of secular nationalism. However, it was during the Suez crisis that Nehru made a decisive impact on the Arab mind. Nehru took the earliest opportunity to make it clear that freedom of navigation in the Suez Canal was not contingent upon its being run by a foreign-owned company. He justified Nasser's decision of nationalising the canal and maintained that Egypt had the sovereign rights over the Suez Canal. Nehru's India lost no time in condemning the Anglo-French-Israeli attack on Egypt. Nehru denounced it as "a naked aggression", reminiscent of the "past colonial methods". India further showed its solidarity to the people of Egypt in their hour of crisis by extending a loan of Rs 50 million to Egypt which was subjected to Western economic blockade. Nehru's role during the Suez crisis won him the respect and admiration of the entire Arab World.

Nehru had rightly predicated in 1958 that "there can be no real peace in the area till this difficult problem (Israel issue) is settled in a satisfactory way." The region witnessed several wars since then. India supported her Arab friends in every hour of crisis, in recent past as the country by and large followed the policy laid down by the man of vision - Jawaharlal Nehru.

From the above discussion it becomes clear that one of the greatest factors in India's foreign relations has been close ties with the Arab world. Its origin and growth was mainly the handiwork of Nehru who in the words of his biographer. Michael Brecher was "the philosopher, the architect, the engineer and the voice of his country's policy towards the outside world". In board terms Nehru's Arab policy was rooted in three converging principles: opposition to imperialism; extension and consolidating of the area of peace; and restoration of India's cultural, economic and commercial links with the Arab world. The Nehru era indeed witnessed an all-round development of Indo-Arab relations. It was during the Nehru period that the foundations of a sound and viable policy were laid. The acid test of the success or failure of the foreign policy of a state is whether the interests of the country have gained or lost. Viewed in this context, it can safely be concluded that India's policy on West Asia as enunciated by Jawaharlal Nehru is logical and far-sighted. The economic, cultural and political interests of India are inexorably linked with the Arabs both in the short term as well as in long term perspectives.

31

Rajiv Gandhi–A Secular Political Leader

Rajiv Gandhi was an outstanding pclitical leader who combined in himself the rare qualities of a visionary and a system builder. He had the unique privilege of having grown up with the cultural and political milieu of Jawaharlal Nehru and Indira Gandhi. This heritage combined with his own orientation towards modern history and values enabled him to have a pragmatic approach to life and politics. He understood India's glorious past, was aware of the demands and compulsions of the present and was concerned about the future. He dreamt of an India of the 21st century. Young and dynamic, Rajiv Gandhi had a fresh approach to problems.

Rajiv Gandhi was quite secular in his outlook like his mother Indira Gandhi and grandfather Jawaharlal Nehru. His faith in and commitment to secularism was not doubted even by his avowed critics. He was more of a humanist than anythingelse. He was deeply concerned for human life and well-being of the individual. The family environment in which he was brought up contributed towards the formulation of his views on religion, politics, man and society. His rationalistic and scientific approach to life made him an ardent follower of a non-religious approach to politics. His understanding of the Indian situation and its history convinced him that in India no nation-building could be possible except that which was based on secularism. As a true heir of Nehru's vision, he acknowledged the fact that inspite of diversity, India is a compact unit. He was not a mere spectator looking from outside, but he was an active participant in the process of promoting the concept of unity in diversity.

Rajiv Gandhi believed very strongly that democracy and secularism were the two pillars on which the Indian edifice could rest itself squarely. He stressed that whereas democracy is one pillar of our nationhood secularism is the second one. Secularism described the sum total of Indian values and principles. As a social revolutionary, he devoted his attention towards a harmonious union of democracy and secularism. Truly faithful to dynamic democracy, he visualized essentials of democracy in secularism as well. Rajiv Gandhi's own exposition of secularism includes all the essentials of humanism in the form of reverence, sympathy, tolerance in the behavioural patterns of different people lead. As he elucidated:

"Democracy is one pillar of our nationhood. The second pillar is secularism which is our contemporary, shorthand word to describe the sumtotal of our values and principles; those values and principles which have ensured the continuity of our civilization for over five thousand years. Secularism for us is the pursuit of truth in conviction that truth will triumph: 'Satyameva Jayate'. Secularism for us is the self-confidence of our civilization which makes us open to the best of influences from elsewhere, to seek a cross-fertilization of cultures and ideas which enables us to move forward. While maintaining our continuity with the past. Through history, we have been the great sympthsisers, so absorbing and assimilating what comes from outside that it gets transformed into our own, not as an alien graft but as a part and parcel of our heritage. Secularism for us is tolerance – the ability to respect the customs and beliefs, the rights and rituals, the philosophy and ways of life of others. Associated with tolerance is compassion, the capacity to sympathize with the suffering of others, to find satisfaction for the self in the selfless service of others. All these human capacities are resumed in the capacity to see all human beings as one large family and all the world as one's own".[1]

Rajiv Gandhi regarded secularism as the cardinal principle of Indian culture. He once observed:

"The essence of our present day nationalism lies in the greatness of our ancient culture. In order to exist as a nation, we will have to preserve our cultural identity. For this we should give equal respect to various aspects of our national life. Therefore, secularism is the cornerstone of our existence as a nation. People of various religions, various languages and various dialects have made India their home. In fact, cultural plurality is what India stands for. Each one of these diverse characteristics is important in its own way. Their identity is inseparable from that of India's identity, rather it is this plurality, this composite culture, which forms the basis of our identity as a nation, and in turn, each one of these parts maintains its uniqueness as part and parcel of this great Indian nation."[2]

The above-cited statement of Rajiv Gandhi makes it abundantly clear that Rajiv Gandhi had a clear understanding of the Indian social structure. Therefore, it was his considered view that secularism with its links with our traditional values of truth, non-violence, tolerance, compassion etc should be the lifestyle of India and political or any other colour should not be given to it.

For Rajiv Gandhi, India was one great land in the lap of which the diverse religious groups have always flourished in vigour. As he once rightly commented:

"Our secular traditions began with the vedas and the epics. The concept of vasudhaiva Kutumvakam, further developed by the Buddha and Mahavira, were the basis for the development of Indian civilization and of our society. We welcomed Judaism in Kerala, we welcomed St. Thomas and Christianity; we welcomed zaroastrianism and today we have the largest Parsi community in the world; we welcomed the great Sikh Gurus from Guru Nanak to Guru Gobind Singh. We synthesized Islam and great Sufi traditions of Amir Khusro and Kabir and Baba Farid and Shah Abdul Latif. Our religious festivals are festivals not of one community but of all Indians and all communities. We celebrate them together."[3]

A multi-religious, multi-lingual and multi-cultural society has a lot to do with the problem of humanism and this is what Rajiv Gandhi considered as the most positive of India's secularism. He reiterated the spirit of humanism for national cohesion in a very characteristic fashion:

The essence of India's civilization is its secularism. Our civilization is unique in its manifestation of the values of compassion and tolerance. These are keys to the unity of our country. These are keys to the continuity our civilization. These constitute the legacy of our freedom fighters and our freedom struggle. They are today the bedrock of our nationhood."[4]

He further stated:

"A secular India alone is an India that can survive. India and secularism must remain synonymous to assure the glory of our civilization and the future of our country. Secularism is a condition of our existence. It is the essence of our tradition. Secularism and nationhood are inseparable."[5] Laying emphasis on "unity in diversity", Rajiv Gandhi once declared:

"We are a multi-religious society, we are a mutli-cultural society, but we are not a multi-national society. We are one people, we are one nation, we are one country and we have one common citizenship. Most civilization posit nationhood and diversity as antithetical. The single greatest contribution of India to world civilization is to demonstrate that there is nothing antithetical between diversity and nationhood. Through five thousand years of long experience, we have demonstrated to the world that our unity in diversity is a robust reality."[6]

Rajiv Gandhi's concept of secularism allowed national cohesion to be murtured in the essential values of huamnism inherent in the dissemination of the inner excellence of mankind. As he said:

"First and foremost, our secularism is not anti-religious or irreligious. We have a deep and abiding appreciation of the rich view of spirtuality that runs through our culture, that runs through every religion of India. It runs through history, it runs through every person who is an Indian. The rich view of spirituality is the source of our moral values, of our ideals and our standards, of our goals and our objectives. We venerate this spiritual tradition. We cherish its moral values. We respect all the different forms in which the spirituality manifests itself. The cardinal principle of our secularism is equal respect for all religions: 'Sarva Dharma Sambhava'."[7]

Rajiv Gandhi was critical of those who approached politics through religion. Even though he was aware of the hold of religion on Indian masses, he was not willing to make use of it for political reason. He stated:

"We cannot replace religion by secularism. There is place for religion, there is place for secularism. Our secularism is not 'non-religion'. Our secularism in 'Sarva Dharama Sambhava', which means a place for every religion, but religion must not be mixed with religion. This is perhaps the most important thing."[8]

Rajiv Gandhi was fully alive to the problem of the scourge of communalism which was carroding the vitals of India's secular fabric. He believed that mixing religion with politics was totally against the wisdom of the Indian constitution and the cannons of civilization. In one of his speeches he stated: "Throughout our history, communalism has weakened us. Our genius throughout the ages has been the way in which we have assimilated, in which we have absorbed, the way in which we have synthesized, how we have tolerated differences, how we have produced a harmony out of different groups of people in our country. Communalism is a danger that is common to all in India. It is a danger that attack all equally, whether big or small, whether big countries or small countries. Our strength will lie not in allowing this to flourish but in seeing that everyone's interest is fulfilled by reducing communlism".[9]

While taking about communal parties, Rajiv Gandhi observed: "Nazism and fascism are two faces of same thing. Communal parties are no better than fascism. And if anyone thinks that these communal fascists are against only one minority, then he is very much mistaken, because after this minority, they will turn to the second minority and, then to the third and this will continue first as Hitler first attacked the Jews, then the communists, the church, and then democrats. We have to put up an allied force against the modern day communal fascists, their defeat is important for the unity of India.."[10]

Rajiv Gandhi was deeply concerned about the communal interpretation of Indian history. Drawing attention to this fact he said:

"Our history is very old but the concept of unity has always dominated it. We had fought the British imperialism which had distorted our history. British imperialism and capitalism had exploited our people and that the, communalism or the two Nation theory was their gift to us. Imperialism had injected the poison of communalism into our educational system. This gave rise to the feeling of separate identity. We Indians have always had faith in secularism, and we cannot forget for a moment that we have, in the poisoned and bloody atmosphere of communalism held the flag of secularism high so that our country does not seek cracks."[11]

Being fully conscious of the communal and divisive forces that eat up the vitalities of humanism, Rajiv Gandhi explicitly observed.

The battle against communalism is not a battle that can be fought strictly and only through constitutional, legal, policy or administrative means. The battle has to be fought primarily in the minds of our people. The values of our constitution, the traditional values, have to be inculcated in the minds of younger Indians, in the minds of a generation that was not touched by the freedom struggle, a generation which unfortunately has not been educated in the values of the freedom struggle and the values of Indian civilization. The battle has to be fought with political actions."[12]

Addressing the teachers of Delhi University, Jawaharlal Nehru University and Jamia Millia Islamia University, Rajiv Gandhi advised that the educational system should never allow communalism to poison it. Communalism should not be allowed to corrupt the younger generation which holds the key to the future. The battle against communalism, as Rajiv Gandhi correctly pointed out has to be fought in the minds of people. It is the battle of mind against all evil and divisive forces of communalism. And for this, India's own characteristics which amply contribute to the positive forces of humanism must be nursed with all care and attention. While underlying the challenges facing Indian polity and pluralistic society, Rajiv Gandhi repeatedly called upon each and every Indian to rise above the narrow barriers of casterism, communalism and parochialism to unite and live in a spirit of brotherhood. The views expressed by him in this regard are worth recalling:

"In modern day world, perhaps India is the first experiment in the form of pluralistic society. You look at any other country. I do not think any other country has accepted such a challenge. Therefore, it is not just as a challenge before us alone, rather it is our example for the whole world that despite all diversities, humanity as a whole can live as a family without any parochial barriers or schism. It is an ideal before the world that the values enshrined in our ancient philosophy depict the best way of life for India and the world as a whole."[13]

Rajiv Gandhi had an eventful five years as the Prime Minister of India. What stood out in his tenure as the Prime Minister was his revulsion against all forms of oppression. His instructive revulsion against any forms of oppression was a trait that he shared with Jawaharlal Nehru and Indira Gandhi. Referring to the qualities of a good Prime Minister, he declared:

"I think dedication and commitment to the nation, being totally non-partisan on any regional, caste religious, linguistic lines and an ability to carry everyone together."[14]

To Rajiv Gandhi nothing was above India's unity and integrity. Thus, after becoming the Prime Minister of India, he initiated the process of strengthening and consolidating the forces that stood for India's unity and integrity and endeavoured to obliterate the forces that were out to sow the seeds of disaffection and disharmony and thus, strike out the vitals of India's unity and integrity. Stressing the significance of a strong and united India, he maintained:

"Nothing is more important than the unity and integrity of our nation. India is invisible. Secularism is the bedrock of our nationhood. It implies more than tolerance. It involves an actives effort for harmony. No religion preaches hatred and intolerance. Vested interests, both external and internal, are inciting and exciting communal passions and violence to divide India. Answering communalism with communalism will help only those subversive and secessionist forces. The combind might of the people and the government will thwart their designs"[15].

As a humanit Rajiv Gandhi never believed in eradicating the disruptive forces of national disintegration through the strategy of fire fighting operation. Rather his humanistic vision was to chalk out plans and prorgrammes for furtherance of national cohesion right from the grass-root level of action. The fundamental strategy of such an action was to launch development programmes of activities in key areas of the country. For instance, elimination of poverty and work opportunities to one and all are the vital strategies he regarded to be introduced in right earnest for national cohesion. He had taken strong note of atrocities committed against the weaker sections. As far the welfare of minorities the real test of a healthy secular democracy, he had been solitious all along. The 15 point programme for the upliftment of the poor and minority communities was aimed at ensuring their fuller participation in all aspects of national life. Special consideration in the recruitment to public services, in the state governments as well as the centre, attending to their educational needs, and receiving all the benefits equally from various development programmes including the 20-point programme. He had been suggesting consistently that the old schemes and programmes which had fallen dormant, had to be revitalized and implemented with vigour. During his stewardship of India, Rajiv Gandhi launched many centrally sponsored and federal schemes for the betterment of the weaker sections of the Indian society, especially in the sphere of education.

To sum up, Rajiv Gandhi firmly stood for a secular India. For him secularism meant the pursuit of truth in the conviction that truth will triumph. He dreamt of and worked for a strong India, a secular India, a humane India and well-developed India where every section of the society would reap the benefits of development. He worked hard to realize there objectives. In his opinion, India stood out as a unique and multi-faceted society, because of its unity in diversity since antiquity. The manifestation of values like compassion and tolerance is matchless. These characteristics are the basis of the continuity of Indian civilization. They are the foundation of Indian nationhood on which democratic traditions have to be built. Rajiv Gandhi's quintessential strength lay in his personal uprightness and a dynamic modern mind. He was earnest to do his best, if need be, single handed to sort out the intricate problems of the largest democracy in the world. For him India was indivisible in whose lap diverse religions, cultural and linguistic groups could blossom with equal vigour and equal right. His vision of India will continue to be a source of inspiration. Rajiv Gandhi was often misunderstood for his down to earth involvement in national solidarity and peaceful change of approach to humanity. In this connection one might endorse the noted historian Professor Bipan Chandra's significant observation:

"Rajiv Gandhi was prescient enough to see dangers ahead. He raised the question of governance and stability as the most important question in India at present. Stability is needed to face the challenge of communalism and casteism and the hatred and violence they have generated. It was needed so that hard decisions on the economic front could be taken and implemented. It was needed above all that popular forces to defend the nation state and to fight for social change and social equity could be energized, mobilized and organized. But precisely the twin slogans of stability and governance were ridiculed by many who saw it as a mere electoral ploy. The more radical intellectuals felt that any programme of governance and stability was bound to mean defence of the status quo and established social order. They were myopic in failing to see the difference between a revolutionary and counter-revolutionary situation, both being product of the breakdown of administrative and political structure. Where is the radical, not to speak of revolutionary challenge in India today? The choice is between keeping united such a diverse and immense society and political break down funneled not by the action of popular forces but by casetist, communal and ethnic conflict and violence leading sooner or later to dictatorship or fascism.."

References

1. Rajiv Gandhi, *Democracy Socialism, Secularism -The Three Pillars of our Nation,* Ministry of Information and Broadcasting, Govt. of India, New Delhi, October 1988, pp. 6-8.
2. *Rajiv Gandhi and Parliament*, Edited by C. K. Jain, Lok Sabha Secretariat, New Delhi, 1992, pp. 63-64.
3. Rajiv Gandhi, *A Secular India Alone can Survive*, Ministry of Information and Broadcasting, Govt., of India New Delhi, May 1989, pp. 5-6.
4. Rajiv Gandhi, *The Battle Against Communalism*, Ministry of Information and Broadcasting, Govt. of India, New Delhi, November 1988, p.1.
5. Rajiv Gandhi, *A Secular India Alone can Survive*, *op.cit.* p. 1.
6. *Ibid.*
7. *Ibid.*, pp. 5-6.
8. Rajiv Gandhi, *The Battle Against Communalism*, *op.cit.*, pp. 6-7.
9. *Lok Sabha Debates*, New Delhi, 28 July 1986. C. 354.
10. *Rajiv Gandhi and Parliament* Edited by C.K. Jain, *op.cit*, pp. 244-45.
11. *Ibid.*
12. Rajiv Gandhi, The Battle Against Communalism, *op.cit.*, pp. 1-2.
13. *Rajiv Gandhi and Parliament*, Edited by C.K. Jain, *op.cit.* pp. 64-65.
14. *The Telegraph*, Calcutta, 25 May 1991.
15. Bipan Chandra, 'Intellectuals Ignored the Positive side of Rajiv Gandhi', *The Telegraph,* Calcutta, May 31, 1991.

Index

B

C

~~14~~

36